14.95

UNIVERSITY OF CAMBRIDGE
DEPARTMENT OF APPLIED ECONOMICS

MONOGRAPH 24

PLANNING PROBLEMS IN THE USSR
THE CONTRIBUTION OF MATHEMATICAL ECONOMICS
TO THEIR SOLUTION 1960–1971

UNIVERSITY OF CAMBRIDGE
DEPARTMENT OF APPLIED ECONOMICS

Monographs

This series consists of investigations conducted by members of the Department's staff and others working in direct collaboration with the Department.

The Department of Applied Economics assumes no responsibility for the views expressed in the Monographs published under its auspices.

The following Monographs are still in print.

PLANNING PROBLEMS
IN THE USSR

THE CONTRIBUTION
OF MATHEMATICAL ECONOMICS
TO THEIR SOLUTION
1960–1971

MICHAEL ELLMAN

Research Officer, Department of Applied Economics, Cambridge

CAMBRIDGE
AT THE UNIVERSITY PRESS

1973

Published by the Syndics of the Cambridge University Press
Bentley House, 200 Euston Road, London NW1 2DB
American Branch: 32 East 57th Street, New York, N.Y.10022

© Cambridge University Press 1973

Library of Congress Catalogue Card Number: 73–75861

ISBN: 0 521 20249 3

Printed in Great Britain
at the University Printing House, Cambridge
(Brooke Crutchley, University Printer)

CONTENTS

[v]

LIST OF TABLES AND FIGURES

PREFACE

The aim of this study is to provide a critical exposition of the contribution to overcoming the problems of the Soviet planning system made by the Soviet school of mathematical economists in the years 1960–71. Hence the book describes some problems of Soviet planning, outlines the theory of the optimally functioning socialist economy, relates the programme of the mathematical economists to that of the State Committee on Science and Technology, and focusses attention on the contributions of the mathematical economists to improving the methods of economic calculation and the economic mechanism. On the other hand, I do not consider many issues which have been raised by the work of the Soviet mathematical economists and which may be of great interest to computer and operational research specialists, sociologists, economic theorists or applied mathematicians, but which do not seem to me essential for appreciating the contribution of the school of Kantorovich and Fedorenko to improving the planning and management of the Soviet economy.

This book is the final report on a programme of research, earlier results of which were reported in a number of articles and in the DAE Occasional Paper *Soviet Planning Today* (Cambridge 1971). The reader who has read that study will find in this one a mass of new material (notably in chapters 4, 5, 6 and 7). The reader who has not read *Soviet Planning Today* will find this study self-contained.

At one time I hoped that this book would contain a definitive account of the work of the Soviet mathematical economists in the 1960s. This goal, however, has not been attained. The book leaves open for further research a number of important questions, ranging from the usefulness of numerical turnpike models, via the difficulties and prospects of introducing rent payments, to the progress of the management information and control system Metall, the relationship between social stratification and economic reform, and the role of the party in a reformed economic system. My defence for broaching so many topics is simply that they all form part of a story which can only be understood if they are related to one another. Another weakness of this study is that I write as an outsider and cannot convey as good a picture of events as many Soviet researchers could.

The reader should bear in mind that this study analyses an ongoing research project. It may be that the course of this research will set some of the issues discussed in the book in a different perspective from that adopted in this study.

The literal translation of the usual Soviet term for the subject of this book is 'economic-mathematical methods', which is rather cumbersome in English. Sometimes, e.g. in the Economics Faculty of Moscow State University, it is referred to as 'economic cybernetics'. It has also been referred to as 'planometrics'. I have translated it throughout as 'mathematical economics'. This seemed the least unsatisfactory term, but the reader should remember that most of the Soviet work is closer to 'operational research' than it is to variations on a theme by Walras. The terms 'mathematical economist' and 'optimal planner' are used interchangeably in the text to describe the research workers in this field.

This study could not have been written but for the opportunity I had of studying at the department of mathematical methods of analysis of the economy of the Economics Faculty of Moscow State University in 1965–7, and the opportunity for research which I have had at the Department of Applied Economics since 1969. My work at the DAE has been financed by the Social Science Research Council. The book is based on a PhD thesis submitted to Cambridge University in 1972. I am very grateful to Charles Feinstein, Bob Rowthorn, David Lane, Tadeusz Kowalik, Christopher Bliss and Martin Cave, for helpful comments and discussion. I have also gained a great deal from the writings of Janos Kornai and David Joravsky. In addition I have benefited greatly from repeated discussions in the last eight years with colleagues in Cambridge, London, Moscow, Leningrad, Novosibirsk, Glasgow and Birmingham, but none of those with whom I have discussed the topics analysed in this book would subscribe to all the arguments advanced therein.

MICHAEL ELLMAN

August 1972

GLOSSARY

The administrative economy The term used by the author to describe *the economic mechanism* (q.v.) which has existed in the USSR since 1929. It corresponds to model 1 in the classification of allocation models by Margolis and Trzeciakowski, and to Kornai's 'suction economy'. The distinguishing feature of the administrative economy is *current planning* (q.v.).

Association Organisation formed by grouping together a number of enterprises, often together with research and design organisations.

Automated management system (ASU) The Soviet term for a management information and control system. For example, the introduction by British Rail of the wagon information system TOPS would be referred to in the USSR as 'the introduction of an automated management system by British Rail'.

Automated system of plan calculations (ASPR) The use of electronic data processing, mathematical models and network planning in economic planning. One of the departmental management information and control systems which constitute the *OGAS* (q.v.).

The break-through The transition from *NEP* (q.v.) to the administrative economy (in 1929).

Capital The value of the capital goods (in the case of fixed capital) and/or materials (in the case of circulating capital) of an enterprise or association as valued in its accounts.

CC The Central Committee of the party.

CPSU The Communist Party of the Soviet Union.

Current planning The system under which enterprises receive instructions as to which products they should produce in the current period (quarter, half year or year) and quotas for the materials which are to be used to meet the production targets, and other instructions concerning their activities in the current period. To be contrasted with medium term planning, which is concerned with compiling and implementing five year plans, and regional planning.

The December (1969) Plenum   Meeting of the CC at which the General Secretary made a report on the economic situation. Marks the end of economic reform as that was understood by some people between the *22nd Congress* (q.v.) and the 1968 events in Czechoslovakia, i.e. of economic reform as part of a process of social change comparable to the transition from *War Communism* (q.v.) to *NEP* (q.v.).

The economic mechanism   The relationship between the parts of the economic system, such as the role of the banks and the existence of allocation or of wholesale trade, which together form a system, such as *War Communism* (q.v.), *NEP* (q.v.) or the administrative economy. In theoretical analysis referred to as the ownership and allocation model.

The efficient allocation of resources   The rational organisation of the *productive forces* (q.v.).

Gosplan   The State Planning Commission, the central planning organ.

Gossnab   The State Committee on Material-Technical Supply, the central organ for the planning of supply, i.e. the allocation of commodities to enable output plans to be implemented.

Gostekhnika   The State Committee on Science and Technology, the central organ for R. & D.

GSVTs   State network of computer centres. Together with the *OGSPD* (q.v.) the technical basis of the *OGAS* (q.v.).

IEOPP   The Institute of Economics and the Organisation of Industrial Production of the Siberian branch of the Academy of Sciences.

Indirect centralisation   Guiding enterprises to socially rational decisions by establishing appropriate rules of enterprise behaviour (e.g. profit maximisation or the present value criterion) and appropriate values of, or rules for determining, the economic parameters (prices, the rate of interest). To be contrasted with direct centralisation, where the authorities try to ensure that the enterprises take socially rational decisions by issuing them with detailed instructions, and decentralisation, where decisions are made by enterprises whose decisions are entirely independent of the wishes of the authorities.

Interdepartmental automated system for the gathering and processing of information for accounting, planning and control of the national economy (OGAS)   Departmental management information and control systems which are compatible with one another.

IPU   The Institute of Management Problems (automation and remote control) of the Academy of Sciences. Formerly the Institute of Automation and Remote Control.

Khozraschet   Word which describes an economic unit which has its own profit and loss account and is run in a businesslike way. Used by extension in phrases such as 'full *khozraschet*' to describe the choice of inputs and outputs by enterprises themselves, flexible prices, and payment for the use of natural resources and capital goods.

The khozraschet economy The term used by the author to describe the economic mechanism of a socialist planned economy without current planning, i.e. an economic mechanism similar to the *NEM* (q.v.) and to the economic mechanism which existed in Yugoslavia in 1954–60 (except that wages are a first charge on the income of enterprises rather than a residual). It corresponds to model 5 in the classification of allocation models by Margolis and Trzeciakowski, to Kornai's 'pressure economy' and Joan Robinson's 'rational price system'.

    The *khozraschet* economy is to be contrasted on the one hand with the administrative economy, and on the other hand with the planless market economy. It differs from the first by the absence of current planning and the widespread use of indirect centralisation, and from the second by the presence of regional planning, medium term planning, and state regulation of the economy to ensure smooth economic growth and a steady rise in living standards, and to ensure the achievement of the social objectives of the party.

The methods of economic calculation The techniques used to arrive at solutions to economic problems (other than socio-economic and organisational-economic problems), e.g. linear programming.

MIF The material incentive fund, one of the enterprise incentive funds introduced as part of *the reform* (q.v.).

Minpribor The Ministry of Instrument Building, Means of Automation and Management Systems.

Narkomfin The People's Commissariat of Finance (since 1946, the Ministry of Finance).

NEM The New Economic Mechanism introduced in Hungary as from 1.1.68. The distinguishing feature of the NEM is the absence of current planning.

NEP The New Economic Policy is the term used to describe the economic mechanism which existed in the USSR in the 1920s.

Objectively determined valuations Kantorovich's term for the multipliers which characterise an optimal plan, which are usually known in English as 'shadow prices'. They are 'objectively determined' in the sense that they result from certain mathematical operations on the original data of the problem, in contrast to the 'subjectively determined valuations' arrived at by planning officials, which all too often represent no more than the arbitrary decision of some official.

OGSPD Interdepartmental system of data processing. Together with the GSVTs, the technical basis of the OGAS.

PDF   The production development fund, one of the enterprise incentive funds introduced as part of the reform.

The productive forces   The technology, skills and resources available to society.

The productive relations   The relationship between people in the process of production, e.g. the exploitation of the workers by the capitalists under capitalism.

The rational organisation of the productive forces   The efficient allocation of resources.

The reform   The economic reform announced at the September (1965) Plenum of the CC and subsequently implemented by stages.

RSFSR   The Russian republic (the largest of the republics which constitute the Union of Soviet Socialist Republics).

SCF   The socio-cultural and housing fund, one of the enterprise incentive funds introduced as part of the reform.

SOPS   The Council for the Study of the Productive Forces, the central organ for regional planning. (SOPS, the Institute of Complex Transport Problems, Gosplan's Institute for Economic Research, its Institute for research on planning and norms, and its Chief Computing Centre, are all organisations attached to Gosplan.)

Tekhpromfinplan   The current (technical-industrial-financial) plan of an enterprise.

TSEMI   The Central Economic Mathematical Institute of the Academy of Sciences.

TsSU   The Central Statistical Administration.

The 20th Congress   The 20th Congress of the CPSU was held in 1956. At this Congress the First Secretary made a report 'On the personality cult and its consequences'.

The 22nd Congress   The 22nd Congress of the CPSU was held in 1961. At this Congress a resolution was passed to remove the body of J. V. Stalin from the Lenin mausoleum.

VASKhNIL   The all-Union Academy of Agricultural Science named after Lenin.

VNIESKh   The all-Union Scientific Research Institute of Agricultural Economics (of the Ministry of Agriculture).

War Communism   Term used to describe the economic mechanism which existed in the USSR in 1918–21.

DRAMATIS PERSONAE

Notes

1 Persons marked * were no longer living in December 1971.
2 '*Kandidat nauk*' has been translated as 'PhD', '*doktor nauk*' as 'D.Sc', and '*dotsent*' as 'Reader'.
3 'b' is an abbreviation for 'born', 'd' for 'died'.

Aganbegyan A. G. Economist. Director of IEOPP. Corresponding Member of the Academy of Sciences. Played a major role in the emergence within Soviet economic science of economists who are able to throw light on urgent policy questions.

Albegov M. M. Economist. Research worker at SOPS. Played an important part in the calculation and utilisation of the optimal prices of fuels at locations throughout the country.

Bachurin A. V. Planner. A Deputy Chairman of Gosplan. D.Sc. Critical of some of the ideas of the optimal planners.

Baranov E. F. Economist. Research worker at TSEMI. Specialist in regional input–output and regional aspects of optimal planning.

Birman I. Ya. Economist. Head of the department of economic-mathematical methods of the Central Scientific Institute for Technical-Economic Research in the Building Materials Industry. Played an important part in calculating and publicising optimal plans for the development and location of industries. Supporter of economic reform.

Boyarsky A. Ya. Economic-statistician. Head of TsSU's Research Institute for the Design of Computing Centres and Systems of Economic Information, and of the department of statistics of the Economics Faculty of Moscow State University. Professor, D.Sc. Opponent of the Kantorovich–TSEMI position on optimal planning. Supported the break-through.

Bunich P. G. Economist. Corresponding Member of the Academy of

Sciences. In the late 1960s a leading specialist at TSEMI on the development of the reform.

Cheremushkin S. D. Agricultural economist. Head of the section on economic problems of land management and the cadastre at VNIESKh. Professor, D.Sc. The leading figure in cadastral work.

Chernyavsky V. O. Planner. Head of a sub-department of Gosplan in the 1960s. D.Sc. Consistent supporter of the use of mathematical methods in planning.

Drogichinsky N. E. Planner. Head of the department for the new methods of planning and economic incentives of Gosplan.

Dudkin L. M. Economist. Deputy head of the plan-economic administration, and head of the department for the utilisation of mathematics and computing technology, of the Ministry of the Chemical Industry, in the 1960s.

Efimov A. N. Economist. Academician. Director of Gosplan's Research Institute. Chairman of the Scientific Council of the Academy of Sciences on The Economic Competition of the Two Systems.

Eidel'man M. R. Economic-statistician. Head of the section for the balance of the national economy of TsSU. Professor, D.Sc. Played a leading role in TsSU's work on input–output.

Fedorenko N. P. Chemical engineer. Specialist in the economics of the chemical industry. Director of TSEMI. Academician. Chairman of the Scientific Council of the Academy of Sciences on Optimal Planning. Member of the Presidium of the Academy of Sciences and Secretary of the Economics Section of the Academy of Sciences. Head of the department of mathematical methods of analysis of the economy of the Economics Faculty of Moscow State University, and of the department of economic-mathematical methods of the Institute for the Management of the National Economy. The organisational leader of the mathematical economists since Nemchinov's death.

*Gerchuk Ya. P. Economist. In the 1920s research worker at Narkomfin's *kon''yunktur* institute[1] (of which Kondratiev was the Director). Wrote a monograph *Seasonal fluctuations in industry* (1930). In 1959–61 popularised linear programming. In 1965 published controversial pamphlet on the limitations of linear programming. Opposed extremist ideas about economic reform. d. 1969.

Glushkov V. M. Applied mathematician, specialist in computers. Academician, Director of the Institute of Cybernetics of the Ukrainian Academy of Sciences, and Vice President of the Ukrainian Academy of Sciences. Author of *The theory of algorithms* (1961), *An introduction to the theory of self improving systems* (1962), *The electronic digital computer*

---

[1] A *kon''yunktur* institute is one which studies the current economic situation, e.g. the National Institute of Economic and Social Research in the UK.

for engineering calculations (1963), *An introduction to cybernetics* (1964) . . . .
Played a leading role both in the development of computers and in
their use in management information and control systems. Head of a
direction in Soviet management science distinct from mathematical
economics.

Kantorovich L. V. Mathematician. Graduated and became university
teacher at age 18, acting professor at 20, awarded title of professor at
22, D.Sc. at 23. Elected Corresponding Member of the Academy of
Sciences in 1958, full Member in 1964. Awarded State Prize in 1949,
decorated with the Order of Lenin, the order 'Mark of honour', the
order 'Red Banner of Labour' (twice), and many medals. Head of
the department of mathematical economics of the Mathematics
Institute of the Siberian branch of the Academy of Sciences in the
1960s. Specialist in functional analysis (e.g. author of the axiomatic
theory of K spaces[1]), computing mathematics (e.g. co-author of
Approximate methods of higher analysis (1936) and an important contributor to the development and use of computers) and mathematical
economics (e.g. discoverer of linear programming). Outstanding
scholar, operational researcher (e.g. played a leading role in introducing optimal production scheduling into the steel industry in the
1960s) and teacher (helped train specialists in computing mathematics from 1948 and mathematical economics from 1958, at the
mathematics faculty of Leningrad State University). The major
intellectual influence on the development of research on optimal
planning and functioning.

Karagedov R. G. Economist. Research worker at IEOPP. D.Sc. Opponent of the idea that perfect competition should be regarded as a
model for the optimal functioning of a socialist planned economy.

Kats A. I. Political economist. D.Sc. Senior Research Officer at the
Institute of the World Economy and International Relations. Critic of
the Kantorovich–TSEMI conception of optimal planning.

Khachaturov T. S. Economist, Academician. The leading figure in the
development of the official investment appraisal methods. Sceptical
about optimal planning.

Klotsvog F. N. Head of a sector of Gosplan's Research Institute. Played
an important part in the work of this Institute on input–output.
Awarded State Prize in 1968 for work on input–output (together
with A. N. Efimov, E. F. Baranov, L. Ya. Berri, E. B. Yershov,
V. V. Kossov, L. E. Mints, S. S. Shatalin and M. R. Eidel'man).

Kossov V. V. Economist. Head of the department of economic planning of the Plekhanov Institute. Professor, D.Sc. Pupil of Nemchinov's.

[1] The linear semi ordered spaces on which Kantorovich worked are called K(antorovich)
spaces in his honour.

Kovalev V. I.   Electrical engineer. PhD (in economics). Head of Gosplan's Chief Computing Centre. Reader at the Academy of Social Sciences attached to the CC, member of the editorial board of the journal of the Institute of Economics. Opponent of the TSEMI position on optimal planning and functioning. d. 1971.

Leibkind Yu. R.   Economist at TSEMI. Head of the laboratory for the design of the ASPR.

Lemeshev M. Ya.   Economist. Head of the section for forecasting the development of agriculture of Gosplan's Research Institute in the 1960s, and author of a book which uses input–output to study the relationship between agriculture and the rest of the economy. Subsequently a research worker at IEOPP and working on the implications of the systems approach to economic planning and management.

Lur'e A. L.   Economist. Professor at Moscow State University, Senior Research Officer at TSEMI. D.Sc. Important contributor to the utilisation of mathematical methods in transport planning and economic theory. Played an important role in the development of the official method for comparing investment projects. Contributed to probability theory. Member of the editorial board of the journal of TSEMI. d. 1970.

Makarov A. A.   Electrical engineer. Research worker at the Siberian Energy Institute. D.Sc. Played a major role in the building of optimisation models of the energy sector of the economy.

Makarov V. L.   Applied mathematician. Head of a laboratory at the Institute of Mathematics of the Siberian branch of the Academy of Sciences in the 1960s. Specialist in linear theory.

Melent'ev L. A.   Engineer. Academician. Director of the Siberian Energy Institute.

Mikhalevsky B. N.   Economist. D.Sc. Research worker at TSEMI and deputy editor of its journal. Author of quantitative growth models aimed at providing a basis for medium and long term planning. Work shows wide knowledge of the literature in English, German and French.

Myasnikov V. A.   Head of the Chief Administration for computers of Gostekhnika. A leading figure in the development of the OGAS.

Nekrasov N. N.   Academician. Chairman of SOPS. Awarded State Prize in 1970 (together with Academician Fedorenko) for work on the economics of the chemical industry. Member of the editorial board of the journal of TSEMI.

Nemchinov V. S.   Economist, specialising for many years in statistics, especially agricultural statistics and statistical theory (in 1946 he published the book *Chebyshev polynomials and mathematical statistics*).

Member of the collegium of TsSU 1926–30. Head of the department of statistics at the Timiryazev agricultural academy 1928–49, and Director of the latter 1940–8. Academician from 1946. Professor at the department of political economy of the Academy of Social Sciences attached to the CC 1947–57. Member of the Bureau of the economics and law section (from 1963 the economics section) of the Academy of Sciences 1949–64. Member of the Presidium of the Academy of Sciences 1953–62. Academician-Secretary of the economics, philosophy and law section of the Academy of Sciences 1954–8. Chairman of SOPS 1949–64. Outstanding organiser, teacher and scholar. Provided the statistical data for Stalin's speech 'On the grain front' (May 1928). *Publicly opposed Lysenko's views on genetics at the August 1948 session of VASKhNIL* (as a result of which he lost his post as Director of the Timiryazev agricultural academy). Struggled against the liquidators in statistics in 1950–5 (he published an article 'Statistics as a science' *in 1952*). Advocated economic reform 1961–4. Played the major organisational role in the emergence of the economic-mathematical direction in Soviet economic science. d. 1964.

**Novozhilov V. V.* Economist. Head of the laboratory of systems of economic evaluation of the Leningrad branch of TSEMI 1965–70. Professor, D.Sc. (his doctoral dissertation, on the choice between investment variants, was defended in 1941). University teacher from 1915 (b. 1892). Member of the Scientific Council of the Academy of Sciences on the use of mathematics in economics and planning, and of the Scientific Council on the scientific bases of planning. Member of the editorial board of the journal of TSEMI. Awarded the Lenin prize in 1965 (together with Kantorovich and Nemchinov). Head of the economics and statistics section and member of the Council of the Leningrad House of Scholars. Worked for many years on the theory of optimal planning and functioning, especially the choice between investment variants (he advocated the present value criterion) and price formation (he emphasised the importance of opportunity costs). d. 1970.

**Oblomsky Ya. A.* Planner. PhD in economics. Worked for many years in the metal industry. For 8 years head of the secretariat of a Deputy Chairman of the Council of Ministers. 1957–60 deputy chief scientific secretary of the Presidium of the Academy of Sciences. In the 1960s head of the department for the introduction of economic-mathematical methods into national economic planning of Gosplan. Member of the editorial board of the journal of TSEMI. d. 1971.

Pashkov A. I. Political economist. Corresponding Member of the Academy of Sciences. Chairman of the Scientific Council of the Academy of Sciences on The Economic Laws of the Growth of

Socialism and its Development into Communism. Critic of the theory of optimal planning and functioning.

Petrakov N. Ya.   Economist at TSEMI. D.Sc. A deputy director of TSEMI. Working on the development of the reform, and in particular on prices.

Pugachev V. F.   Head of a laboratory at TSEMI. A leading theorist of optimal planning and functioning.

Rakovsky M. E.   Planner. A Deputy Chairman of Gosplan. Member of the editorial board of the journal of TSEMI. An influential figure in the development of the ASPR.

Shatilov N. F.   Economist at IEOPP. The leading figure in IEOPP's work on numerical dynamic interindustry models.

Strumilin S. G.   Economist. Academician. Doyen of Soviet economists. Participant in the revolutionary movement (b. 1877). Active supporter of the party in the 1920s. Supported the breakthrough. Sceptical about the Kantorovich–TSEMI position on optimal planning.

Trapeznikov V. A.   Engineer. Academician. Director of IPU. A Deputy Chairman of Gostekhnika. Chairman USSR national committee on automation. The leading Soviet specialist on automation and the head of a direction within Soviet management science distinct from mathematical economics.

**Vainshtein A. L.*   Economist. Specialist on national wealth and national income. Professor, D.Sc. Research worker at Narkomfin's *kon''yunktur* institute in the 1920s, where he specialised in agricultural economics. In detention 1937–55. Prominent research worker at TSEMI in the 1960s. d. 1970.

Val'tukh K. K.   Economist. Research worker at IEOPP. Critic of one sided economic interpretation of programming theory.

Volchkov B. A.   Planner. A chief specialist at Gosplan. A leading figure in the development of the ASPR.

Volkonsky V. A.   Research worker at TSEMI. Head of the laboratory of mathematical problems of national economic planning. D.Sc. A leading theorist of optimal planning and functioning. Member of the editorial board of the journal of TSEMI.

**Yushkov L. P.*   Author of 1928 paper which contains the basic ideas of optimal planning and functioning.

IMPORTANT DATES

1928 (October)   Yushkov publishes 'The basic question of planning methodology'. He criticises the view that the existence of a planning organisation is adequate to ensure that socialism is more efficient than capitalism. He suggests a method of comparing investment variants, and the use of interest, rent and prices, to ensure that it is more efficient.

1929   The break-through.

1929 (December)   Stalin addresses the agricultural economists. Political economy becomes the 'theoretical' justification of 'practical' decisions already taken.

1952   Stalin publishes *Economic problems of socialism in the USSR*.

1956 (February)   Stalin's theoretical legacy criticised at the 20th Congress. Way open for the reestablishment of a science which can help resolve questions of planning practice.

1957–9   Nemchinov campaigns for the utilisation of mathematical methods in economics and planning.

1958   Laboratory for economic-mathematical methods created in the Academy of Sciences.

1959   Kantorovich's book *Economic calculation of the best use of resources* at last published.

1960 (April)   Conference on the utilisation of mathematical methods in economic research and planning held in Moscow.

1961 (October)   Stalin's policies criticised at the 22nd Congress. Way open for the discussion of alternatives to the administrative economy.

1962–4   Nemchinov advocates economic reform.

1963 (May)   Government adopts a decision to improve the introduction of computers and automated management systems into the national economy.
TSEMI established.

1965 (September)   Meeting of the CC at which the economic reform is approved.

[xix]

1966 (November)   2 day debate on optimal planning in the Academy of Sciences.

1967 (August)   CC decree emphasises the importance of research on optimal planning and functioning.

Scientific Council of the Academy of Sciences on optimal planning and management of the national economy set up.

1968 (August)   USSR supports socialism in Czechoslovakia.

1969 (December)   Meeting of the CC at which the General Secretary delivers speech on the economic situation which shows that economic reform of the Hungarian type in the USSR is unacceptable to the authorities.

1971 (December)   First all-Union conference on optimal planning and management of the national economy.

There exist in the USSR several institutes and many research workers engaged in the application of mathematical methods to improving the planning and management of the economy. Mathematical methods are being widely used in the planning organs.

What does the operations researcher do? Here he is, faced by his fundamental difficulty. The future is uncertain. Nature is unpredictable, and enemies and allies are even more so. He has no good general purpose technique, neither maximizing expected somethings, nor *max-min*ing, nor gaming it, to reveal his preferred strategy. How can he find the optimal course of action to recommend to his decisionmaker?

The simple answer is that he probably cannot. The same answer is also the beginning of wisdom in this business. There has been altogether too much obsession with optimizing on the part of operations researchers, and I include both grand optimizing and sub-optimizing. Most of our relations are so unpredictable that we do well to get the right sign and order of magnitude of first differentials. In most of our attempted optimizations we are kidding our customers or ourselves or both. If we can show our customer how to make a better decision than he would otherwise have made, we are doing well, and all that can reasonably be expected of us.

And this much we frequently can do.

C. J. Hitch
(*Operations Research*, 1960 pp. 443–4)

Using mathematical programming methods, the programme computed is of course 'optimal' in the mathematical sense, it is a constrained maximum or minimum solution of a given mathematical extremum problem. This optimality, however, is a *relative* one, valid only under given simplifying assumptions, regarding definite political targets and expressed in the constraints and in the objective function of the model. In a series of computations we determine 10 or 50 'optimal' plans, each of them is *relatively* optimal. The significance of mathematical planning is not the search for 'optimality', which is only the blue bird of economic theory, but the exploration of feasibilities; the explanation of interdependencies between conflicting goals; and the improvement of efficiency.

J. Kornai
(*Economics of Planning*, 1970, pp. 12–13)

INTRODUCTION: THE USE OF MATHEMATICS IN SOVIET ECONOMICS – AN HISTORICAL SURVEY

It would be difficult to name another branch of knowledge, with the possible exception of biology, that suffered more from the personality cult than economics.

Report of the 1964 round table of economists and mathematicians
(*Ekonomisty i matematiki* [1965], p. 9.)

During the 1920s vigorous discussion of the problems involved in the rapid socialist industrialisation of backward Russia took place among Soviet economists. Much of the 'new' Western economics of the post World War II period, such as the discussion of the economic problems of the developing countries, growth models and input–output, was simply the rediscovery and development of the fruitful Soviet work of the 1920s.[1]

During this heroic period the use of mathematical methods was widespread. Indeed, in an article published in 1928, L. P. Yushkov discussed what later became a central problem of the theory of the optimally functioning socialist economy; how to create a system of planning that would provide the 'semi-automatic optimality' of the development of the national economy, combining optimal national economic development with maximal operational independence for the separate parts of the economic system (Yushkov [1928]). After 1929, however, the situation changed. In a speech on the relationship between agricultural economics and agricultural policy delivered in December 1929, at the time of the bitter struggle to impose collectivisation on the peasants, Stalin criticised those 'Soviet' economists who had failed to realise that the function of agricultural economics was to provide arguments for his agricultural policies. He criticised Chayanov, Groman and Bazarov by name, and referred to TsSU's pioneering balance of the national economy for 1923–4 as a mere 'game with figures'. The only economist mentioned favourably in this speech was Nemchinov, who had supplied Stalin with useful statistics on agriculture (Stalin [1929b]). Subsequently many able economists, such as

[1] See the Soviet essays of the 1920s collected and translated in Spulber [1964].

Kondratiev, Groman, Feldman, Chayanov, Preobrazhensky and Vainshtein, were arrested, and exiled or sent to prisons and concentration camps, many never to return. The censorship during the period of the personality cult was far stricter than under NEP. The view that economists should confine themselves to finding arguments in favour of the Government's economic policies – or to use the terminology of the time, that 'in the dialectical unity of theory and practice theory guides practice but practice is the criterion of theoretical truth' – remained orthodox for the rest of Stalin's lifetime. In a work written at the end of his life Stalin decisively rejected the view that the function of political economy 'is to elaborate and develop a scientific theory of the productive forces in social production, a theory of the planning of economic development . . . . The rational organisation of the productive forces, economic planning etc. are not problems of political economy but problems of the economic policy of the directing bodies. These are two different provinces, which must not be confused . . . . Political economy investigates the laws of development of men's relations of production. Economic policy draws practical conclusions from this, gives them concrete shape, and builds its day to day work on them. To foist upon political economy problems of economic policy is to kill it as a science.'

As Yaroshenko, one of the participants in the discussion of the draft textbook of political economy to which Stalin was reacting, put it, in a passage quoted by Stalin: 'healthy discussion of the rational organisation of the productive forces in social production, scientific demonstration of the validity of such organisation' is to be replaced by 'scholastic disputes as to the role of particular categories of socialist political economy – value, commodity, money, credit etc'.[1]

Their task confined in this way, Soviet political economists were mainly engaged in agit-prop, and in particular in demonstrating the virtues of socialism in general and of the latest statement by Stalin in particular, and in enlarging on the sins of capitalism (the height of research was to find a hitherto unused quotation from one of the classics of Marxism–Leninism); and the economic practitioners (engineers and politicians) made decisions on the basis of rules of thumb (as was done in contemporary British and American firms). When in spite of all these obstacles, serious contributions to economic analysis were published, such as the well-known works of Kantorovich and Novozhilov, they were ignored.

[1] All these quotations are from Stalin's essay, 'Concerning the errors of Comrade Yaroshenko', in Stalin [1952]. The subjects which Yaroshenko thought political economy should discuss (the rational organisations of the productive forces, economic planning, formation of social funds etc.), but which Stalin regarded as outside the competence of academics, are precisely those which the present day theory of the optimally functioning socialist economy discusses.

At the 20th Congress Mikoyan[1] criticised Soviet economics. He even compared the number of Soviet economists working on the development of the Soviet economy adversely with the number of American economists working in this field. He recognised that this unfortunate situation was not solely the fault of the economists. He explicitly criticised, some propositions in *Economic problems of socialism in the USSR*, the closing of some research institutes during the period of the personality cult, and the paucity of published economic statistics. After the 20th Congress the number of economists and economic institutes increased,[2] the availability of economic statistics was much expanded, and the range of subjects open to research by economists widened. The study by economists of the rational organisation of the productive forces revived. From 1957 onwards Academician Nemchinov, who had proved his usefulness and reliability in the 1920s, repeatedly advocated the use of quantitative methods of analysis of economic phenomena. Using the 1950 British input–output table as a basis, he began popularising the idea of input–output in the USSR. By emphasising its Russian roots, Marxist orthodoxy and usefulness for planning, Nemchinov played an important role in disseminating the idea of input–output in the USSR. His position within the Academy of Sciences, and his post as Chairman of SOPS, provided a solid organisational basis for action. He himself organised a team of enthusiastic young economists who compiled a regional input–output table. He also provided an institutional framework for this new development in Soviet economics, the economic-mathematical laboratory of the Academy of Sciences, which was founded in 1958 and which subsequently grew into the Central Economic Mathematical Institute. Not only Nemchinov, but also other economists who had made contributions to Soviet economics before 1929, such as Novozhilov, Vainshtein and Konüs, played a prominent role in the development of the economic-mathematical direction within Soviet economic science after the 20th Congress.[3]

In 1958 Kantorovich was elected a Corresponding Member of the Academy of Sciences and became head of the laboratory for the utilisation of statistical and mathematical methods in economics of the Computer Centre of the newly established Siberian branch of the Academy of Sciences. In 1959 his famous and very influential book *Economic calculation of the best use of resources* edited and with a preface by Nemchinov, was published. This book had been written in the first half of the 1940s, and papers containing its main theses were read at the

[1] Mikoyan was a prominent party leader in the 1950s.
[2] Gosplan's Research Institute was founded already at the end of 1955.
[3] The standard English language surveys of the development are ECE [1960], Ward [1960], Johansen [1966], Zauberman [1967], Hardt [1967].

Leningrad Polytechnical Institute in 1940 and at the Institute of Economics in 1943, but its publication had to wait for more propitious times (Vainshtein [1966] p. 25). The purpose of this book was to explain to economists, in a simple non-mathematical way, the relevance of linear programming for economic planning in the USSR. In spite of the fact that the book contains numerous references to party documents, Marx and the labour theory of value, it was greeted by hostile reviews.[1]

Also in 1959 there was published under the editorship of Nemchinov a volume entitled *The use of mathematics in economic research*. This book contains an extensive work, practically a book in itself, by Novozhilov, on the problems of rational decision making in a socialist economy, together with a reprint of Kantorovich's pioneering paper of 1959 on linear programming, and a number of other articles. In 1961 and 1965 two further volumes appeared, with the same title and the same editor.

In April 1960 a conference was held in Moscow to discuss the use of mathematical methods in economic research and planning. Its proceedings were published in a number of volumes. A wide discussion took place, with numerous points of view expressed. Whereas at first the mathematical economists were a small minority struggling to put their views forward in the face both of official inertia and of attacks from the representatives of orthodoxy, the position rapidly changed. In May 1963 the government took a decision to improve the organisation of the introduction of computers and automated management systems into the national economy. The task of introducing mathematical methods and computers in planning was assigned to Gosplan; in the planning and management of supply, and the development of automated management systems, to the USSR Sovnarkhoz, and in accounting and statistics, to TsSU. The Computing Centre of Gosplan was enlarged and reorganised into the Chief Computing Centre of Gosplan, TsSU's research institute for the design of computing centres and systems of economic information was established, and TSEMI was founded.

At the 1964 round table of economists and mathematicians it was the orthodox political economists who were on the defensive, and the report of this meeting was edited in a way critical of the political economists. In 1965 the Lenin prize was awarded to Kantorovich, Novozhilov and Nemchinov, and *Ekonomika i matematicheskie metody*, the journal of TSEMI (published six times a year) commenced publication. At the 1966 debate on optimal planning TSEMI put forward the theory of optimal planning and functioning (outlined in chapter 3), which implied radical changes in the organisation of the economy, and

[1] *Planovoe khozyaistvo* 1960 No. 1, *Kommunist* 1960 No. 15, *Voprosy ekonomiki* 1961 No. 2.

challenged the position of political economy. In 1967, a CC decree on the development of the social sciences drew attention to the importance of 'the development of the theory and methods of optimal planning and functioning of the socialist national economy ... the wide utilisation of computing technology in planning and management', and the Scientific Council of the Academy of Sciences on optimal planning and management of the national economy was established. After the 1968 events in Czechoslovakia had shown what incorrect theoretical views could mean in practice, TSEMI had to desist from its criticism of political economy, while continuing its work on improving planning techniques.[1] The directives of the 24th Congress (April 1971) stated the intention to develop an 'interdepartmental automated system for the gathering and processing of information for accounting, planning and control of the national economy'. An integral part of this programme is the development of an automated system of plan calculations, in which field TSEMI is the leading research organisation. In December 1971 a conference was held in Moscow on optimal planning.[2] Whereas the 1960 conference was largely concerned with visions about the gains in efficiency to be had if computers and mathematical methods were to be widely applied, the 1971 conference was able not only to look to their future uses, but also to survey the numerous fields in which they had already been applied.

Four main themes can be distinguished in the lengthy debate which accompanied the rise of mathematical economics in the USSR. First, many of the old school of political economists regarded the 'mathematical' theory of prices, in which prices are numbers which help a decision maker to arrive at optimal solutions, as contrary to the labour

---

[1] In a paper published in 1968 between the January and the August events in Czechoslovakia, Academician Strumilin even made an ominous comparison between some of the views then being put forward by advocates of an optimally functioning socialist economy, and the views of Groman and Bazarov (Strumilin [1968]). (Groman and Bazarov were prominent, but non-Bolshevik, economists of the 1920s. Groman was tried and found guilty of wrecking activities in 1931. Bazarov was arrested in 1930 and then disappeared.) It was not only in the USSR that the transition to the administrative economy was accompanied by the removal of many of the leading, but non-Bolshevik, economists and planners. In Poland the formulation of the six year plan 1950–5 was preceded by the 'CUP debate' – CUP stands for Central Planning Office – and the removal of the authors of the 1947–9 Reconstruction Plan. (One of the architects of the Reconstruction Plan, Professor C. Bobrowski, then Chairman of the CUP, left Poland in 1949.)

Strumilin's scepticism about optimal planning is scarcely surprising. Novozhilov, who dedicated so many years to working out the theory of optimal planning and functioning, was an orthodox academic economist who in the 1920s suggested curing the 'goods famine' by raising prices. Strumilin, on the other hand, is a Bolshevik who already in 1925 (Strumilin [1925] p. 32) anticipated the thesis that 'We do not need just any growth of productivity of the people's labour. We need a *definite* growth of productivity of the people's labour, namely the growth which ensures a *systematic preponderance* of the socialist sector of the economy over the capitalist sector.' (Stalin [1929].)

[2] This conference was originally scheduled for the autumn of 1969.

theory of value. Secondly, there arose the intellectual and organisational question of the relationship between the new discipline of mathematical economics and the traditional subject of political economy, which continued to be taught and to be an integral part of the Marxist–Leninist world outlook. Thirdly, there arose the question of the quality of the traditional planning methods. Fourthly, there arose the question of the practicability of the proposals of the mathematical economists.

When the models of Kantorovich and Novozhilov were first expounded they were attacked because, as Boyarsky put it, 'in the place of value in the Marxist sense he [Kantorovich] places the relationship of cost on the "last" unit of this or that product and against his will reproduces several propositions of so-called "marginalism"'. (Boyarsky [1960] p. 95). The discussion of the relationship between Marxism and mathematical economics gave rise to a wide debate, both inside and outside the USSR.[1] In this connection the following observations are relevant.

The problem investigated by Marx and those investigated by Soviet mathematical economists are entirely different. Marx was concerned with an analysis of the productive relations of capitalism, with the conflict between social groups, with discovering the laws of motion of capitalism. Soviet mathematical economists are concerned with the rational organisation of the productive forces of a socialist economy. As Kantorovich has clearly explained:

Marxist analysis of the capitalist economy aimed at a more general, fundamental investigation of capitalist production and the study of its basic laws, and for this reason could, of course, abstract from all the temporary transient factors and influences.

Economic calculation (and analysis) in a socialist economy serves as a basis for practical solutions and for this reason it must be more accurate and detailed. It must take into consideration the concrete situation including temporary and accidental circumstances. (Kantorovich [1965b] p. 218.)

The analysis of equilibrium growth paths and the analysis of the factors affecting the prices of particular goods at particular times involve very different considerations, and it is scarcely surprising that different conceptual apparatuses are required.

Marxists have always objected to the marginal productivity theory of distribution because it attempted to explain the distribution of income under capitalism by technological factors (the marginal products of the factors of production) rather than by social ones (i.e. exploitation). Soviet mathematical economists are not developing an apologetic

---

[1] See for example Campbell [1961], Johansen [1963a], [1963b], Dickinson [1963], Konüs [1964], *Ekonomisty i matematiki* [1965].

theory which hides the fact that capitalism is a mode of production based on the exploitation of labour, but are concerned with raising the efficiency of socialism.

In so far as the mathematical economists confine themselves to the development of improved methods of economic calculation, there is no real conflict between their ideas and orthodoxy (although it is still necessary to wage a difficult struggle to get the improved methods of economic calculation adopted on a large scale). In so far as the mathematical economists draw conclusions from the study of the rational organisation of the productive forces for the economic mechanism, it is undoubtedly true that their ideas about the economic mechanism are at variance with orthodox ideas about the economic mechanism. (In this connection one should bear in mind that orthodoxy is not immutable.) The usefulness of the ideas of the mathematical economists for improving the economic mechanism is examined in chapter 6, and the relationship between their work and the economic reform actually being implemented in the USSR is explained in chapter 8.

It is true that the emphasis placed by the mathematical economists on the allocative function of prices and on the usefulness of prices and other value relations, such as rent, quasi rent and the rate of interest as guides to the efficient allocation of resources, is the repetition of an argument much emphasised by the Lausanne school. The conception of value relations as guides to efficient decision making was not originated by Walras, however. It is simply a generalisation of the Ricardian concept of comparative costs as a guide to rational decision making in international trade, and the Ricardian analysis of rent. Emphasis on the allocative function of prices is a wholly understandable reaction to the problems of the administrative economy (some of which are explained in chapters 1 and 2). Moreover, the Ricardo–Pasinetti argument that it is misleading to extend the concept of scarcity prices from non-reproducible to reproducible commodities, and that the function of prices and other value relations in an economy can only be understood in terms of a dynamic model, has been forcefully stated by a number of Soviet mathematical economists (Novozhilov [1963] p. 49, Val'tukh [1970a]). In addition, the institutional framework which most of the optimal planners assume is very different from that assumed by the Lausanne school. Most of the latter study systems in which the enterprises themselves choose their own production plan guided by some rules of the game (such as profit maximisation) and prices determined by tâtonnement or some equivalent process. Novozhilov ([1966] p. 366), on the other hand, considers that the information embodied in prices is 'inadequate for important alterations to the plan, still less for the compilation of perspective plans' but is useful for 'the decentralised fulfilment of a given plan on the basis of *khozraschet* and for small alterations to the plan'. This idea of the usefulness of prices is based upon an argument of Kantorovich's which is considered in general in chapter 5 and with specific reference to the steel industry in chapter 6. In both cases it will be argued that the cases where it is possible to use prices in the way suggested are only a subset of all possible cases. The validity of the conclusions about the economic mechanism which the mathematical economists have drawn from the study of linear programming will be analysed in chapter 5.

There has in fact been some penetrating criticism published in the socialist countries of the work of Kantorovich and his followers, but it has not been produced by those who criticised 'marginalism'. On the practical level, a telling criticism of the policy ideas of the mathematical economists, and well thought out alternative proposals for deepening the economic reform, have come from Ya. G. Liberman. On the theoretical level, the most penetrating criticism has come from mathematical economists such as Gerchuk [1965], who criticised exaggerated ideas in some circles about the applicability of linear programming; Lur'e [1969], who criticised the idea that the rate of interest to be used in investment planning should be identified with the marginal product of capital in an aggregate production function, and put forward an alternative way of determining it; Mikhalevsky [1971], who criticised the assumptions of the general equilibrium approach; and Kornai [1971], who launched an extensive attack on the application of general equilibrium ideas to the economic mechanism.

From a Marxist point of view, the main weakness of the work of the mathematical economists is that it concentrates on the rational organisation of the productive forces and neglects the need to develop the productive relations, thus reviving the Yaroshenko conception of the political economy of socialism. As Kowalik has pointed out, the latter was progressive relative to the Stalinist conception, that it should be concerned with disseminating the false consciousness of a socialist society, but for a Marxist it is the building of socialism, rather than the improvement of the techniques of planning, which is of decisive importance (Kowalik [1964]).

A major issue resulting from the emergence of mathematical economics was the organisational and doctrinal fate of political economy. Before the emergence of mathematical economics, political economy, which is an integral part of the official doctrine of the USSR – Marxism–Leninism – and is disseminated at all levels from evening classes for workers via *Pravda* editorials to the Academy of Social Sciences attached to the CC, had held an unchallenged position in the USSR. Its function was, and had been ever since Stalin's 1929 speech, to provide an ex post 'theoretical' justification of 'practice'.[1] Its inability to assist in the resolution of economic problems was notorious, and was repeatedly pointed out in official statements after Stalin's death. The evident need for a science which could assist in the resolution of economic problems, combined with the inability of political economy to do this, explains the support given to mathematical economics by the authorities in the 1960s.

The mathematical economists considered that whereas the political economists were quite unable to provide guidance as to how to improve the methods of planning and the economic mechanism, they were able to do this. At the November 1966 debate on optimal planning the rivalry between mathematical economics and political economy was clear. At that debate Academician Fedorenko distinguished between two approaches to economics, the descriptive and the constructive. He suggested that the time had come to abandon the descriptive approach, implicitly identified with political economy, in favour of the constructive approach, i.e. the theory of optimal planning, which alone could serve as a source of useful ideas on how to improve the planning and management of the economy. Lur'e added that it would not be so bad if the political economists were in fact descriptive (description is a useful activity), but the trouble was that they were often destructive, hindering the analysis of such problems as how to raise efficiency and how to utilise such levers as profit and rent.

Fedorenko's argument, not surprisingly, aroused much controversy. Professor Tsagolov in rebuttal argued that to distinguish between a descriptive political economy and a constructive political economy was incorrect. There was only one political economy, which was not a mere descriptive science because it formulated the laws characterising the essence of socialism (the basic law of socialism, the law of planned proportional development and so on). In addition there were some suggestions for improving planning practice. It was in this pigeon hole that he placed research on optimal planning. The compilers of the record of this debate in the journal of TSEMI indignantly note that to accept this subordinate role for the theory of optimal planning would mean practically abandoning it as a scientific theory. At the same meeting Pashkov also advocated maintaining the subordination of economic-mathematical modelling to political economy.

The reason why optimal planning challenged the position of political economy is that it is not much use calculating optimal plans if the economy functions in such a way that the optimal plans are not imple-

---

[1] As Fedorenko has quite rightly written, 'Until recently economic science was often used, not so much as the theoretical basis for working out the most efficient economic policy, but for commenting on decisions which had already been taken.' (Fedorenko [1968a] p. 7.)

mented and non-optimal decisions are made instead. In an instructive article (Belkin [1964]), Belkin and Birman wrote that:

Electronics has brought no really tangible benefit to the planning and management of the economy, mostly because the existing practice of planning and management is not adapted to the devising and particularly the effecting of optimal decisions.

Just one example. It is widely known that the compilation of optimal schemes of freight shipment can yield a quite tangible saving. This is not a complicated task. Many articles and books have been written and not a few dissertations defended, but almost no freight is shipped by the optimal schemes. Why? Simply because the transport organisations are given plans based on ton kilometres. One can establish computer centres, and conceive superb algorithms, but nothing will come of it as long as the transport organisations reckon plan fulfilment in ton kilometres.

Precisely because the administrative economy often operates in such a way as to frustrate attempts to implement optimal plans, an important part of the work on replacing the traditional planning methods by optimal planning must be concerned with proposals for transforming the existing economic system into an optimally functioning economic system, that is an economic system which operates in such a way as to facilitate, rather than hinder, the implementation of optimal plans. TSEMI considers that it is impossible to work out such proposals, for example payment for the use of natural resources, without a scientific theory which explains both the need for such categories and how to calculate their numerical magnitude. This is the role which the theory of the optimally functioning economic system aspires to fill, and there naturally arises the question of its relationship with the already existing discipline of political economy. TSEMI's point of view was clearly explained by one of its deputy directors at the November 1966 debate on optimal planning.

Let us take motor transport. How can it use the index of profit and expand direct contacts, when the tariffs take account neither of the type of freight, nor the capacity of the lorries, nor the limitation of transport? Is it possible, for example, to establish the same tariff for the delivery of bread to bakers at the usual time and at the peak with limited transport resources? How is it possible without taking all these aspects into account in prices to harmonise the interests of the enterprises with the interest of the whole national economy?

I have been working on the use of mathematical models in the economy since 1958. I have to recognise, unfortunately, that up till now in the industry in which I am working (motor transport) the real saving from the introduction of the new methods has been considerably less than we expected. But this is not the fault of the officials in transport, and it is not the fault of the models. Because of inadequacies in price formation the minimisation of costs leads to the worsening of practically all the indices of the work of motor transport. The same is observed in other fields.

Precisely for this reason we say: a radical improvement in the practice of planning and management of the national economy is impossible without the creation of a consistent economic theory, in which the system of prices, the principles of incentives, the forms of relationships between the various levels of the national economy etc. find their logical explanation.

Some participants in the discussion say that 'some of your practical suggestions are very good, we completely accept them.' V. P. Dyachenko noted a number of points of contact in the field of practical suggestions, regarding payment for the use of natural resources, taking account of scarcities. But how is it possible to explain the necessity for payment for capital and natural resources and to give methods for their practical calculation starting from the conception of the average costs of an industry as the basis for price formation? In our opinion it is impossible to do this. That is why we are struggling not only for the acceptance of concrete suggestions but also for giving them a precise theoretical basis, which is very important for the construction of a strict and integrated system of an optimally functioning economy. (*Diskussiya* [1968] pp. 120–1.)

The criticism of political economy by the optimal planners appears to have had a positive effect on the work of the Institute of Economics, which is shown both by its publications and by its research interests. In 1967–70 some of the most interesting studies of the economic reform were produced by the Institute of Economics, at a time when TSEMI was publishing works on optimal prices and methods for iterative aggregation which can scarcely be regarded as a contribution to the understanding of economic reform. Rakitsky [1968], which was sponsored by the Institute of Economics, advocates an economic reform which combines an improvement in the organisation of the productive forces with an improvement of productive relations. Ya. Liberman [1970], which was also sponsored by the Institute of Economics, contains useful suggestions for the further development of the reform, and its criticism of TSEMI's ideas about the role of optimal prices in the economy is not dogmatic but powerful and well argued. Similarly, the Institute of Economics is playing an important role in research on the economic aspects of technical progress. By 1970 the position of the Institute of Economics had evolved so far that it sponsored a book (Zhamin [1970]) which fully accepted the key doctrines of the optimal planners. A further sign of the end of the rift between these two institutes was the publication in 1971 of a book on forecasting (Gatovsky [1971b]), edited by the Director of the Institute of Economics and containing papers by authors from the Institute of Economics, TSEMI, IEOPP and other institutes.

In a book published in 1968, two years after he made his speech calling in effect for the replacement of political economy by economic cybernetics, Academician Fedorenko stated that:

In the complex and continuously developing system of economic sciences the decisive place belongs to political economy. Marxist–Leninist political economy, which reveals the objective laws of development of economic life, plays an immense role in forming and strengthening the scientific world outlook of the Soviet people. At the same time it is the theoretical basis for the actual running of the socialist national economy, for the building of a socialist and communist national economy, for the analysis of world developments and the relationship between our country and other countries. (Fedorenko [1968a] p. 7.)

Academician Fedorenko envisaged in this book the writing of a fundamental work, *The political economy of socialism*, a most important part of which would be the theoretical bases of the system of an optimally functioning economy (Fedorenko [1968a] p. 16). In 1970, TSEMI's views on the economic mechanism appeared in a book (Fedorenko [1970a]) the first chapter of which was pure orthodoxy.

By the end of the period a *modus vivendi* had been reached, along the lines suggested by Professor Tsagolov at the 1966 debate, in which TSEMI's right to put forward ideas on improving planning practice was generally accepted, and TSEMI had disavowed its earlier critical attitude to political economy. TSEMI had recognised that only Marxist–Leninist political economy can form the theoretical basis of the economic policy of the party and the socialist state. Political economy was discussed in the press, lectures were given on it in the factories, and it was taught to students throughout the higher educational system. Mathematical economics was a specialised academic discipline taught to future planners.[1]

The extreme position, implicit in TSEMI's stance at the 1966 debate, but subsequently recognised to be incorrect, was that optimal policy conclusions could only be derived from a study of the conditions for the maximisation of the national economic objective function. This is regarded in the USSR as incorrect for two reasons.

First, correct policy conclusions can only be derived by analysing the concrete problems from the standpoint of the policy objectives of the party. As the late director of Gosplan's Chief Computing Centre has clearly explained, in the course of a critique of the idea of deriving policy conclusions from a national economic objective function:

The aims of social production at any stage of the historical process always have a socio-economic character, expressing the motion of the productive and social relations, the development of the productive forces. These cannot be fully formalised and are always determined, and will be determined, by society. You see with the help of a formal apparatus it is impossible to determine these aims concretely, for example what material and other resources are necessary for the fulfilment by society of its international duty, what measures it is necessary to put into practice for improving the physical and intellectual development of the members of society, the communist upbringing of the masses, how to organise the pre-school upbringing of children, the leisure of the working people and so on. All these and other non-political actions of the socialist state are determined not by formal schemes and models, but on the basis of scientific foresight of the processes of social development, including the objective

---

[1] The significance of the challenge to political economy by optimal planning is analysed in chapter 7.

economic laws. This is a creative process. Any law, including the basic economic law, taken in its most general form, does not determine a concrete aim. The latter is born, made concrete and obtains real features, as a result of the analysis, generalisation and scientific foresight of the development of all sides of social life. The working out of such an aim is the highest achievement of scientific thought, which synthesises the achievements of all sciences, and not just one branch of scientific knowledge, still less one of the applied sciences. It is therefore no accident that the concrete goals of social development are worked out by the Communist party on the basis of its pro- gramme, scientifically formulating the general goals and tasks of social development. Already V. I. Lenin, speaking about the tasks of Gosplan, underlined that they consist of working out ways and means of achieving those goals, which the party places before the national economy. (Kovalev [1970] p. 38.)

From this it follows that Marxist–Leninist political economy, which is that part of Marxism–Leninism which formulates the economic laws of socialism, and which provides some of the tools for the analysis, generalisation and scientific foresight of social processes, must have primacy over optimal planning, which is simply a branch of applied mathematics which enables some of the party's concrete objectives to be attained in the most efficient way. Throughout this period the official view was that economics (including mathematical economics) was a party (*partiinii*) science, and that fruitful work was only possible on the basis of the principle of party mindedness (*partiinost'*). This point was made at the beginning of the period by Boyarsky ([1961] p. 61) and at the end of it in the explanations that followed the CC's December 1971 criticism of the Institute of Economics.

Secondly, as Schumpeter, Wiles and Pasinetti argued long ago, 'growth' is more important than 'choice'. This argument has been strongly emphasised by Karagedov. It has also been stated by Kats. In their policy proposals the optimal planners stress one half of the Ricardian legacy, the scarcity of resources and the importance of rent. The party stresses the other half, produced goods, technical progress and capital accumulation, i.e. precisely those factors which have prevented the gloomy prophecies of the dismal science from being realised and have ensured unparalleled prosperity for ever increasing numbers.

The favourable evaluation of the work of TSEMI by the Presidium of the Academy of Sciences in 1969 made it clear that by the end of 1969 the Academy of Sciences regarded TSEMI, which was only founded in 1963, as being one of the two leading economics institutes, and the chairman of the commission looking into the work of these two institutes particularly approved of TSEMI's quest for an optimally functioning economic system (*Razvitie* [1970]). In 1971 Academician Fedorenko became a member of the Presidium of the Academy of Sciences and secretary of its economics section, clear indications of the strong position which TSEMI had acquired, within a few years of its foundation, in the

Academy of Sciences. Another sign of the strong position which the mathematical economists had acquired within Soviet economic science by the end of this period was the fact that in the CC decree of December 1971 criticising the work of the Institute of Economics the latter was instructed, inter alia, to pay more attention to 'the contemporary achievements of economic science and the new methods of research, in particular economic-mathematical modelling'. (*O rabote* [1972] p. 5.)

The attitude of the optimal planners to the traditional planning methods was made very clear at the March 1968 conference on problems of growth and improved planning, organised by the scientific council of the Academy of Sciences on the laws governing the transition from socialism to communism. At this conference S. Shatalin, a deputy director of TSEMI, put forward the thesis of the three conceptions of planning.

The essence of this thesis is the proposition that at the present time there are being worked out and developed three conceptions of planning the national economy. The first conception exists and is realised in the process of working out the national economic plans. This conception, in the opinion of S. Shatalin, is non-scientific, because it starts off from goals for the output of the most important means of production. The second conception is beginning to be introduced into planning. It is based on the utilisation of the input–output model and it starts from goals for final output. Finally, the third conception of planning, which S. Shatalin regards as the only really scientific one, 'adequate for the essence of a socialist economy', is the conception of optimal planning. (Bor [1969] p. 5.)

This thesis has come in for sharp criticism from Professor M. Z. Bor of the economics department of the Academy of Social Sciences attached to the CC. Bor argues that Soviet plans have always aimed at the efficient allocation of resources, and that they have always had a scientific basis. 'The supporters of the so-called theory of optimal planning, however, in their articles and books treat national economic planning as in essence not scientific but empirical. From this follows their false premise about the necessity for creating a theory of scientific planning under the head "the theory of optimal planning".' (Bor [1969] p. 7.)

In 1969 Bachurin, a deputy chairman of Gosplan, expressed his irritation at the attitude of the optimal planners to the traditional methods of planning. (Bachurin [1969].) 'In the opinion of the authors of the system of an optimally functioning economy it turns out that really scientific planning will only become possible with the introduction of the system of working out an optimal plan suggested by them. From this it follows that the practice of planning in the USSR as it has existed for many years was based only on intuition, on subjective decisions, and did not have a scientific basis.' He replied to the accusation that Gosplan's methods were unscientific by accusing the supporters of the theory of optimal planning of a lack of orthodoxy, of having a position on some issues similar to that of supporters of 'market socialism'. In 1970 Kovalev, then head of Gosplan's Chief Computing Centre, strongly attacked 'the nihilistic approach to planning the national economy and especially to centralised planning, which exists among some supporters of the "theory of optimal planning".' (Kovalev [1970].)

Why the supporters of optimal planning consider that the traditional planning methods are 'unscientific', and that it is necessary to replace them by optimal planning, will become clearer by analysing whether or not the balance method is capable of leading to the compilation of consistent plans.[1] Such an analysis is contained in chapter 1.

In 1971, a book produced by officials of the department of Gosplan USSR responsible for the reform explicitly endorsed the central conception of the theory of the optimally functioning socialist economy, the fact that the solution to an optimal planning problem yields not only physical indices but also value indices (prices, rent, quasi rent, the rate of interest) and that the use of these value indices permits the harmonisation of the interests of national economic development with the maximisation of its local optimality criterion by each enterprise. (Drogichinsky [1971] pp. 180–1 and p. 192.[2]) With a lag of thirty years Kantorovich's key proposition about the implications for the economic mechanism of the theorem of the characteristics of an optimal plan had received the imprimatur of Gosplan. (In chapters 5 and 6 it will be argued that this key idea is not in general valid, and in chapters 7 and 8 it will be argued that the economic mechanism should be derived on entirely different grounds.)

During the 1960s the proposals of the mathematical economists were repeatedly attacked (and still more ignored) by economists and administrators on the ground that, whatever their theoretical merits, they were so far removed from the real problems of the economy as to be quite impracticable. For example, in a working commission on prices of the all-union conference on the application of economic-mathematical methods in the planning and management of branches of the economy (1966), a plenary session of which was addressed by Academician Kantorovich, when an official of the Ukrainian price fixing apparatus was reproached with ignoring the ideas of the optimal planners in her outline of how work on the forthcoming price revision

---

[1] The criticism by the Soviet mathematical economists in the 1960s of the traditional planning methods is analogous to the criticisms by British econometricians in the same period of the methods used by the Treasury for forecasting and controlling the economy. In both cases the criticism has had considerable impact on the techniques used.

[2] These passages were written by Kossov.

was being organised, she replied 'well of course all that has nothing to do with practical matters'. It is undoubtedly true that the ideas expounded by TSEMI in the middle 1960s were far removed from the problems of the Soviet economic mechanism. TSEMI dealt with this criticism by establishing a laboratory for the study of the role of *khozraschet* in an optimally managed socialist economy, and by attracting to TSEMI people such as Petrakov and Bunich, who are economists but not mathematical economists. By 1971 both some of the works published by TSEMI (such as Bunich [1970]) and TSEMI's concrete proposals for the further development of the reform were concerned with the real problems of the Soviet economy.

At the beginning of the 1970s the position of mathematical economics within Soviet economic science is entirely different from that at the beginning of the 1960s.

Formerly it was necessary to argue, demonstrate, substantiate, convince. Today it would seem that everyone is convinced, openly at any rate they do not argue, and many even help us. Conditions have been created for the development of the economic-mathematical direction in Soviet economic science: there exist scientific institutes and special faculties [within higher educational establishments]; books and journals are published, dissertations are defended; prizes are awarded. But, and this is the chief difficulty, practical contributions are awaited from our work, real benefits are required from us, we are required to give answers to numerous important and difficult questions. (I. Birman [1970] p. 5.)

The kinds of answers the mathematical economists are giving to the 'numerous important and difficult questions' of planning and economic management and the extent to which they can be regarded as 'practical contributions' will be considered in chapters 4 and 6 below. Before examining these answers however, it is necessary to consider some of the non-optimalities of the administrative economy, a study of which makes very clear why some individuals and organisations lay so much stress on the need for the optimisation of the economy, and then to describe and analyse the theoretical framework within which the proposals of the optimal planners are being made, the theory of the optimally functioning socialist economy.

The mathematical economists are not the only group of research workers offering answers to the 'numerous important and difficult questions' of planning and management. Work on improving the management and planning of the national economy, stimulating technical progress, raising labour productivity and improving the organisation of labour is proceeding in a large number of scientific research institutes, both departmental (such as the Scientific Research Institutes of the Ministry of Finance, the State Committee on Labour and Wages, the Ministry of Agriculture, Gosplan and Gossnab) and academic (such as the Ukrainian Cybernetics Institute and IPU). Some departmental institutes, such as the State Committee on Labour and Wages' scientific research institute and Gossnab's scientific research institute, have worked closely with TSEMI. On the other hand, the Ministry of Agriculture's scientific research institute is pursuing a policy with respect to land valuation opposed to that of TSEMI. The outlook of the Ukrainian Cybernetics Institute is not identical with that of TSEMI, and its Director, Academician Glushkov, has contrasted the ability to use computers to solve practical problems of the mathematical economists unfavourably with that of researchers at his own institute (Glushkov [1970]). An aspect of the relationship between the work of TSEMI and that of IPU is briefly explained in chapter 3.

SUMMARY

The use of quantitative methods in Soviet economics was common in the 1920s. During the period of the personality cult the ideas of economists about the economic mechanism and the methods of economic calculation were not welcome, and decisions were made by politicians and engineers using a limited arsenal of methods of economic calculation. Economists were expected to confine themselves to apologetics.

After the 20th Congress the application of quantitative methods in economic analysis and planning developed rapidly. The ideas of Kantorovich and TSEMI were controversial throughout this period, and their application proceeded slowly, but by the end of it they were being taught on a wide scale and had attained a solid organisational position within Soviet economic science. Research on optimal planning was coordinated by a Scientific Council of the Academy of Sciences, a central academic research institute existed, there were other institutes partly engaged on work in this field, and research workers aimed at applying the theory of optimal planning and functioning to particular problems were working in numerous departments and departmental institutes.

By 1971 the important questions were, to what extent could the application of mathematical methods help raise the efficiency of economic planning and management? Could TSEMI throw more or less light on how to raise efficiency, stimulate technical progress and improve the management of enterprises, associations and the national economy as a whole than other organisations working in this field?

1. THE CONSISTENCY OF THE CURRENT PLANS

THE PROBLEM

If there existed the universal mind – that projected itself into the scientific fancy of Laplace; a mind that would register simultaneously all the processes of nature and of society, that could measure the dynamics of their motion, that could forecast the results of their interactions, such a mind, of course, could *a priori* draw up a faultless and exhaustive economic plan, beginning with the number of hectares of wheat and coming down to the last button for a vest. In truth, the bureaucracy often conceives that just such a mind is at its disposal; that is why it so easily frees itself from the control of the market and of Soviet democracy.

L. D. Trotsky (1932) (Trotsky [1932] p. 8.)

All Soviet enterprises have a *tekhpromfinplan* which prescribes in detail their activity during the planned year. It is divided into ten sections:

1   Basic indices (summary table)
2   Plan of production and sales
3   Plan for raising the efficiency of production
4   Plan norms
5   Investment plan
6   Supply plan
7   Labour and wages plan
8   Plan for profit, cost and profitability
9   Plan for economic incentive funds
10 Financial plan

The *tekhpromfinplan* is worked out by a process of administrative iteration between the enterprise and its administrative superiors during the planning year (the year preceding the planned year). In the light of its own possibilities and its knowledge of the goals of the higher bodies, each enterprise sends in suggestions to its ministry. The ministry receives two streams of suggestions for its plan, from the enterprises and from Gosplan USSR. The suggestions from Gosplan USSR take into account inter-industry proportions and national economic requirements.

On the basis of control figures received from the ministry, each enterprise works out its draft *tekhpromfinplan*. The first stage of the planning process is scheduled for completion in September. The second stage in the compilation of the *tekhpromfinplan* comes with the receipt of the confirmed tasks of the enterprise, arising from the national economic plan, and consists of making the draft *tekhpromfinplan* detailed and precise. This second stage should be completed within a month of receiving the confirmed plan tasks, and in no event later than the end of the year.

It is clearly desirable that these *tekhpromfinplany* be consistent in the twofold sense that for each enterprise the planned outputs are feasible with the planned inputs, and that for the country as a whole the planned requirements for each commodity are no greater than the availability of that commodity. If the plans are not consistent in the first sense, then some enterprises will be unable to fulfil their plans. This may have unfortunate effects on enterprises which planned to use the good which was not produced as an input or on final consumers for whom the good was intended. If the plans are inconsistent in the second sense, that is if for example steel-using enterprises plan to consume 130 million tons of steel and steel producing enterprises to produce 100 million tons, then this will lead to the non-production of commodities which it had been planned to make available either as inputs to other enterprises or for final uses, and the splitting up of the economy into a priority sector whose needs are met and a non-priority sector whose needs are not met.

It is well known that 'The plans for production, labour, finance and supply are often inconsistent.' (Nemchinov [1965] p. 56.) The purpose of this chapter is to explain why this is so and what effects it has on the economy. To keep the argument within a reasonable compass attention will be focussed on one section of the consistency problem, that of drawing up consistent supply and production plans.

From the point of view of the planning of supply,[1] commodities are considered both in a specified and in an aggregated classification. The aggregated classification is used for working out the national economic supply plan, the material balances, distribution plans and quotas. The specified classification is a detailed one which lists commodities according to their types, qualities and standards. It is this classification, in which enterprises express their detailed requirements (within the limits of the quotas which they have been allocated), in which contracts are concluded, and to which the price lists relate. In the process of the planning of supply, commodities differ according to the organ which

---

[1] The classic account of the planning of supply in the English language literature is Levine [1959].

allocates them. A convenient distinction is between centrally distributed and non-centrally distributed products. The centrally distributed products include those distributed by Gosplan, Gossnab, and some of the ministries. (Of the commodities for which material balances and distribution plans are worked out by Gosplan, the balances and distribution plans for some, the so-called funded commodities, have to be confirmed by the Council of Ministers.) The non-centrally distributed commodities include those for which distribution plans are worked out by the territorial organs of Gossnab for all consumers in their region irrespective of their departmental status. In 1969 in the aggregated nomenclature, about 2000 products were centrally distributed (of which the balances and distribution plans for about 300 were confirmed by the Council of Ministers) and about 12,000 products were non-centrally distributed.

Consider a commodity distributed by Gosplan. During the planning year the consumer enterprises submit their estimated requirements (indents) to the appropriate administration (their administrative superior). The administration checks them, possibly adjusts them, adds them up and sends them to the chief administration of supply of the ministry. The latter sends them to the corresponding department of Gosplan. In Gosplan they are carefully examined, and then a material balance, which is designed to ensure that requirements during the planned year will be consistent with production, is drawn up, and a production plan and a distribution plan based on it are worked out. The distribution plan is a detailed version of the requirements side of a material balance, which subdivides 'production needs' and 'capital construction' by organ (e.g. a ministry).

In the distribution plan for 1972, 169 quota holders were listed (a quota holder is an organisation, such as a ministry, which has been allocated a quota of a commodity), of which 44 were small consumers which were grouped together under the heading 'other consumers'. Each of the quota holders listed in the distribution plan subdivides its quota among its subordinate organs, which subdivide them into quotas for the enterprises. When the enterprises receive their quotas they specify their requirements in detail (within the limits of the quota) and submit them to the supply organs. On the basis of these specified quotas the supply organs distribute orders between the producer enterprises and organise the attachment of producers to consumers.

From the point of view of the planning of production, commodities are divided into the most important ones, for which plans are included in the state plan for the development of the national economy, and the less important ones, whose output is planned by the ministries. For example in 1968 the nomenclature of industrial products in the state plan was 615, and the total number of centrally planned products (i.e. products planned by a central organ such as a ministry) was about 40,000. 'The starting point for the planning of the volumes of production *in physical terms* is the determination of the requirements of the national economy for particular types of products.' (Kotov [1969] p. 41.) The calculation of requirements for intermediate goods is based on the sum of the indents of consumers, which are based on norms for the utilisation of materials. The calculation of requirements for consumer goods is based on consumption norms and estimates of demand for particular goods. The calculation of requirements for machines and equipment is based on the plans for *komplektirovanie*.[1] Simultaneously with calculations of requirements, calculations of productive possibilities are being undertaken. The following basic types of calculation are performed: of the availability of deficit raw materials; of the utilisation of deficit raw materials; of productive capacities and their utilisation; of the equipment required for the replacement of old equipment and the expansion of capacity; and of the labour force and the possibilities of attracting additional workers.

Comparing and analysing all these calculations, the planning organs determine the maximum possible volume of output feasible with the materials and equipment available. For coordinating requirements and output the following methods are used: searching for possibilities of economising on materials and substituting less scarce materials for scarce ones; investigating the possibility of increasing production by expanding productive capacities and using the existing capacity more effectively; more rational utilisation of materials and a reduction in the output of less scarce products; importing scarce materials and equipment; and if it is impossible to increase the volume of resources, determining which are the priority needs to be met in full, and the degree of fulfilment of the non-priority needs.

The results of all these calculations are expressed in the material balances, which are worked out for the more important products, and in the plans for production and distribution.

From the point of view of the enterprise, the planning process ends with the working out of the final version of the *tekhpromfinplan*. From the point of view of the relations between producers and consumers it ends with the conclusion of contracts between the supply organs and the producer, and the supply organs and the consumer, or directly between

---

[1] *Komplektirovanie* is the process of ensuring that complementary machines and equipment are available in the necessary sets and are not supplied in an individual, uncoordinated and useless way. Attached to Gossnab are a number of chief administrations for the *komplektirovanie* of particular sorts of equipment, such as Soyuzglavneftekomplekt for oil industry equipment, which are mainly concerned with the supply of sets of equipment to new enterprises or to enterprises which are being reconstructed.

the consumer and the producer. From the point of view of the chief administrations of Gossnab, it ends with the working out of the final versions of the attachment plans and the production schedules. From the point of view of the ministry it ends with the splitting up of the production plan and the quotas between its enterprises. From the point of view of Gosplan USSR it ends with the working out of the final version of the production plans, the distribution plans, the plans for inter-republican deliveries and the plan for the delivery of output for all-Union needs (i.e. plans for the supply of resources to consumers having all-Union significance) for all of the commodities for which Gosplan is responsible. During the planned period it is necessary to ensure that the plan is fulfilled. After the planning period is over it is necessary to report on the extent of fulfilment to the statistical organs.

From a formal point of view, the long process of planning and counter-planning, which begins with the elaboration of control figures by Gosplan USSR and the submission to the ministries by the enterprises of suggestions for the plan, and ends with the working out of the final version of the plan, can be regarded as an informal iterative process designed to solve the following problem. Consider a multi-commodity multi-enterprise economy where production takes place in discrete time periods. The problem of drawing up a consistent national economic plan for any period can be represented as the problem of finding numbers.

$$\begin{matrix} a_{11}\, a_{12} \ldots a_{1n} \\ \vdots \qquad\qquad \vdots \\ a_{m1}\, a_{m2} \ldots a_{mn} \end{matrix} \qquad (m \to \infty,\, n = 60{,}000)[1]$$

where a_{ij} is the amount of the ith good produced at the jth enterprise (if $a_{ij} > 0$) or required (if $a_{ij} < 0$) in the process of production by the jth enterprise.

Subject to the conditions

$$a_j \in A_j \quad (j = 1 \ldots n), \qquad\qquad (1)$$

where a_j is the vector $(a_{1j}, a_{2j} \ldots a_{mj})$ and
A_j is the set of feasible plans for the jth enterprise; and

$$\sum_{j=1}^{n} a_{ij} + b_i = b_i' \qquad i = 1 \ldots m \qquad\qquad (2)$$

where b_i is the stock of the ith good at the start of the period, and
b_i' is the desired stock at the end of the period.

---

[1] The textbook Berri [1968] in its chapter on the planning of supply gives a figure of 42,000 industrial enterprises and 19,000 construction sites as the number whose supply has to be planned (ibid, p. 409). A. and N. Kobrinskii give a figure of 20,000,000 as the number of commodities distinguished in the all-Union industrial classification in their book A. and N. Kobrinskii [1969].

Condition (1) is that no enterprise receives an impossible plan. A plan may be impossible for technical reasons (because the planned input–output pattern is technologically not feasible) or for economic reasons (because the planned inputs cannot be made available or the planned outputs cannot be sold). If condition (1) is violated this will show itself during the planned period as a breakdown in the supply system, or as difficulties with marketing, or in the need to alter enterprise plans, or some combination of these undesirable, but frequent, phenomena. Condition (2) is that the output of each commodity, together with the initial stocks, be equal to the requirements of the system. If condition (2) is violated this will show itself during the planned period as a breakdown in the supply system, the alteration of the plans, the de facto creation of non-priority sectors which have to do as best they can, the accumulation of unwanted stocks, or some combination of these undesirable, but frequent, phenomena.

Define a 'consistent plan' as a matrix A which satisfies conditions (1) and (2). The chief difficulties in compiling a consistent plan are:

I Collecting the necessary data. The data on requirements available to the central planners are based on the indents of the enterprises, adjusted and aggregated by the intermediate bodies. These data are not very reliable for the following reasons:

a The indents are sent in before the enterprises know their output plans, at a time therefore when they are unable to state their requirements precisely. As a recent study has observed, '. . . it is impossible to base the determination of real requirements for material resources on the indents because the indents are based on preliminary volumes of output, which are altered to a considerable extent in the process of working out the plan'. (Lebed' [1969] p. 54.)

b The indents of the enterprises are adjusted, in an essentially arbitrary manner, by the intermediate bodies. 'Analysis of the practice of the supply of enterprises subordinated to the regional economic councils, and also the material published in the press, indicates that the planning organs not infrequently pay little attention to the indents of the consumers . . . .' There are three reasons for refusal to satisfy an indent:

1 insufficient resources;
2 the discovery as a result of economic analysis that the consumer has internal reserves, is exceeding the norms;
3 arbitrary reductions in the indent. (Tanchuk [1965] pp. 80–1.)

c In view of (b) and of the disadvantages of underfulfilment of the plan, enterprises are tempted to overstate their needs (and understate their productive possibilities) in reports to the centre.

d The process of aggregating requirements, and subsequently of dis-aggregating the production and distribution plans, destroys some of the information on the times, places and quantities in which particular commodities are required. I have analysed this in Ellman [1969].

II Processing the necessary data. A limited number of officials, divided into numerous departments, and armed with telephones, pens and abacuses – or more sophisticated equipment – have only a limited time to solve the problem, which is very complex both because of its huge dimensions and because the variables are interrelated. When, during the course of plan calculations, the output of one commodity is altered, it is necessary to alter the output of other commodities which are direct inputs into the process of production of the commodity whose output has been altered. This involves altering the output of the commodities which are indirect inputs into the process of production of the commodity whose output has been altered.

As Aganbegyan ([1964] p. 66) has observed 'every year it becomes more difficult to balance the economy, to complete a plan for its development, to control it ... the chief difficulty is that with the existing system of planning and control, based on manual calculations and the perception of a limited amount of information by a planner, it is difficult not only to find an optimal solution to the development of the economy, but physically impossible to balance the plan. For the com-pilation of such a plan for the tens of thousands of products for which the USSR state plan sets targets, requires the carrying out of milliards of calculations (mathematically this is a problem of solving a system of linear equations) whereas a man, equipped with a desk calculator can only do 1000–2000 calculations per day. Even if the splitting up of the work were possible (which is impossible with these relationships) the whole apparatus of Gosplan could not do one-hundredth of the necessary calculations for this group of plan indices.'

The data processing problems involved in drawing up a consistent plan take the following form:

a The planning of production and supply for the entire economy is regarded as too large for any one organisation, and accordingly is split up among many organisations. This creates three sorts of problems:

1 The organisations other than Gosplan USSR which allocate resources, such as the territorial administrations of Gossnab, scarcely use the method of balance for securing consistency. They rely pre-dominantly on the 'method' of planning from the achieved level. 'This leads, and must inevitably lead, to mistakes.' (*Reforma* [1968] p. 152.)

2 If the various organisations concerned make incompatible assump-tions, then inconsistent plans will emerge.

3 Because the planning of production and supply is split up between numerous organisations and because de facto an enterprise is obliged to accept the instructions of all the higher bodies, it often happens that an enterprise receives conflicting or impossible plans. In particular, when the production plan and the quotas for the scarcest materials are received from Gosplan and the ministry, and the requirements for the less scarce goods are supposed to be satisfied by the local supply organs, it may well happen that the local supply organs are unable to supply those commodities which are essential for meeting the production plans.

b The planning of production and supply for all the commodities produced and consumed in the economy is regarded as too big a problem to be solved, and accordingly the authorities concern themselves only with the more important commodities (16,000 in 1968). This reduces the size of the problem from millions to thousands of equations, but it introduces into the planning process aggregation errors, the possibility of a shortage or the waste of an unplanned commodity and hidden shortages. When the planning work is finished and the balances appear to be balanced, there may well be a hidden shortage of products whose output is not planned centrally but which are used as inputs into the production of centrally planned products. This is because the requirements for these non-centrally planned products, implicit in the output plans of the centrally planned products, are greater than their output (which is not centrally planned). As the deputy head of one of the departments of Gosplan USSR has put it: 'One of the reasons for inconsistencies is that materials which are necessary for the production of centrally planned products are themselves not completely included in the list of centrally planned products, and therefore the balancing of production and requirement in the planning organs is not completed.' (Kotov [1969] p. 43.)

c The process of specifying the quotas, that is of obtaining through the supply organs or by direct contacts the precise goods needed (which are stated only in broad terms in the quotas) often gives rise to considerable difficulties. 'Under this system the production plan often does not fully correspond to the specified orders, and the latter are satisfied either not fully, or in a different assortment to that required.' (Kotov [1969] pp. 43–4.) Five types of problem in particular arise during the process of specifying the quotas.

1 Suppliers may not wish to supply goods of the type required. For example, when planning is in tons, metallurgical enterprises are not very keen on producing thin steel sheets, which may be useful to consumers but which are costly to produce and do not contribute much to plan fulfilment. As an official of the Byelorussian supply organisation has observed: 'There are many complaints about shortages of special

steels, rolled products, cold rolled sheet steel etc. At the same time there is a certain surplus of ordinary steel, thick construction and hot rolled sheet steel etc. One of the reasons for this inconsistency is that the production of steel is planned in tons. Under this system of planning the metallurgical enterprises are not interested in producing thin sheet steel, because it is light in weight and labour intensive to produce.' (Zakruzhny [1966] p. 53.) In the administrative economy, with its permanent sellers' market, producer enterprises are in a strong position and are often able to act in their own interests regardless of the effect of their actions on consumer enterprises.

2 The producer enterprise may not be able to produce the goods required, because it lacks the necessary inputs. Months earlier, when it sent in its indent, it did not know what its production plan would be. If it turns out that the orders it is now receiving differ substantially from those it anticipated, it will be impossible to fulfil them because of the lack of the necessary inputs.

3 The producer enterprise may not be able to produce the goods required because the plan, although balanced in aggregate terms, is unbalanced in disaggregated terms, that is the demand for some goods exceeds productive possibilities as a result of aggregation errors. Take tubes (of the type used in oil pipelines). In terms of tons of tubes, supply and demand may appear to be in equilibrium, but the demand for a particular sort of tube may far exceed the supply possibilities.

4 A producer enterprise may find itself with insufficient orders to fulfil its production plan. This often happens as a result of enterprises stating at the end of the planning process that they do not want goods which they ordered earlier. The following example indicates how this can happen. Take an enterprise producing a good required for investment projects, e.g. cranes. It may appear to have an assured demand for cranes, based on the investment plans of its customers. The last plan to be confirmed is the investment plan. It may well happen, as a result of a central campaign to reduce the wasteful spreading of investment resources over numerous unfinished projects, that many of these investment plans are rejected. The enterprises concerned then inform the crane plant that they no longer want cranes. The crane plant, which seemed to have an assured demand, now finds, at the beginning of the planned year, that it is in serious danger of underfulfilling its production plan. Another reason for enterprises not having enough orders is that quota holders may not need all the products listed in their quota – they only applied for them so as to have a margin in hand against a reduction in their supply requests or an increase in their production plan by the higher bodies. (Zakruzhny [1966] p. 86.)

5 The enterprises may begin the year without a final *tekhpromfinplan*

because the planning process has not been completed within the planning year.

The main technique used to try to achieve efficiency of the plans is the system of norms. The main techniques used to try to achieve consistency of the plans is the system of material balances.

MATERIAL BALANCES

The method of material balances is the basic method of planning not only the volume of production but also the distribution of the means of production between the separate consumers, that is the planning of supply for the national economy.

A Soviet textbook (*Ekonomika* [1963] p. 313.)

An essential requirement for successful Government regulation of an economy is a statistical picture of the economy arranged in a way compatible with the instruments of regulation which the Government uses. In Britain such a statistical picture is provided by the national accounts, which provide the information necessary for the regulation of the economy by fiscal means, and by financial statistics which provide the information necessary for the regulation of the economy by monetary methods. In the Soviet Union the necessary statistical information is arranged in a series of 'balances', the 'balance of the national economy' and its subdivisions.[1] The material balances are part of this system. The use of material balances in planning has been well described in the literature.[2]

The method of material balances cannot lead to the compilation of consistent plans because the material balances are not complete, nor universal, nor do they form an integrated system, nor does technology correspond to the strong technological assumptions implicit in the use of material balances.

Often material balances do not cover the entire output of the good in question. For many kinds of product material balances embrace little more than 60 % of production. (Efimov [1965] p. 8.) When commodity A is produced as a subsidiary product of enterprise X belonging to industry B, then X's output of A may not be known to the central planners or to the sectoral planners responsible for the A industry.

Material balances are compiled for far fewer commodities than are produced in the economy. For most commodities balance calculations are not performed, either because they are included in a very aggregated way in balances which are calculated, or because they are altogether excluded from the balance calculations.

[1] Some of the balances record stocks, others show flows. For a description see Basic [1971].
[2] See for example Koldomasov [1959], Grebtsov [1960], Karpov [1970] pp. 98-59, Montias [1959], and Chandra [1965], especially chapter 6.

The compilers of material balances are primarily concerned with balancing output and requirements for a single commodity. Diagrammatically compilers of material balances are doing calculations of the type:

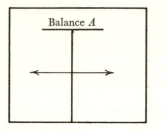
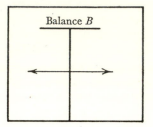

rather than calculations of the type:[1]

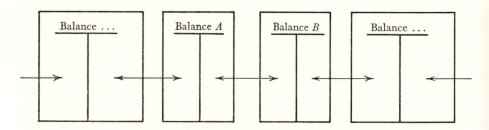

When during the course of the material balance calculations the output of one product is altered, consistency requires that the outputs of all the products that directly or indirectly are used in the production of that commodity should also be altered. For example an increase in the production of cars entails an increase in the production of steel, which in its turn entails an increase in the production of electricity, which in its turn . . . . In practice however, Academician Efimov has explained that:

Because of the great labour intensity of the calculation of changes in the material balances and the insufficiency of time for the completion of such work in practice, sometimes only those balances which are linked by first order relationships are changed. As regards relationships of the second order, and especially of the third and fourth order, changes in the balance are made only in those cases where the changes are conspicuous.

(Efimov [1957] p. 107.)

In other words, whereas consistency requires the evaluation of the convergent series

$$X = (I + A + A^2 + A^3 \ldots) Y$$

---

[1] For this contrast see Isaev [1969] p. 271.

it often happens that X is approximated by considering the first two terms only. In view of the fact that the process of calculation is often cut short, inconsistencies are to be expected, in principle. The practical importance of this depends on the ratio of direct inputs to full inputs and the number of iterations required for consistency. TsSU, working on the 1959 input–output table for the USSR in value terms, found that usually the ratio between direct input and full input was between 1 and 2, but that much larger values occurred quite frequently, ranging up to 54.7! The number of iterations required for the estimated value of X to approach the true value of X has been estimated by Levine at between 6 and 13.

On the other hand it has been shown, using Soviet data, that in many cases two rounds of iteration were enough to bring direct input coefficients quite close to full input coefficients. (Kvasha [1961].) Furthermore, the number of iterations required is reduced by the existence of bottlenecks. The planners can arrive at a consistent plan without matrix inversion, through iteration, provided that the outputs in the excess capacity sectors are adapted to the potentials of the bottleneck sectors. (Montias [1962b] pp. 339–42 and [1962a].) In addition the number of iterations required for consistency can also be reduced if the input–output matrix has certain special properties, e.g. if it can be triangulated. Soviet experience has shown that in many industries a small number of coefficients account for a large proportion of the inputs, which reduces the number of feedback effects which it is necessary to take into account during the plan calculations.[1]

The method of material balances assumes that the process of production can be represented by a matrix of fixed coefficients (the norms). For each commodity requirements are assumed to be represented by the relation

$$x_i = \sum_{j=1}^{n} a_{ij} x_j + y_i \qquad i = 1 \ldots n$$

where x_i is the output of the ith product,
$\qquad a_{ij}$ is the norm of requirements of the ith product per unit of output of the jth product, and
$\qquad y_i$ is the requirement of the ith product for final demand.

This is a very strong assumption, which rules out substitutability, non-proportional inputs, learning by doing and non-constant returns to scale, and there is no reason to suppose that it is in general true. Hence one would not expect the material balance calculations to produce accurate results. The practical importance of this problem is reduced by the fact that in planning practice the assumption of fixed coefficients

---

[1] Attention has been drawn to this by Dobb [1966] p. 359.

is not strictly adhered to, and the production schedulers suggest substitutes for scarce inputs.

The norms used in the calculations are generally averages weighted in favour of the more efficient producers. This creates two problems. First, for efficient producers the norms may be too soft and provide no incentive for efficiency; and conversely, for inefficient producers they may be impossible. Secondly, when during the process of plan calculations the relative output of plants with different input–output relationships is altered, this alters the actual mean input–output relationship. If the planners continue to use a given norm, then inconsistencies will result. (This is an example of an aggregation error.)

INPUT–OUTPUT

Experience has shown that at the preliminary stage of planning the static input–output table can be an active instrument of analysis, but that at the concluding stage of the plan calculations its role is limited, it serves only as a method illustrating the interindustry relations envisaged by the draft plan.
A. Dorovskikh (head of a subdepartment of Gosplan USSR) (Dorovskikh [1967] p. 39.)

An input–output table is a way of arranging the national accounts which focusses attention on the productive relationships between industries. In Soviet statistical practice input–output has become an integral part of the system of balances of the national economy.

The concept of an economy as a circular flow of commodities goes back to Quesnay's *Tableau Economique*. The first set of national accounts providing data on productive relationships between industries was that compiled by TsSU for 1923–4 (Popov [1926].) After Stalin's unfavourable reference to this 'game with figures' in his speech of December 1929, Soviet work in this field gradually faded away. Meanwhile, Leontief, aware of the Soviet work,[1] developed, in the United States, a mathematical model which provides a convenient way of arranging, and a useful way of analysing and extrapolating, statistics on interindustry relations.

Soviet interest in input–output revived after the 20th Congress, as part of the general development of mathematical economics which took place then. Since the Government's instruction to Gosplan and TsSU of November 1959, a great deal of work has been done on input–output in the USSR. TsSU has compiled accounting input–output tables for the USSR as a whole for 1959 and 1966 in both value and labour units, and an accounting capital stock matrix for 1966. Gosplan's research institute has compiled several planning input–output tables in value

---

[1] He reviewed some of it in a German journal. For a contemporary Russian translation of his review see Leontief [1925]. There is an English translation in Spulber [1964] pp. 88–94.

terms, and Gosplan's Chief Computing Centre has compiled several planning input–output tables in physical units. Numerous regional input–output tables have been compiled, a field in which TSEMI has been active. IEOPP has done some work for Gosplan on dynamic input–output models.

Elsewhere I have described some of the problems that arise in the compilation and utilisation of input–output tables, and their usefulness as sources of data and as tools which enable variant calculations to be undertaken in perspective planning (Ellman [1971] chapter 6). Here I propose to consider only the question of whether the use of input–output enables the consistency problem to be solved.

Above it was argued that the use of material balances cannot lead to the compilation of consistent plans because the material balances are not complete, nor universal, nor do they form an integrated system, nor does technology correspond to the strong assumptions implicit in the use of material balances. Input–output tables are complete, that is they do include all the output of particular industries. This however raises a number of problems concerning the comparability of the indices of the input–output table and the national economic plan. In particular, the indices of an input–output table, which refer to the outputs of 'pure' industries, violate the important plan principle of *adresnost*'[1] and have to be recalculated to fit the plan industries, which is not difficult but does not enhance the reliability of the results. Unlike material balances, input–output does form an integrated system. This fact enables the full implications of possible output changes to be worked out, and numerous plan variants to be experimented with. As is the case with material balances, the technological assumptions of input–output – fixed co-efficients – do not accord with reality, ruling out such phenomena as alternative techniques of production, non-proportional inputs, learning by doing and non-constant returns to scale. In fact the technological assumptions of input–output are more restrictive than those of material balances, because in planning practice the norms of the material balances are flexible. Considered as a technique for drawing up consistent plans the most important defect of an input–output table is that it is not universal. The number of industries in the largest input–output table – 600 – is much smaller than the number of products for which material balances are regularly drawn up, and is so small as to be scarcely relevant to the problem of drawing up consistent plans for 20,000,000 commodities.[2]

---

[1] The principle of *adresnost*' is that there should be no plan targets which are the responsibility of no-one in particular. To each plan target there should correspond an organisation (address) responsible for implementing it.

[2] The fact that input–output would be unable to solve the consistency problem for this reason was pointed out by Nove in 1963 (Nove [1964a] pp. 124–5).

THE SIGNIFICANCE OF, AND THE SOLUTION TO,

INCONSISTENCIES

In general, with the existing nomenclature of balances it is impracticable to take account of all the direct and indirect links in the economy. As a result of this the balancing of all the links in the production of the social product is in practice not achieved, which leads to the violation of the proportional development of the economy.
N. E. Kobrinskii and A. M. Matlin (Kobrinskii and Matlin [1968] p. 17.)

It is suggested that the development of mathematical methods of planning will enable the troubles of the planning of supply to be overcome. Deviations from normal economic activity, including non-productive costs, which result from breakdowns in supply can be completely liquidated, however, only by raising *khozraschet* to the required level, when *khozraschet* will create between enterprises healthy productive relations, when the responsibility of personnel, and of enterprises will be raised.
E. O. Kaitsa (Kaitsa [1965] p. 6.)

It has not been possible to ensure that the plans for all the many thousands of administratively allocated commodities are consistent, using material balances or input–output or a combination of these techniques. The fact that the economy is run on the basis of inconsistent plans has a number of deleterious effects.

1 It leads to inattention to non-priority sectors, such as personal consumption. As inconsistencies come to light, and shortages are revealed, priority sectors receive what they need and non-priority sectors have to accept what they are given.[1]

2 It leads to repeated alterations to the plans. As inconsistencies come to light, plans have to be altered to deal with them.

3 It leads to difficulties with supply, which result in the idleness of men and machines.[2] According to one estimate (*Khozyaistvennaya reforma* [1968] p. 36), 25 % of all working time is lost through difficulties with the supply system. It also results in cost increases (resulting for example from the cost of sending *tolkachi* to find materials,[3] the cost of sending telegrams, the additional cost incurred in the procurement and

---

[1] A recent article has explained how this works out in the case of tubes (of the type used in oil pipelines). 'In accordance with the quotas which they have received the consumers send in orders for the necessary assortment. It now turns out that the planned output of some kinds of tube is less than requirements and that some kinds of tube were almost excluded from the plan. There arises a shortage. In order somehow or other to make ends meet it is necessary to divide the industries of the national economy into priority and secondary. Willy nilly the secondary industries have to adapt their needs to the existing situation, and take not those tubes which they need but those tubes which they are given.' (Osada [1969].)

[2] Urban unemployment and unused capacity, resulting from lack of aggregate demand, are important sources of idleness of men and machines in market economies, which do not arise in the administrative economy.

[3] *Tolkachi* are supply agents. Their role is created by the permanent sellers' market and corresponds *mutatis mutandis* to that of salesmen in an economy with a permanent buyers' market.

use of unsatisfactory substitute materials, and the use of commodities obtained from the auxiliary enterprises of collective farms or from local industry which may be substantially more costly than the same commodities produced by large scale industry). In addition it results in difficulties in meeting the requirements of customers (because the necessary materials are not available).

4 It leads to difficulties with marketing. Enterprises may find that there is no demand for the products that they have been instructed to produce.

5 It contributes to the unresponsiveness of output to demand. Take commodities whose output is not balanced by the central planners, such as shoe polish or spares for machinery. Unless resources are left for the production of these goods, and an economic mechanism is available which will ensure that the resources are used in accordance with the needs of customers, then these useful commodities will not be produced in the required types and quantities.

6 It is one of the factors explaining the length of time taken to build new plants – a notorious feature of Soviet investment planning.[1]

7 It is one of the factors hindering the development of agriculture. Machinery and equipment goes not to those farms which need it, but to those to whom it has been allocated, and the opportunity for the farms to determine the output patterns of the plants producing machinery and materials for agriculture is limited. (Lemeshev [1968] chapter 5, part 3.)

8 It is one of the factors explaining the low level of specialisation in production. Enterprises and ministries, fearing that they will be unable to secure through the supply system the components that they need, produce their own at higher cost, and the development of low cost component enterprises is hindered.

9 It is one of the factors explaining the existence of shortages, both of consumer goods and of producer goods, which is such a characteristic feature of the Soviet economy. Take large suitcases. Equilibrium in the large suitcase market ought to be maintained by balancing. But in fact this cannot be done, and in an environment characterised by suppressed inflation and the determination of the production plans of consumer goods factories by planners rather than in accordance with the needs of the retail trade, large suitcases become a scarce good (*deficitnyi tovar*). (If the planners do notice the shortage they are likely to over-react, and

---

[1] 'Big difficulties arise in investment as a result of the incomplete balancing in the plan of the requirements of the construction sites and the quotas allocated to them, in particular for equipment, ferrous metals, cable production etc. Often when allocating these materials to the construction sites it turns out that the quotas which they have received do not correspond to the specifications which they have requested, which leads to the over-expenditure of materials, the irrational utilisation of labour, to redoing already completed work, and as a consequence, to the dragging out of construction periods.' (Krasovsky [1967] p. 60.)

large suitcases will become a surplus commodity, like the reduction gears which I described in Ellman [1971], chapter 6, appendix 2.)

10 It leads to the irrational distribution of stocks. Under conditions of strict rationing and given the practice of reducing quotas allocated in the future if current quotas are underutilised, enterprises have a strong incentive to hoard materials. Stocks accumulate at those enterprises which are relatively good at exaggerating their real requirements, and production is hampered by shortages of materials at those enterprises which play the game according to the official procedure.

Even if the plans were consistent, they might still be wasteful. In fact it often happens that the attachment plans involve irrational hauls of materials. The reason for this is that the officials in the Soyuzglavs-nabsbyty[1] are primarily concerned with ensuring that the indents are met without exceeding the production possibilities of the suppliers, and neither have the time, nor use the methods, necessary to ensure that the attachment plans and production schedules are optimal. (Towards the end of the period this began to be remedied.)

It is generally recognised that the existing system of working out and implementing the plans for the administrative allocation of resources is unsatisfactory. At the present time there are five main directions, not mutually exclusive, in which an improvement in the situation is being sought: the enlargement of stocks; the decentralisation of the planning of supply; an improvement in planning techniques; a greater emphasis on direct contacts within the supply system; and the gradual transition from the planning of supply to wholesale trade.

If consumers had adequate stocks, then many of the adverse consequences of the inadequacies of the supply system would be eliminated. In that case, the failure of necessary goods to arrive would not cause a plant to come to a halt, or result in dearer materials being substituted, or necessitate obtaining materials from another plant on an informal basis, as happens now. It would simply be dealt with by running down stocks. This would be an example of what in the literature on systems is called decoupling by means of a buffer. It is not a new idea. Almost half a century ago, in his famous *Notes of an economist*, Bukharin[2] pointed out the difficulty of constructing buildings with bricks that had not yet been produced, and the need for reserves, but his views were rejected at that time on the ground that one should plan to 'widen' a bottleneck, not 'on' the bottleneck. The desirability of an increase in stocks has been argued by a number of writers (Probst [1967], Smekhov

---

[1] The Soyuzglavsnabsbyty, such as Soyuzglavmetal, are the Chief Administrations for supply and marketing of Gossnab, each responsible for a particular group of commodities.
[2] Bukharin was a prominent Soviet politician of the 1920s. He opposed the breakthrough, and *Notes of an economist* is an article in *Pravda* in which he put his views publicly.

Table 1.1. *Number of products allocated by various organs*

Year	Total nomenclature	Gosplan USSR	SNKh USSR	Gossnab	Chief administrations (centralised by ministries)	Territorial administrations
1966	21,677	1,904	1,243	—	18,530	—
1968	14,498	1,969	—	103	3,198	9,228
1970	15,043	1,908	—	178	1,070	11,887

SOURCE: Karpov [1972] p. 59.

[1968], Krylov [1969]); considerable attention was paid to the question of stocks at the January 1968 conference on problems of improving material-technical supply at the Scientific Research Institute of the Economics and Organisation of Supply, and the importance of adequate reserves was recognised in the decree of the Council of Ministers of 28 April 1969 entitled 'On measures for the further improvement of the material-technical supply system of the national economy.'[1]

An important feature of the reform has been the decentralisation of the planning of supply which has resulted from the increased importance of the territorial supply organs. The purpose of this is to bring resource allocation more into line with real requirements and possibilities. The increased role of the local supply organs (the territorial administrations of Gossnab) is shown in table 1.1. There are a number of important organisations to whom this decentralisation of the planning of supply has not been applied. The enterprises of the Ministries of energy and electric power stations, defence, the gas industry, and transport construction, Mosgorispolkom (i.e. Moscow city council), Lengorispolkom (i.e. Leningrad city council) and a number of other organisations send in their specified quotas not to the territorial supply organs but to their own ministry or to the central supply organs.

In some circles it is considered that the way to overcome the problems of the supply system is to improve planning by widening the detail of the plan and making extensive use of computers and mathematical

---

[1] This decree is reprinted in *Khozyaistvennaya reforma* [1969] pp. 159–66. The importance of reserves is recognised in 1(c). Chapter 4 of Lagutkin [1970] is devoted to the question of stocks. See also Kvasha [1971].

The traditional view of the authorities was that large stocks were a sign of waste, and efforts were devoted to maintaining stocks at a low level and if possible reducing them. Low stocks, or stocks irrationally distributed, ensure that breakdowns in the supply system have the maximum effect in disrupting production, and the changed attitude of the authorities is an important development.

For a Western study of the role of stocks in improving the balance method of planning, see Weitzman [1971].

methods. According to an advocate of wholesale trade (Lemeshev [1968] p. 228):

The supporters of the existing system of supply of socialist enterprises generally explain its character by reference to the supposed interest of centralised planning and the shortages of separate types of products. Moreover, they are inclined to see the reason for all these shortcomings in the supply of means of production and materials to the factories, mines, construction sites, collective farms and state farms, and of food products and consumption goods to the population, in the inadequate detail of national economic planning.

Economists supporting this point of view believe that if, for example, how much a collective or state farm should receive, not just in the way of tractors and combines, lorries and mineral fertilisers, but also pitchforks, spades, string for packing tomatoes and shavings for packing eggs, were determined in a centralised way, or at any rate by an order from the higher organs, then, in the opinion of these planning officials, the material needs of every enterprise would be fully met. If, on the other hand, these collective and state farms received plans for the sale to the state not only of grain and meat, milk and potatoes, but also beans, bristles, parsley and celery, then the supply of food products to the population, and raw materials to industry, would be guaranteed.

Such a description of the position of the supporters of unlimited centralisation may seem like an exaggeration. This is not so, however. The proof of this is the fact that at the present time many economists and planning officials place great hope on the creation with the help of computers of a single automated system for the management of the national economy. With the help of an all-embracing all-Union classification of indices for the management and planning of production it is proposed to take account of the needs of every enterprise for all requirements and determine down to the last detail the production programme of every enterprise, beginning with turbines and ending with fishhooks.

Great efforts were devoted towards the end of this period to improving the techniques used in current planning, and in particular to improving the calculation of requirements. By the end of the period the requirements for material resources were worked out directly by the Ministry without reliance on the unreliable indents in the Ministry of Building and Road Engineering, and in the Ministry of Oil Refining (Lebed' [1969] p. 54, Solomonovich [1970] p. 93). Soyuzglavtosel'mash, which is responsible for the supply of components for motor vehicles for agriculture, had also done away with the unreliable indent system. Information on the component requirements of each of the 4000 types of machines was stored on the memory of its computer. An enterprise which produced motor vehicles simply informed Soyuzglavtosel'mash of its output plan and of any changes in the norms for the number of components required per vehicle. This avoided the problems created by the need to send in indents before the production plan was known, and it also saved tens of thousands of man-days per year. It is not, however, suitable where the assortment and/or the norms are changing rapidly. In 1971–2 a discussion took place in the journal of Gossnab about the possibility of the general abolition of the error–generating indent system. In Soyuzglavtyazhmash the indent system had been retained, but the indents were put on forms which could be read by machines, transferred to tape and fed into a computer. In 1970, when this system had been only partly introduced, it saved Soyuzglavtyazhmash 40,000 man-days. In the Kiev territorial supply organisation, forecasting methods were used to estimate future requirements. The Soyuzglavsnabsbyty are charged with the efficient distribution of orders between plants. Soyuzglavmetal was using linear programming to work out optimal production schedules and attachment plans (this is described in chapter 4), and Soyuzglavkhim and Soyuzglavstroimaterialy (in collaboration with TSEMI) were applying the transport problem of linear programming to the task of calculating optimal attachment plans (Lagutkin [1970] chapter 6, section 2, Nesterov [1971].) Methods of iterative aggregation had been suggested, with the help of which one could go from consistent plans for a highly aggregated group of commodities to consistent plans for all the commodities. (Dudkin [1965], [1966], [1968], Shchennikov [1966].) In 1971 Dudkin and Shchennikov put forward their ideas on this question in *Pravda* (Dudkin [1971]). The process of planning was itself planned, by means of network planning (e.g. the critical path method). The rapid growth in the professionalism of planning was one of the most striking features of planning in the 1960s. Whereas in 1960 input–output was a strange new device, by 1970 input–output, linear programming and network planning had all been incorporated into planning practice.

The idea that the use of mathematical methods will be sufficient to overcome the problems of current planning is most implausible, and while it has some support among the officials of the central economic organs, it has none among research workers in the field of the application of mathematical methods to current planning. Three research workers in the field of the application of linear programming to oil refining (this is a classic field for the application of linear programming and useful results were achieved in the United States as early as the 1950s) have described their work on the current planning of five oil refineries in the Ukraine. The optimal plan which they computed diverged substantially from the actual plan. This did not mean that the optimal planners are able to bring about substantial savings, but simply that with the present price system a plan that minimises costs is not necessarily optimal from the national economic point of view. What these calculations showed was not that mathematical methods can save current planning, but that the price system requires further improvement. The researchers' general conclusion about the significance of optimising models for current planning is that they do not resolve the important, perhaps the most important, problem – how to interest the direct producers, that is the enterprises, in the maximum display of their reserves, in the most efficient utilisation of their own resources, so that they produce more, better and cheaper.

The economic reform envisages the expansion of direct contacts between suppliers and consumers. In this case Gosplan and the Ministry should switch over from current planning to perspective questions, to determining the directions of technical policy in the industry. The role of the central organs in current regulation should be reduced to the planning of state reserves, the satisfaction of non-economic needs and export–import operations. The purpose of the models of current planning should be altered – they will probably be used not for the establishment of directive output indices for producers and the establishment of quota limits for consumers, but for the discovery of bottlenecks in the balance of production and consumption, in order that the state reserves be manoeuvred in the best way. The role of the optimisation models in the calculations of indices of indirect regulation and *khozraschet*, in particular objectively determined valuations, will also be increased. (I. Birman [1970] p. 143.)

Similarly both TSEMI as an organisation and those of its research workers who have been concerned with the introduction of optimal attachment planning into the work of Soyuzglavkhim and Soyuzglavstroimaterialy, advocate the transition from supply to trade. An all-Union symposium on problems of creating automated management systems for the management of supply, organised by the section on problems of the management of supply of the Scientific Council on Optimal Planning of the Academy of Sciences, TSEMI and the Scientific Research Institute on the Economics and the Organisation of Supply, was held in Moscow in the autumn of 1970. Its recommendations included the statement that 'In the elaboration of automated management systems insufficient attention has been paid to the problems of the gradual transition to the planned distribution of producer goods by means of wholesale trade.' (*Simpozium* [1971] p. 96.)

Great efforts have been devoted in recent years to building up long term contacts within the supply system between producers and consumers. The point of this is to develop long term coordination of the plans of complementary enterprises. In 1967–8 Gossnab linked up on a long term basis more than 5.5 thousand consumer enterprises and 1.5 thousand producer enterprises. In practice the development of direct contacts alters little, because those enterprises which are linked in this way are precisely those which in any case had permanent business contacts. The main effect is to reduce the volume of work which Gossnab has to do in the course of the planning of supply. One should not exaggerate this point however. The long term linking is done on the basis of the aggregated nomenclature and without a detailed breakdown by period of delivery. The supplier and the consumer themselves then agree on the specification and the concrete periods of delivery. In this way there is a certain transition from 'production for plan' to 'production for use'.

A number of economists consider that the conclusion to be drawn from the impossibility of drawing up a consistent plan for the national economy and the harmful effects this has on the economy is to abolish current planning and move over to the determination of current production programmes on the basis of orders received and wholesale trade.[1] For example, Matlin realises that it is impossible to draw up consistent plans for all the commodities, and concludes that what is required is to utilise flexible prices, supply and demand and the market. (Matlin [1968], chapter 6.) A number of steps in this direction have been taken, but the idea of a rapid and complete transition from the planning of supply to wholesale trade has little support either among policy makers or among officials of Gossnab. At the section on supply of the 1968 all-Union economics conference the majority of planning officials argued that it was necessary to limit alterations in the planning of supply to overcoming particular defects in the system of centralised supply, in order to strengthen and improve it. I. M. Gruzdev, deputy chairman of Gosplan RSFSR, stated that it was 'mistaken to exaggerate' the role of wholesale trade and 'to suppose that one day it will replace centralised distribution. The overwhelming majority of means of production, such as rolled metal products, steel tubes, fuel, wood products, boilers and other types of equipment will never be distributed by wholesale trade (except for small consumers).' (*Vystupleniya* [1968] p. 50.)

In the following chapter I consider some further problems created by the system of current planning, as a preliminary to analysing the work of those who advocate the transition to an optimally functioning socialist economy.

---

[1] Even before the reform, trade between enterprises was *de facto* quite important. The need for it arose as a result of the inadequacy of the planning process. For a description see chapter 3 section 2 (Poluchenie materialov iz sluchainykh istochnikov) of Kaitsa [1965].

2. SOME PROBLEMS OF CURRENT PLANNING

The optimisation of the national economy means above all the optimisation of the economic relations. Therefore optimal planning requires not only the use of mathematical methods and electronic computing technology, but also the improvement of the forms of socialist productive relations, including legal forms. The choice of these forms lies beyond the boundaries of mathematical programming, but no doubt mathematical approaches to their optimisation will be found in the not too distant future. Such possibilities have already been noted, and the search for, and utilisation of, them is prompted by the requirements of practice.

In particular, the correct combination of the interests of the controlling and the controlled levels of production is one of the most important tasks of an optimally controlled economy. It is quite possible (and even highly probable!) that the liquidation of the striving of the lower levels to hide their productive possibilities, the orientation of the interests of the masses to the search for new, better variants of production and many other consequences of such a combination, at the present time conceals bigger reserves for the growth of the socialist economy, than the use of mathematical programming with the preservation of the former relations between the controlling and the controlled levels of the economy.

V. V. Novozhilov (Novozhilov [1969] p. 32.)

An integral feature of the administrative economy is the determination by the planners of obligatory values of a large number of variables in the *tekhpromfinplan* of every enterprise. It is now being argued by a number of Soviet economists that this process is wasteful and that the planners ought to confine themselves to high-level goals, such as the perspective development of the national economy, and abandon the practice of setting numerous obligatory values of variables in the *tekhpromfinplan* of every enterprise. As two Soviet economists, one of whom is a leading figure in the field of economic cybernetics, have argued in a book entitled *Economic-mathematical models in planning.*

It is extremely important to underline that planning, as the social regulation of the proportions of production, has two substantially different aspects. First, the determination of the perspective development of the national economy (starting from the goals of future development) and the determination of the means of their achievement – the economic macroproportions. Secondly, the regulation of current production, the current physical microproportions, which are defined within the limits of the annual plans or the plans worked out for still shorter periods.

The realisation of the perspective plans is based on the utilisation of such highly efficient methods of influencing the economy as investment policy; credit, financial and foreign currency policy; wages policy and so on. With the help of the indicated methods the big socio-economic tasks are efficiently resolved in our country, scientific-technical progress and economic growth are assured.

However, as is clear from the preceding discussion,[1] the basic work of the planning organs, now, lies in the fields of the current regulation of the proportions, solving problems which are different in principle and using other methods. The successes of planning in this field are more or less modest. (Kobrinskii and Matlin [1968] pp. 19–21.)

Similarly, a Hungarian economist justifying the decision of his government to abolish the system of setting compulsory indices to enterprises has written that

These indicators were, in some way or other, derived from the national economic plan but were mostly, by the nature of things only indirectly related to the latter. They restricted the scope of decision of enterprise leaders, restricted their chances of, and their inclination to, initiative, their ambitions and sense of responsibility. The indicators did not, and in fact could not reckon with the local endowments and requirements of the enterprises, and, therefore did not help and sometimes even hindered the choice of the most favourable, economically most efficient solutions, i.e. the most rational utilisations of resources. (Friss [1969] p. 11.)

Some of the ways in which current planning hinders the most rational utilisation of resources are as follows.[2]

Slack plans

A notorious feature of the administrative economy is the tendency by enterprises to strive for a slack plan. The fact that in a socialist economy, which is supposed to have eliminated the contradiction between the productive forces and the productive relations which Marxists consider to be the reason for the inevitable downfall of capitalism, enterprises should seek to conceal their productive possibilities has long been regarded as undesirable by many Soviet economists, and a major feature of the reform was a new incentive system designed to motivate enterprises to aim at taut plans.[3] The reasons why enterprises strive to secure

---

[1] 'The preceding discussion' is a brief description of the traditional system of planning by material balances, which, the authors consider, can not even lead to consistent plans, let alone optimal ones.

[2] The ways in which current planning hinders the most rational utilisation of resources have been extensively described in the Western literature, notably in Berliner [1957]. The Western literature is summed up in Bergson [1964].

[3] The fact that the traditional system provides an incentive to adopt slack plans, and the case for incentives for adopting taut plans and for the use of profit as a fund forming index, were argued by E. Liberman in his 1950 book.

a slack plan when the economic mechanism is of the administrative type, seem to be as follows.

First, slack plans are an insurance against undesirable consequences of the 'administrative uncertainty' which characterises the administrative economy.[1] There is uncertainty about the value of the plan for the following year, resulting from the absence of firm plans for a number of years ahead and the practice of planning from the achieved level. Uncertainty about the value of the plan for the following year is a major disincentive to adopt a taut plan, as such a plan may merely result in the receipt of a more difficult plan in the following year. There is uncertainty about the final value of the plan for the 'planned' period, resulting from the instability of the plans. When a *Pravda* correspondent enquired of the chief accountant of an enterprise working under the *new* system why enterprises were still adopting slack plans, he was shown by way of reply a letter from Rosglavkhlopkoprom of the Ministry of light industry of the RSFSR received on 27 December raising the annual profits plan (of the year about to end) by 275 thousand roubles. (Kuz'michev [1968].) The instability of the operational 'plans' is an obstacle to the adoption of taut plans. Another type of uncertainty is uncertainty about the timely arrival of inputs resulting from the way that the supply system operates. A slack plan provides the enterprise with a buffer to absorb any increase in the plan or breakdown in supply during the planned period.

Secondly, the incentive system adopted may stimulate enterprises to aim at slack plans. It is convenient to distinguish between three types of incentive system: incentives related to plan fulfilment, incentives for adopting a taut plan, and incentives for high results.[2] The first system is the one traditionally employed in the Soviet Union; the second was introduced in Czechoslovakia and Poland at the end of the 1950s and the beginning of the 1960s and its adoption was an important feature of the reform in the Soviet economy; the third is customary under managerial capitalism.

The system of incentives for plan fulfilment and overfulfilment can be written

$$B = a + b(Q_a - Q_p) \qquad \text{When } Q_a \geqslant Q_p$$
$$B = 0 \qquad \text{When } Q_a < Q_p$$

$a, b > 0$

---

[1] The absence of the uncertainty which supposedly characterises capitalism is sometimes adduced as a major advantage of socialist planning, at any rate of investment. (See Dobb [1969] passim especially pp. 122–3, and Nuti [1970] p. 370.) Those who argue in this way never pause to consider whether the uncertainty generated by the market mechanism is greater or less than the uncertainty generated by the administrative economy. Indeed, they write as if they were unaware of the uncertainty generated by the administrative economy, which is in fact, one of its most characteristic features.

[2] This threefold distinction is Veselkov's. See Veselkov [1968] p. 3.

where B is the value of the bonus,

Q_p is the planned value of the bonus forming index, and
Q_a is the actual value of the bonus forming index.

This system is a strong disincentive for a risk averting enterprise to adopt a taut plan (because there is a risk that it might be underfulfilled, which would lead to the total forfeiture of bonus payments), and would be a strong incentive to secure a high $(Q_a - Q_p)$, which can be achieved both by securing a high value of the bonus forming index (achieving a high Q_a) and by securing a slack plan (obtaining a low Q_p) or by some combination of these strategies, were the values of a, b and Q_p in period $t+1$ independent of the value of Q_a in period t. Generally Q_p in period $t+1$ is related to Q_a in period t. (This is known as 'planning from the achieved level'.) This provides a powerful disincentive for aiming at a high $(Q_a - Q_p)$ because such a result will simply make life more difficult in the following plan period.

It is important to realise that not only material but also moral incentives are related to plan fulfilment and overfulfilment. Bazarova has pointed out that in cases of plan underfulfilment 'the moral consequences are far from being unimportant. The enterprise which has not fulfilled its plan is responsible to the ministry or chief administration, to the regional (or district) committee of the party, to those shops and workers who did fulfil their obligations.' (Bazarova [1968] p. 138.) For a Soviet manager, the attitude of his administrative superiors and controllers towards him is of great importance. This creates a situation in which a *Pravda* journalist gave as a reason for the failure of the reform to lead to the adoption of taut plans the fact that: 'It is no secret that the following idea is still firmly established in the consciousness of many managers: 110 % means honour, a banner, a bonus and a place in the presidium, but 99 % means scowls, reproaches and a stern talk in the district committee.' (Kuz'michev [1968].)

The system of incentives for taut plans can be written

$$B = aQ_p + ka(Q_a - Q_p)$$
$$a, k > 0.$$

The first term provides an incentive to adopt a high plan. The higher the planned value of the bonus forming index, the higher the bonus. If

$$Q_a > Q_p \qquad k < 1.$$

This condition ensures that an increase in the plan of e produces a greater bonus than overfulfilment of the plan by e, and hence provides a disincentive for the enterprise to conceal its possibilities and aim at a low plan when the plan is being drawn up and an incentive for it to aim at the highest possible plan, a so-called 'taut' (*napryazhennyi*) plan.[1] Once the plan has been adopted there is still an incentive to overfulfil it, because $k > 0$ (although there is also an incentive, because $k < 1$, if any additional productive possibilities are discovered in the planned period, not to take advantage of them but to incorporate them in the plan for the following period).

If
$$Q_a < Q_p \qquad k > 1.$$

This condition ensures that underfulfilment of the plan by e reduces the bonus by more than the same reduction in the plan, and hence provides enterprises with a disincentive to adopt high plans which they are subsequently unable to fulfil, and provides them with a disincentive to underfulfil the plan.

Ceteris paribus, this type of incentive scheme is an incentive to adopt taut plans and a disincentive to underfulfil them.

The system of incentives for high results can be written

$$B = aQ_a.$$

This is the system normal under managerial capitalism (e.g. when executives receive bonuses tied to the level of the firm's profits). Ceteris paribus, this type of bonus system is an incentive to achieve a high value of the bonus forming index.

These formulae can easily be extended to the case where the bonus is related to several bonus forming indices, or to cases where non-proportional incentive schemes are used.

The process of formulating an enterprise plan can be regarded as a game between the authorities (e.g. the *glavk*), who do not know the productive possibilities of the enterprise, and the enterprise, which is interested in obtaining a slack plan. It is therefore scarcely surprising that the plans are often slack or impossible (impossible plans can arise if the *glavk* makes excessive corrections to the plan suggestions of the enterprise on the ground that the enterprise is aiming at a slack plan) both resulting in waste.

Prior to the reform the incentives used were of the first type, and had the negative effect one would expect. This was an important reason for the reform, a major feature of which was a switch from incentive systems of the first type to incentive systems of the second type.

---

[1] 'In the economic literature there is still not a sufficiently well founded answer to the question, what is a taut plan.' (Poltorygin [1969] p. 41.) A taut plan is often identified with an efficient plan. As both Ames and Poltorygin have pointed out, however, if the enterprise has a U-shaped cost curve then there is a difference between the least cost output and the maximum output. (Ames [1965] p. 54, Poltorygin [1969].) Is a taut plan for the production of goods which are not needed 'efficient'?

Criteria

The national economy is a complex hierarchical system whose objective is to maximise national economic welfare. At each level of the hierarchy it is necessary to adopt an appropriate criterion to guide decision makers to optimal solutions. Because maximisation of national economic welfare is too vague a criterion some more precise criterion must be adopted as a proxy for it.[1] The criteria used in the Soviet Union often stimulate waste. The central planners, concerned with maximising output, often ignore the cost of the output and its usefulness. Although the Soviet Union has caught up with the United States in the production of a number of important intermediate goods, they are often produced less efficiently, and the volume of final products derived from them is often lower, than in the United States (Efimov [1967], pp. 248–9). In some of the experiments which preceded the reform it was found that instructing clothing factories to produce according to the requirements of shops led to a fall in the growth rate. But this did not signify that the experiments were a failure. It simply resulted from the fact that when given a choice the shops ordered a wider assortment of clothes than the planners would have ordered, as a result of which production runs were shorter and 'output' (measured in constant prices rather than in units measuring consumer satisfaction) lower. (Khanin [1967a].) The Ministries are primarily concerned with plan fulfilment and hence sometimes ignore proposals which would raise national economic efficiency but might jeopardise a Ministry's plan, such as the construction of specialised enterprises to provide low cost components for enterprises belonging to several ministries.[2] The enterprises are primarily concerned with securing a low plan for the production of goods with which they are familiar, and have little incentive to pay attention to the needs of customers, or innovate or make the most efficient use of the resources which they have.

The enterprise plan specifies the value of a large number of target variables. This may well be a source of waste. If there are targets for the use of inputs this may encourage their wasteful use. If gross output is a target variable then costs may be unnecessarily high or the assortment pattern undesirable.

A characteristic of enterprise operations is storming, that is a tremendous burst of effort towards the end of the planned period in order to fulfill the plan. This may well have adverse effects on quality.

---

[1] The importance of choosing the right criterion in planning has been emphasised by C. J. Hitch and R. N. McKean (Hitch [1960] pp. 158–81). The classic western account of the criterion problem in Soviet planning is Nove [1958b].

[2] For a striking example of this see Selyunin [1968].

The introduction of a new technology, to produce an old product in a more efficient way, or to produce a new product, tends to have an immediate adverse effect on plan fulfilment. Innovation is discouraged by a system that places so much stress on quarterly plan fulfilment (and where prices are unrelated to the usefulness of commodities).

Incentives for the efficient use of inputs are weak. It was to overcome the weak incentives for the efficient use of capital that payments for capital and the use of profitability as a fund forming index were introduced as part of the reform. It was to provide an incentive for the efficient use of labour that the CC in a decree of 9 October 1969 recommended the experience of the Shchekino *kombinat* to party committees throughout the country. It is to overcome the weak incentives for the efficient use of natural resources that the introduction of payments for using them is being discussed.

It is precisely because of the long experience of unsatisfactory criteria for guiding and evaluating the work of enterprises that the idea of using profit as a synthetic success indicator gained ground in the Soviet Union in the early 1960s.[1]

Instability of the plans

A characteristic feature of enterprise plans which has a severe adverse effect on the work of enterprises, is their instability.[2] The operational (quarterly and annual) plans of enterprises are often altered repeatedly during the course of the 'planned' period, and sometimes even retrospectively. The main cause of this is the fact, the reasons for which were explained in chapter 1, that the plans received by the enterprises are always inconsistent. As these inconsistencies come to light during the planned period, it is necessary to alter the plan to allow the economy to function. A typical example of an inconsistency leading to the alteration of a plan is the impossibility of fulfilling a plan because of the lack of a necessary input. It often happens that plans have to be altered because of inconsistencies between the current and perspective plans, for example the current plan assumed that there would be available as an input the products produced by a plant that has not yet been completed. The alterations made by the planners to correct imbalances in the plans may well create the need for further alterations.

The above alterations in the plans result from the fact that the methods used in compiling them are such that the plans are always arithmetic-

---

[1] The classic account of the criterion problem in the USSR is the humourous essay published in *Pravda* in 1926 by G. E. Ryklin about the firemen who were paid according to the length of the fire. The classic account in a capitalist context is G. B. Shaw's criticism of the fact that doctors and dentists are paid according to the work they do.

[2] For a discussion of the instability of Soviet plans see Smekhov [1968].

ally inconsistent and alterations to them inevitable. There is, however, another cause of alterations, the fact that when the plans were drawn up insufficient account was taken of the possibilities for expanding output which then existed. The alterations in the plans for agricultural output which followed the September (1953) and the March (1965) Plena were a result of the failure of the CC prior to these plena to pursue policies which would lead to the development of agriculture. Similarly, it often happens that designs (e.g. for equipment or for entire enterprises) are altered after they have been adopted as a result of a decision to use a superior technology, which existed at the time the design was adopted and which should have been adopted in the first place.

There is also a third cause of alterations to the plans, namely changes in the situation (e.g. in technology, the weather or consumer tastes) after the plan is compiled. This type of alteration in the plan is not at all reprehensible (if the plan were left unchanged despite changes in the situation that would be reprehensible).

Clearly one way of minimising the need for changes in the plans would be for enterprises to have substantial reserves of inputs. This was mentioned at the end of the previous chapter as one of the ways of reducing the harmful effects on the economy of the inconsistency of the plans.

The fact that a method for solving the consistency problem does not exist, combined with the tendency to run the economy with a considerable degree of planners' tension, means that the instability of the enterprise operating plans is an integral feature of the administrative economy. This has an adverse effect on the work of enterprises, and is one of the reasons why enterprises try to obtain slack plans.

Rationing of producer goods

The material inputs which enterprises need for production are not simply purchased from producers as they would be in a market economy, but are allocated to consumer enterprises by the state supply organs. In effect this is a rationing system for producer goods. This system hinders the efficient working of enterprises and encourages enterprises to make wasteful decisions.

The efficient working of enterprises is hindered by the permanent shortage of all or almost all commodities which is associated with the supply system.[1] The supply system is such that goods often arrive late,

---

[1] To a considerable extent, it is not the shortages that create the need for the supply system, but the supply system that creates the shortages. Devons has observed that in the British aircraft industry in World War II 'a real but quite small shortage was soon inflated into a desperate and enormous scarcity. For as soon as the users found out that there was a shortage, they would conceal any stocks they already possessed and would put in exag-

resulting in the idleness of men and machines, and when they do arrive are of unsatisfactory quality. The difficulties to which the supply system gives rise are felt particularly harshly by the non-priority sectors of the economy. A 1969 court case provides a vivid example of the problems which the supply system creates for these sectors. A state farm needed wood to build cow sheds and pig styes. Wood is one of the commodities that is centrally allocated, but unfortunately the farm received through the supply system only 10 % of the wood that it needed. Without cow sheds and pig styes the animals were scarcely likely to survive the winter. The deputy director of the farm for building obtained the necessary wood by buying it from a local quarry which was about to burn the trees on some land in order to clear it before starting quarrying. The deputy director of the farm and the director of the quarry were subsequently arrested, tried and found guilty. In his speech the prosecutor dismissed the defence that this example of enterprise initiative and direct contacts was in the interests of the state. 'This was done, in the interpretation of the defendants, in the interest of the state, although it seems to me that the state would have gained more if the quarry had kept to its business and the farm to its, to produce agricultural products, in particular in view of the fact that wood is supplied to it in a centralised way.'[1] Hence the administrative economy, which works satisfactorily (from the point of view of the leaders' objectives) when there is a large non-priority sector of the economy (such as agriculture and personal consumption) which feels the brunt of shortages and waste, becomes less satisfactory when as a result of policy changes it is no longer possible to regard personal consumption as a residual, and formerly residual areas of the economy such as agriculture and housing construction come to be regarded as priority sectors, in addition to the already existing priority sectors (defence, space, industrial investment).

In order to insulate themselves from the fallible supply system, enterprises often produce their own inputs, raising the cost of production by not benefiting from economies of scale, and ministries try to become self-sufficient.

gerated demands for further supplies, in order to ensure that they got the maximum share of the limited supplies available. This applied not only to the manufacturers using the component, but also to the squadrons both at home and overseas. And this paper shortage would not be deflated until the users were so flooded with supplies that they felt confident that they could get what they wanted without building up their own private hoards. And then the inflated demand would collapse overnight.' (Devons [1950] p. 79.)

[1] The trial was reported in Klarov [1969]. The defendants were also guilty of other crimes; for example, because spare parts, though theoretically supplied through the supply system were in practice unobtainable, the farm bought some stolen parts on the black market. In addition it was necessary to fake some documents for all these expenditures to appear as legitimate transactions in the books of the farm.

Prices

The present system of wholesale prices in industry is such that in many cases they can not be used to guide enterprises to socially rational decisions. For example, a substantial part of industrial production is priced according to an individual cost plus formula. This provides no incentives for the efficient use of inputs. It may even create a situation in which the demand curve for inputs slopes up to the right.[1] Similarly, the so-called 'prices of economic events'[2] are poorly developed. By these are meant the prices of goods or services used or delivered under special circumstances, e.g. higher prices of electric power during peak hours, higher interest rates for overdue credit payments, penalties for delayed unloading of railway wagons. The permanent sellers' market, combined with the absence of competition, places customers in a weak position.[3]

A graphic example of the difficulties which this creates for the economy is provided by an enterprise in Tambov which was making obsolete, though adequate, machines for vulcanising tyres. This gave it a 1968 sales plan of 8,600,000 roubles. It was proposed that in 1969 it should switch over to a new automatic line which vulcanises at much greater speed and with considerable economy of labour. Prices, however, are such that sales in 1969 would be only 5,000,000 roubles if the new machine were produced.

'Isn't national economic efficiency taken into account in determining the prices of new products?'
'The price of new chemical equipment depends primarily on its weight.' (Belyaev [1968].)

[1] Attention has been drawn to the importance of individual cost plus prices and their adverse effects on efficiency, by Zielinski [1967]. The same point has also been made in Sitnin [1969] pp. 152–8, Garetovsky [1969] pp. 153–5, and Salimzhanov [1969] pp. 23–4.
  'Individual cost plus price' is an analytical term. In Soviet practice such prices are known variously as settlement prices or temporary prices. Wakar and Zielinski have referred to the process by which planning drives out cheap inputs and replaces them by more expensive ones as 'Gresham's law in reverse'. (Wakar [1963].)
[2] The phrase is Zielinski's. See Zielinski [1967].
[3] The decree of the CC and the Council of Ministers of 4 October 1965 'On the improvement of planning and the strengthening of the economic stimulation of industrial production' stated the intention to raise the material responsibility of enterprises which violated contract discipline in particular by making them compensate consumer enterprises for losses resulting from such violations, and subsequent decrees outlined a procedure for the calculation and payment of compensation. It does not seem to have been very effective in raising contract discipline. In many cases consumer enterprises which have suffered as a result of contract violation 'amnesty' the supplier and press, not for compensation for losses incurred, but for the speediest possible fulfilment of the contract, a phenomenon which is partly a result of the permanent sellers' market. In addition it is often unclear how to calculate the losses. Moreover the compensation, when paid, often does not cover more than a small proportion of the losses.

Hence it is not in the interest of the plant to produce the new machinery. This would reduce its sales and thus its incentive funds. This difficulty in adapting output to requirements results from the combination of the existing price system, the absence of competition, the permanent sellers' market, and the fact that enterprises are judged not by the extent to which they satisfy demand but by the extent to which they fulfil the plan.

If the planners had sufficient information and time to make socially rational decisions throughout the economy, and enterprises simply carried out their instructions, then these problems would not arise. The planners would determine the socially rational decisions for the enterprises and the latter would execute them. The problems arise because the planners do not have sufficient information and time to make such decisions and the enterprises have considerable freedom in decision making. The advocates of an optimally functioning economic system consider that whereas instructions from the planners, and prices determined by administrators at lengthy intervals, are unable to bring about rational decision making throughout the economy (because the planners lack the time and information to issue the necessary instructions, and administratively determined prices reflect the situation at some more or less distant date in the past) this function could be performed by prices which are determined on the basis of the correct formula and which are flexible.

The September (1965) Plenum resolved that the existing wholesale prices should be revised, and the new prices were introduced as from 1 January 1967 in the light and food industries, and in the rest of industry as from 1 July 1967. (The scope for revising the price system was limited by the government's insistence, on political grounds, that retail prices, and the price of industrial commodities purchased by the agricultural sector,[1] remain unchanged.) The main differences of principle between the new prices and those prevailing previously are that with the revised prices the proportion of industry which is loss making has fallen considerably, the rates of profit in different industries have been brought closer together, and that, at the level of the industry, the new prices include a substantial profit margin (generally it is 15 %) expressed as a percentage of capital employed.[2] (The old prices included a lower profit margin, expressed as a percentage of cost.)

[1] The prices received by industry for products sold to the collective and state farms were increased, but the prices paid by the collective and state farms remained at the old level. The resulting loss was borne by Selkhoztekhnika (the wholesale organisation for industrial products sold to the farms) which received subsidies from the state budget for this purpose.

[2] As far as the prices of individual goods are concerned, under the 1967 price reform they did include a profit margin, but it was still often calculated as a percentage of cost (because it was often difficult to calculate the capital intensity of particular goods). After the 1967 reform methods were drawn up in research institutes to enable the prices of individual goods to include profit proportional to capital employed.

The new prices are undoubtedly an improvement on the old, but they are still often unable to guide enterprises to socially rational decisions (e.g. many prices are still based on weight), and it is widely recognised that both the price formation formula and the price formation method require further improvement.

Personal consumption

An important negative aspect of the administrative economy is inattention to personal consumption. Aspects of the inattention to personal consumption in the USSR are the restricted assortment of consumer goods and services available (this shows itself in such phenomena as the inadequate arrangements for maintenance of the housing stock, and the fact that it is customary for persons going abroad and subsequently returning to the USSR to be asked to bring back commodities unavailable in the USSR, such as certain medicines, ski wax, and multi-coloured biros); the poor quality of many of the goods that are available (e.g. many of the potatoes and apples); the intermittent supply of consumer goods (it often happens that basic goods such as eggs are simply unavailable for several days); and the poor supply of consumer goods in provincial towns and villages.

Queues and shortages are characteristic features of the administrative economy. It often happens that a particular commodity is unavailable in a particular place, or can only be obtained by queueing, because the commodity has been priced below the equilibrium price (and the activities of the trade and production organs are determined not by consumer demand as expressed in the market but by administrative considerations). This gives rise to irritation among frustrated purchasers and those who have to stand in queues, and to black marketeering. An important theme in the writings of Novozhilov was the argument that shortages and queues are not inevitable, that by suitable use of the price mechanism they can be overcome. In 1926 he published an article (Novozhilov [1926]) in which he criticised the idea being propagated at that time by politicians and newspapers that the Soviet Union was suffering from a 'goods famine', and argued that it was actually suffering from a suppressed inflation and that the way to deal with the problem was to raise prices. In his famous 1959 paper (Novozhilov [1959] pp. 199–200) he reverted to this theme and explained that the underpricing of goods leads to the expenditure of 'time and effort on the search for scarce goods and standing in queues. At the same time unproductive and even criminal actions (speculation in scarce goods, under the counter sales by assistants of the scarce goods etc.) become the source of unjustified enrichment.' Novozhilov's repeated variations on

Table 2.1. *Sales and stocks: 1965 as percentage of 1960*

Commodity	Sales	Stocks in retail net work
Cotton fabrics	78.7	227.9
Woollen fabrics	81.6	130.0
Iron beds	76.2	128.5
Sewing machines	48.4	226.0

SOURCE: Lashchinsky [1968].

the theme of the price mechanism as the most efficient way of allocating scarce goods between consumers have been repeatedly rejected by the authorities on the ground that the way to overcome shortages is not to raise prices but to expand output. Commenting on Fedorenko's 1968 book, a deputy chairman of Gosplan USSR explained once more that 'It is very easy it turns out, to overcome a shortage of this or that product – it is sufficient to raise their prices . . . [However] the raising of prices consciously places limits on the possibilities of satisfying the needs of the members of society instead of devoting all our efforts to their satisfaction by means of growth (increasing investment) and raising labour productivity.' (Bachurin [1969] p. 15.) Ignoring Marshall's distinction between the short run and the long run leads, for example, to a shortage of crockery in the biggest department store in the country, and to long queues in factory canteens in Bryansk because plates are a scarce good. (Leshchevskii [1970], Konenko [1970].)

In the administrative economy the production of consumer goods does not respond quickly to changes in demand. For example, in the period 1962–5 above the norm stocks in the retail network were never less than two milliard roubles (about 1 % of the national income). Table 2.1 shows how the stocks of some goods continued to rise as demand fell.

The result of planning from the achieved level, combined with inflexible prices and plans for output rather than sales, was that when demand for some goods was saturated, instead of producing different, desired, commodities, the unwanted goods were produced as before and piled up in warehouses. Simultaneously there were other goods the output of which increased at a slower rate than the demand for them. In 1965 the demand for leather footwear increased by 11 % over 1964 and stocks fell by 13.5 %; the demand for furniture increased by 10.3 % and stocks fell by 15.7 %. A similar situation existed with respect to ready-made clothes. In other words, supply diverged sharply from demand. For those goods for which demand was falling supply

Table 2.2. *Alterations in the production plan of the Beloomutski Clothing Factory (Moscow Region) in 2nd half of 1965*

Article	Production (thousands of articles)		
	According to plan drawn up in the traditional way	According to plan drawn up on the basis of direct contacts	Output according to new plan as % of output according to old plan
Winter clothes for school children	66.6	116.8	175.4
Half-length winter coats for school children	20.0	13.2	66.0
Spring coats for school children	53.3	98.9	185.5
Children's raincoats	61.7	20.9	33.9
Coats for nursery school children	18.6	4.4	23.7
Winter coats for pre-school children	41.3	15.5	37.5

SOURCE: Lyovin [1967] p. 74.

continued to increase and unwanted goods accumulated. For those goods for which demand was rapidly increasing supply increased less rapidly.

A major feature of the reform was a change in the method of determining the production plans of many enterprises producing consumer goods. Whereas formerly these plans were determined by the higher administrative bodies, under the reform they are determined, in part, by agreement between producer enterprises and the retail trade. In many cases this has led to major changes in the assortment pattern, as table 2.2 illustrates.

The striking divergence between the assortment pattern based on instructions from the planners, and that based on orders from the retail trade corroborates the observation of two Poles: 'The adaption of production to needs can be made only by the market buyer – ultimately by the consumer – but never by the central planner who fixes the prices of goods by himself and without reference to the market and who judges an enterprise by its execution of central directive indices ....' (Kuron [n.d.].)

Bureaucratisation

In 1937 Lange argued that 'the real danger of socialism is that of a bureaucratisation of economic life, and not the impossibility of coping with the problem of allocation of resources.' (Lange [1937] pp. 127–8.)

The experience of the Soviet Union and other socialist countries supports the argument that the bureaucratisation of economic life is a serious danger under socialism, and a major reason for the transition from the administrative economy in Yugoslavia and Hungary, the abortive transition in Czechoslovakia, and the discussion of economic reform in the USSR has been to reduce the bureaucratic elements in economic life. (Horvat [1964] p. 225, Kornai [1959] chapter 5.)

Whereas in a market economy decisions are made by managers in response to economic signals, in an administrative economy they are made by officials in accordance with official procedure. The programme of the optimal planners to reduce the bureaucratisation of economic life is twofold. First, many of the decisions currently being made by the planners in an arbitrary, voluntaristic way, should be made by the use of objective, scientific methods. The optimal planners have devoted great efforts to developing objective, rational methods for decision making, for example in the field of the optimal development and location of industries. Secondly, whereas at the present time many decisions by enterprise management require the approval of some higher official,[1] the optimal planners propose that such decisions should be made by enterprise management in response to economic criteria.

CONCLUSION

This study discusses many unfavourable aspects of our economic mechanism. But we must not forget that planning has made it possible to ensure full employment and the rapid increase in the quantity of production which has been described above. Hence, improvements in administering the economy must be brought about in such a way as to ensure that any changes will develop further these advantageous aspects of our economic mechanism rather than endangering them.

J. Kornai (Kornai [1959] p. 121.)

In conclusion it may be noted:

1 It is important not to contrast the situation actually existing now with an idealised situation that might exist. If enterprises were simply instructed to maximise profits and given a free hand, the experience of capitalist firms suggests that they might well operate with considerable waste and inefficiency.

2 Although the administrative economy clearly has costs, it is important when contemplating possible reforms to offset possible gains in efficiency against possible adverse effects on major policy objectives (such as the ability of the state to determine the main directions of development, price stability, the level of employment, the distribution of income and regional policy).

[1] For a striking example see Yudina [1969].

3 Where decentralisation is advocated because the enterprises have better knowledge than the planners of their own possibilities, it is important to bear in mind the general planning rule that 'Because centralisation restricts lower-level actions, it should be justified only on the grounds that the restrictions lead to better overall behaviour of the organisation. This is true only when significant interactions exist between lower level units. If a sub-unit interacts very weakly with other parts of the organisation, it is desirable to assign the sub-unit only loose goals consistent with those of the organisation as a whole (a "suitable" return on investment, say). In this way, the sub-unit is free to exploit its own detailed knowledge of its operations and environment.' (Emery [1969] p. 121.) In other words, centralise where, and only where, this is necessary in order to internalise what would appear as externalities at some lower level.[1]

4 The elements of the economic system are closely linked together, and this must be borne in mind when introducing reforms. The price system, the supply system, the incentive system, the criteria used, and the degree of centralisation are inseparably interconnected. For example, to give the enterprise more autonomy in determining its assortment pattern, given the existing price system, is scarcely likely to increase efficiency.

The Hungarian economist Kornai long ago observed that

One cannot exchange a cog in an integrated, functioning machine for another one of quite a different type. The latter may be new, but it will obstruct the working of the machine nevertheless . . . . A solution can only be found by taking a comprehensive view of both centralization and decentralization and by renouncing the idea of piecemeal tinkering with the economic mechanism in the course of efforts to change it . . . . The reforms we need are of a kind which will improve all the major methods and institutions of our economic mechanism in a systematic, parallel and harmonious manner. In other words, the job of transforming the system of plan index numbers should be matched by an overhaul of the system of incentives and prices, as well as of the functioning of the monetary and credit systems etc.

It is not necessary that all these changes should be brought about all at once in every sphere; this would probably create too much of an upheaval. It is possible to carry out the reforms that are needed in a number of stages. What is essential is that the changes brought about in various spheres should complement one another in an organic manner. They should constitute parts of a thoroughly thought out, centrally coordinated series of reforms based on a unified conception. (Kornai [1959] pp. 225–6.)

5 The changes in the economic mechanism brought about in recent years have not 'complemented one another in an organic manner'. They have not 'constituted part of a thoroughly thought out, centrally

---

[1] As Lichfield has observed, 'Externalities exist only because of the institutional limitations on the costs and benefits which the decision makers choose to take into their reckoning.' (Margolis [1965] p. 247.) For a discussion of this point see Nove [1969b].

coordinated series of reforms based on a uniform conception'. This explains the fact that the measures announced at the September (1965) Plenum did not overcome the problems outlined in this chapter and the preceding one. The failure of the reform to live up to the hopes of its keenest supporters was a major factor leading to the decisions of the December (1969) Plenum, which sought an increase in efficiency not by expanding *khozraschet* but by increasing discipline.[1]

6 The theory of the optimally functioning socialist economy was developed precisely to serve as the 'unified conception' which could form the basis of a 'thoroughly thought out, centrally coordinated series of reforms'. This theory is examined in subsequent chapters.

---

[1] Similarly the Bulgarian experiment with the use of profit as the chief criterion for guiding and evaluating the work of enterprises in an economy which retained administrative price determination (which took place in 1964–6 and involved 240 enterprises) was abandoned partly because enterprises were able to increase their profit by unjustified increases in prices (for example by the introduction of 'new' products), and because enterprises, in particular in light industry, shifted their assortment pattern towards more profitable, but not necessarily more socially desirable, products.

3. THE OPTIMALLY FUNCTIONING SOCIALIST ECONOMY – A THEORY OF IMPROVED METHODS OF ECONOMIC CALCULATION AND ECONOMIC REFORM

The theory of the optimally functioning socialist economy is an incomplete, developing and controversial theory which arose as a result of a process of interaction between the new techniques of planning and control developed in the last four decades by mathematicians, engineers and economists, and the requirements and problems of the traditional planning system.

It has been developed by TSEMI, with support from Academician Kantorovich, IEOPP, the late Professor Novozhilov, and some of the research workers in the various industrial research institutes, such as I. Ya. Birman. Even among supporters of this theory, however, there exist 'various, and on some points mutually exclusive opinions. It could not be otherwise as this is a developing theory.' (*Diskussiya* [1968] p. 39 – Aganbegyan.) Within TSEMI there are disagreements between those who regard profit as a suitable local optimality criterion and those who do not, between those who approach the question of optimal functioning from linear programming and general equilibrium theory, from technical systems, and from the standpoint of the problems of the administrative economy.

A major source of ideas for the theory has been linear programming. From the work which has been done on the use of linear programming to calculate optimal plans the adherents of this theory have learnt that there is little practical advantage to be gained by the calculation of optimal plans if the economy is organised in such a way that they are not implemented (see Introduction, p. 10). From the theorem of the characteristics of an optimal plan the theory has derived the idea that the calculations of optimal plans and optimal prices are intimately linked, and that price calculations should not be isolated from plan calculations. The theory has also derived from the theorem the idea that associated with the optimal plan are value relations (such as prices, quasi rent and profit), which can be used to guide enterprises aiming to maximise their own optimality criterion to socially rational decisions in the event of small changes in the data since the original optimal plan was drawn up. From linear programming the theory has also derived the idea that the scarcity of resources is a fundamental aspect of reality and that national economic planning can fruitfully be treated as an extremal problem.

From systems engineering[1] the theory derives the idea of the national economy as a complex hierarchical system, in which some decisions should be taken at the level of the national economy, some at the level of the industry or region and some at the level of the association or enterprise. It also derives from systems engineering the idea of planning as a complex hierarchical process, in which the first stage is the elaboration of long term forecasts of the development of technology, natural resources, consumption and population. (A considerable volume of research has been undertaken in recent years, at TSEMI and at other institutes, on forecasting.) The next stages are the elaboration of the national economic perspective plan and of the national economic medium term plan. (A major contribution by the optimal planners to Soviet planning has been the use of input–output for variant calculations in medium term planning, a topic discussed in the following chapter.) The separate industries each compile optimal perspective and medium term plans, whose variables are such questions as the location of enterprises, the capacity of enterprises, the technology to be used, and the best way of using deficit materials for which there are substitutes. Up till now 'The most tangible results in the field of the introduction of economico-mathematical methods into the practice of planning have been achieved in the optimisation of the perspective plans for the development and location of industries.' (Chernyavsky [1969] p. 86.) (This work is discussed in the following chapter.) The separate enterprises or associations each compile optimal medium term plans and use the methods of operational research to ensure that their current plans are optimal.

As far as current planning is concerned, TSEMI's general theoretical framework is a fairly conventional application of general equilibrium theory to a planned economy. The central planners work out a highly aggregated plan for the outputs and prices of the chief commodities. Each industry, on the basis of its own optimality criterion, works out a plan for the output and price of its key products. Each enterprise receives from above plans for the output of its key products, plans for the supply to it of its key inputs, and certain financial parameters, such as prices for key goods, wage rates, payments for the use of natural resources and capital goods, and the rate of interest on bank loans.

---

[1] See for example Mesarovic [1970]. (A Soviet edition of this book was scheduled to appear in 1973.)

Subject to these obligations, the enterprise or association is free to maximise its local optimality criterion. As far as concrete policy measures are concerned, TSEMI emphasises the importance of developing wholesale trade in producer goods (as opposed to their rationing), the grouping of enterprises into associations, and an increased flexibility of prices, for example by establishing three groups of prices, fixed, limited and contractual. The fixed prices would be for the most important goods and would be fixed by the centre uniformly for the whole country. The limited prices would be maxima established by the centre. Transactions below the maxima would be permitted. The contractual prices would be free prices established by agreement between buyer and seller. As far as retail prices are concerned, TSEMI advocates equilibrium prices, in order to eliminate shortages and queues. Rather than provide a detailed description of TSEMI's view about how current planning should be organised, I have translated the most important sections of Academician Fedorenko's speech at the 1966 debate and appended them to this chapter, so that the reader may see for himself the proposals outlined by the Director of TSEMI at a crucial debate.

From the experience of the traditional planning system the adherents of the theory derive the conviction that it is necessary to do better, that the problems discussed in the two preceding chapters are not inevitable, that the economy can be organised in such a way as to overcome them. 'The old system of management', Ya. G. Liberman argued in an article published in the journal of TSEMI,

was well suited to the attainment of its chief aims, to mobilise resources and concentrate them on the satisfaction of the most urgent needs of the state. It was mainly aimed at the quantitative, extensive growth of production (this showed itself for example in the practice of awarding bonuses for overfulfilment of the physical indices of the plan) and feebly stimulated raising the efficiency of production (this gave rise to the formerly well known formula: 'the fulfilment of the plan at any price'). This had if not a theoretical, then at any rate historical justification in the specific conditions of that period in which the system arose (the permanent threat from the imperialist states, and also the existence of colossal natural and labour resources together with a chronic deficiency of all or almost all commodities). (Ya. Liberman [1968] pp. 691–2.)

The advocates of an optimally functioning economic system would like to replace this system by an alternative one which stimulates efficiency and in which all decisions are made on rational (objective, scientific) grounds. This involves both a replacement of much administrative decision making by the use of market forces, and an all round improvement in the quality of decision making to be brought about by the use of mathematical methods. In this way it is hoped, in the words of a critic, 'to guarantee planning against bureaucratism, voluntarism and so on'. (*Diskussiya* [1968] p. 190.) Whereas in the past policy making has tended to be a series of ad hoc, and often contradictory, responses to changing circumstances, lacking any scientific basis, the advocates of an optimally functioning economic system consider that 'Improving the methods of planning and management should take place not by way of sporadic alterations of separate parts of the existing system of planning and management, but by the improvement of the entire economy of the country as a whole and the gradual putting into effect of a single conception objectively reflecting the laws of development of a socialist economy.' (Fedorenko [1968a] p. 43.)

In advocating an improvement in both the methods of economic calculation and the economic mechanism, TSEMI is following in the footsteps of the late Academician Nemchinov, who played a major role not only in the rise of mathematical economics in the USSR and in encouraging the use of mathematical methods in planning, but also in the discussion in the Academy of Sciences which preceded the publication in *Pravda* in September 1962 of the much publicised article by E. G. Liberman, and himself published in *Kommunist* (1964 No. 5) a powerful statement of the case for economic reform.

The theory of the optimally functioning socialist economy provides a framework for the activities of the optimal planners, which can conveniently be considered under three heads, teaching, methodological guidance and research.

To ensure that the knowledge of, and techniques used by, the planners rise pari passu with the increased possibilities which modern technology is creating, a vigorous programme of education is necessary. Undergraduate and graduate education in mathematical economics is now provided in numerous universities and institutes. In addition the leading research institutes (such as TSEMI) function to some extent as graduate schools by providing opportunities for (higher) degrees to be earned. A steady stream of recent *kandidats* (PhDs) leaves TSEMI for responsible posts in the planning apparatus. In 1971 an Institute for the Management of the National Economy, whose students are senior officials of the central and republican Ministries and departments, and which teaches, inter alia, the use of optimising techniques in planning, was opened in Moscow. (It is attached to Gostekhnika.) Academician Kantorovich moved to this Institute from the Institute of Mathematics of the Siberian branch of the Academy of Sciences, and TSEMI has established close links with it. The department of economic-mathematical methods at this Institute is headed by Academician Fedorenko, and research workers at TSEMI are available to guide the work of students at the Institute.

TSEMI, as the chief research organisation in the field of optimal planning, provides methodological guidance to workers in other institutes and departments on how to apply optimal planning to particular problems. The wide range of its work is indicated by the titles of the Methods it has circulated in recent years. They include the two editions of the *Osnovnye polozheniya optimizatsii razvitiya i razmeshcheniya proizvodstva* (Basic principles of the optimisation of the development and location of production), *Metodika po primeneniyu ekonomiko-matematicheskikh metodov dlya operativnogo planirovaniya perevozok gruzov* (Method for the utilisation of economic-mathematical methods for the real time planning of freight transport), *Mezhotraslevye rukovodyashchie materialy po proektirovaniya avtomatizirovannykh sistem upravleniya predpriyatiyami* (Interindustry guide for the design of automated management systems for enterprises – jointly with Gostekhnika and Minpribor), *Tipovaya metodika rascheta optimal'nykh planov prikrepleniya potrebitelei k postavskchikam* (Standard method for the calculation of optimal attachment plans – jointly with Gosplan and Gostekhnika), *Metodicheskie materialy po sozdaniyu avtomatizirovannoi sistemy upravleniya na predpriyatiyakh* (Methodological material for the creation of automated management systems at enterprises) and *Osnovnye polozheniya metodiki ekonomicheskoi otsenki prirodnykh resursov* (Basic principles of a method for the economic evaluation of natural resources).[1]

The research done in this field can conveniently be considered under eight heads: the periodisation of planning, variant calculations in planning, the consistency of the plans, the optimisation of the plans, the relationship between physical and value planning, the provision of information for planning and management, the organisational structure of the economy and improving the functioning of the economy.

National economic planning is thought of in the USSR as a complex system of plans, embracing annual plans, five year plans, a fifteen to twenty year general plan and long term forecasts. The optimal planners accept this conception, and have done considerable work in all these fields.

The desirability of making variant calculations in planning, as a step in the direction of the calculation of optimal plans, has been stressed by the optimal planners, and they provided the technique which enables Gosplan's research institute to incorporate variant calculations into the construction of five year plans (this is explained in chapter 4).

The usefulness of input–output for improving the consistency of planning and its superiority in this respect to material balances have been repeatedly stressed by the optimal planners. They have done a great deal of work on input–output, and during the 1960s this technique was incorporated into planning and statistical practice. In chapter 1 it

---

[1] The writing of such Methods is analogous to the writing of the UNIDO *Guidelines for Project Evaluation* (NY 1972).

was argued that input–output, like material balances, is unable to ensure the calculation of consistent operational current plans. The main gain from the use of input–output in planning has been that it has enabled variant calculations of the structure of production to be made in perspective planning, and the main gain from the use of input–output in statistics has been as a valuable source of data about the economy. For example, analysis of the 1959 all-Union table provided the material for a vigorous critique of the inadequate support which agriculture is receiving from industry (Lemeshev [1968]). Similarly, analysis of the 1961 input–output table for Lithuania showed that only a very small proportion of Lithuanian industrial production flowed into Lithuanian agriculture. Since Lithuania is mainly an agricultural republic, it was decided that this was unsatisfactory and that the proportion ought to be increased.[1]

During the 1960s the optimal planners not only performed numerous experimental calculations on the optimisation of planning, but actually introduced optimal planning into various branches of the economy. Two important examples of the implementation of optimal plans are given in chapter 4. Another important area for the calculation of optimal plans is stock control.

The optimal planners have persistently argued that the traditional planning system suffers from a dichotomy between physical and value planning and that it is necessary to integrate the two, to calculate physical and value plans simultaneously. Their ideas on how to re-organise the Soviet system of national accounts so as to facilitate this are set out, for example, in Isaev [1969] and Isaev [1971].

They have also argued that under the traditional planning system the enterprises have to send to the central administrative and statistical organs a mass of unnecessary information, whereas much of the information which the planners really need, in particular if the new methods of economic calculations are to be used, is not available (Chernyak [1964]). The optimal planners have devoted considerable efforts to the study of information flows in the economy and efforts to improve them.[2] In chapter 4 it is pointed out that a major result of their work on investment planning was an improvement in the information on transport costs available to the planners. In the late 1960s there was initiated a major reorganisation of the process of collecting and processing data in the central planning organs (this is part of the creation of an automated system of plan calculations[3]). The reduction in the unnecessary information which the enterprises have to transmit to the

---

[1] Information supplied at interview in Gosplan Lithuania, Vilna (February 1967).
[2] For examples of such studies see Fedorenko [1967b], *Issledovanie* [1968], *Ekonomicheskaya* [1970], or *Integrirovannye* [1970].   [3] See p. 65 below.

central authorities, the securing of the information which the planners really need, and the replacement of manual methods of data collection and processing by electronic data processing have been important fields for research and proposals by the optimal planners.

At the present time a major development in the organisational structure of the economy is the creation of associations. The optimal planners have supported this and Academician Fedorenko was a member of the commission working out the Statute of the association at the end of the period.

The optimal planners are very much concerned with improving the functioning of the economy. This involves such questions as the role of prices, incentives and credit in the economy. The theoretical basis of their ideas on optimal functioning are considered in chapter 5, and some specific applications of these ideas are analysed in chapter 6.

To direct and coordinate work on optimal planning the USSR Academy of Sciences has set up a Scientific Council on the optimal planning and management of the economy. This Council has 89 members and 29 sections, 13 devoted to particular planning problems and 16 to the problems of particular economic regions. The sections concerned with planning problems include one concerned with long term forecasting, another with the use of economic-mathematical methods for the study of the economies of foreign countries, and another on transport problems. The chairman of the Council is Academician Fedorenko, the Director of TSEMI.

The mathematical economists completely reject the idea that the transition from the administrative economy to the optimally functioning economy will be a once and for all process. They conceive of it as a process stretching over many years, in which the economic mechanism and the methods of economic calculation are steadily improved, a process which some might be tempted to call 'piecemeal social engineering' but which Volkonsky refers to as the 'deepening of optimisation'. (Volkonsky [1967] p. 8.)

In 1970 an editorial article in the journal of TSEMI (*Nauchno* [1970] p. 491) explained that:

'The construction of communism' it is stated in the Theses of the CC CPSU *On the hundredth anniversary of the birth of Lenin* 'is our general perspective .... Going along the Leninist path the CPSU sees the chief task of the building of communism as the creation of its material-technical base'. One of the decisive preconditions for the fulfilment of this grandiose task is the transformation of the existing economy of the country into an optimally functioning one. This means the achievement of such a high level of the organisation and planning of social labour that the fullest possible utilisation of all resources in the interests of raising the living standards of the working people, and also satisfying other requirements of society, would be provided.

Only a country with a socialist planned economy has the objective possibilities for the real optimisation of the national economy. In this is the principal advantage of the socialist system over the capitalist.

Transforming objective possibilities into reality does not take place and can not take place, however, automatically. It requires a gigantic organisational work . . . .

The supporters of the theory of the optimally functioning socialist economy are opposed to the idea that the transition to an optimally planned economy is simply a matter of creating a network of computer centres that will transmit information from the enterprises to the centre, and orders from the centre to the enterprises; they also oppose a one sided emphasis on the role of the market and value relations at the expense of the state plan.

At the present time extensive work is under way on the development of automated management systems. The directives of the 24th Congress (1971) on the 1971–5 five year plan clearly state the intention:

To ensure *the wide application of economic-mathematical methods, the use of electronic computers and organisational technology and means of communication* in order to improve the planning and management of the national economy. To improve substantially the system of accounting and control, to improve statistics.

To develop work on the creation and introduction of automated management systems for the planning and control of industries, territorial organisations, associations, and enterprises, with the intention of creating an interdepartmental automated system for the collection and processing of information for accounting, planning and management of the national economy on the basis of a state network of computer centres and a unified automated communications system for the country. To provide from the very beginning for the organisational, methodological and technical unity of this system.

It is important to be clear as to the relationship between the wide application of automated management systems and the transition to an optimally planned and functioning economic system.[1] The two differ in organisation, in personnel and intellectually. The development of automated management systems is a state matter, on which work is coordinated by a State Committee (Gostekhnika). Optimal planning is a field for academic research, on which work is coordinated by a Scientific Council of the Academy of Sciences. The people who work in the former area are computer and operational research specialists and the chief research institutes are Gostekhnika's all-Union research institute for problems of organisation and management (founded in 1972) and IPU. The people who work in the latter area are mathe-

---

[1] A sympathetic reviewer (*TLS* [1972]) of Ellman [1971] identified the establishment of automated management systems with optimal planning and ascribed the paternity of the programme for the creation of an interdepartmental automated management system to the optimal planners. The real position is more complex.

matical economists and the chief research institute is TSEMI. The stress by the optimal planners on the importance of value relations (prices, profit, payments for resources) as guides to efficiency is not a feature of the development of automated management systems. The two fields are related in the following ways.

First, the development of management information and control systems sometimes incorporates work done by the mathematical economists. For example, as explained in the following chapter, the work done by Kantorovich in introducing optimal production scheduling into the steel industry is being incorporated into the management information and control system Metall.

Secondly, one of the departmental automated management systems which is being developed as part of the programme for creating the OGAS is the ASPR. The project for replacing the traditional methods of drawing up plans by an automated system of plan calculations was launched in the late 1960s.[1] It entails the replacement of the traditional information flows between the enterprises and the planners by electronic data processing, so as to reduce the labour involved in the work and to ensure that the planners have all the information which they need; the introduction of mathematical planning methods; and the control of the planning process by network planning. TSEMI is the leading research organisation in this field.[2] The utilisation of input–output in national, regional and republican planning (an example of which is given in the following chapter) and the calculation and implementation of optimal plans for the development and location of industries (which is described in the following chapter) are part of the development of the ASPR.

Thirdly, TSEMI is playing a role in the development of automated management systems elsewhere, for example in industrial enterprises.

Fourthly, some of the research workers in the field of automated management systems (such as Academician Trapeznikov) share TSEMI's view that improving the planning and management of the economy requires not just the use of better techniques but also alterations in the economic relations between its parts.

In some circles the development of automated management systems and a unified state network of computer centres have hypertrophied at

[1] For reports on the conferences held to discuss this work see Samokhin [1967] (a report of the January 1967 conference), Gurvich [1969] (a report of the May 1969 conference), and *Seminar* [1970] (a report of the May 1970 seminar). For a report of the meeting of the Scientific Council on optimal planning of 4 February 1969, at which the main items on the agenda was the development of the ASPR, see *Plenum* [1969]. For a description of the work by a specialist at Gosplan see Volchkov [1970].

[2] TSEMI's conception of the theoretical basis of the ASPR is set out in Fedorenko [1972a]. For a popular exposition see Fedorenko [1972b].

the expense of the development of economic relations, and the optimal planners have persistently argued against this tendency, for the reason given on page 57. In other circles the opposite danger is encountered, an exaggeration of the role of value relations and an underestimation of the advantages of central planning. The optimal planners do not share this position. They are the ones who have introduced input–output into national economic planning, calculated optimal production schedules, optimal attachment plans and optimal plans for the development and location of industries. At the October 1970 expanded meeting of the Scientific Council on optimal planning Khachaturov argued that the adoption of Academician Fedorenko's ideas on price formation might lead to open inflation on Yugoslav lines. Fedorenko replied that in his conception prices were intimately linked with the plan, and that central planning is a major advantage of socialism. (*Diskussiya po problemam* [1971] p. 308.)

Summary

The theory of the optimally functioning socialist economy is a theory of improved methods of economic calculation and economic reform which was developed in the 1960s by TSEMI. It is based on ideas derived from linear programming, systems engineering and the experience of Soviet planning. This theory provides a framework for a large volume of research. This research is closely related to, but distinct from, the work now under way on a massive scale for introducing automated management systems. The adherents of this theory are opposed both to a one sided emphasis on the technological aspects of the optimisation of planning and management, and to a one sided emphasis on the role of value relations at the expense of the plan.

Appendix   Optimal planning and functioning – extracts from Academician Fedorenko's speech at the 1966 debate.[1]

WORKING OUT THE PLAN

The starting point for working out the optimal plan is the data of the lowest levels of the economy about their productive possibilities. These data are communicated to the adjacent level of the hierarchical system (for example an industry) in the form of input coefficients for various possible ways of producing the articles which are already produced or which it is intended to produce. In principle the initial choice of these articles can be whatever one likes, in particular they can be those actually produced in the pre-plan period. The choice, both of the articles, and of their relative quantities, will be made more precise in the optimal plan by the process of successive approximations. Simultaneously with this action by the enterprises the design organ-

[1] *Diskussiya* [1968] pp. 13–15 and pp. 23–4.

isations inform their higher organ of all the variants of new technically possible decisions. The questions what will be the volume of output by these new methods, where and when the new enterprises will be built or the existing ones reconstructed, will be solved in the optimal plan.

At the level of the industry the intra-industrial constraints (the relations between enterprises) on the output and consumption of various kinds of products are analysed, the physical indices for the enterprises are aggregated, and possible ways of carrying out production are established.

The information of the industry is transmitted further, to a higher level of the hierarchy. In a three level scheme this would be the national economy as a whole, in a four level one some level intermediate between the industry and the economic system as a whole. At this level the inter-industry constraints on the production and consumption of the outputs of the industries are determined. In this way all the conditions necessary for the calculation of the first variant of the plan at the highest level of the national economic system have been met. They are, the availability of the technological coefficients, the inter-industry constraints and the national economic optimality criterion for the development of the economy. As a result of the solution at the highest level of an extremal problem the aggregated physical indices (the resources consumed and the output produced) and the corresponding prices, for each industry, are determined. These prices show the increment to the optimality criterion resulting from a small alteration in the given constraint.

On the basis of these prices the industry solves its local problem for the maximisation of profit. Similar interrelations exist between the industry and the enterprise. In accordance with the optimal prices 'handed down' by the industry, the enterprises solve their optimisation problem for the maximisation of profit and obtain a variant of the plan which harmonises their interests with the interests of the higher levels and the whole national economy. This is how the local optimality criterion is harmonised with the national economic optimality criterion. If such harmonisation does not occur, then either an optimal regime for the functioning of the whole economy can not be maintained, or the wide interference of the higher organs in the activity of the lower levels of management will become inevitable, i.e. purely administrative methods of management will become primary.

It should be underlined that finding the optimal variant of the plan requires not one but several cycles of calculations. The variant of the plan calculated by the enterprise in accordance with the system of prices received in the first cycles is communicated to the higher level, which on the basis of this data again solves an extremal problem (this is the second iteration). Similarly at higher levels of the national economy. As a result of such successive calculations (iterations) (on rapid electronic computers it is possible to do this in a comparatively short period) the optimal national economic plan, which takes account of the social goal formulated at that level and also of the available material natural and labour resources and technical knowledge, is found.

OPTIMAL PRICES

It follows from the scheme of optimal planning just outlined that each level of the national economy receives from the higher level, at each step in the iterative process, prices for its outputs, prices which to some extent or other are aggregated. This gives the corresponding level, and in particular the enterprises, definite scope for exercising their initiative. Using the prices of the optimal plan, the economic objects on the same level establish direct contacts, and make more precise the assortment, quality and the prices themselves (within the limits of the aggregated optimal prices) for the numerous kinds of output produced. Under these conditions the enterprises will be interested in the introduction of new technology, of new more technically progressive methods of production, because this will increase the valuation of their work and hence their incomes.

It is absolutely clear that all the levels of management, other than the highest, cannot be directly guided by the national economic optimality criterion. They need more partial indices of the value of all the types of resources which fall in their field of activity, i.e. prices of resources. If these prices are determined *a priori* and do not reflect the actual influences of each resource on the general goal of the socialist economy, do not characterise the real contribution of each resource to the satisfaction of the needs of society, then such prices cannot serve as an instrument for taking correct economic decisions. Consequently without optimal prices it is possible to harmonise efficiently centralised and decentralised management of the economy.

Striving to maximise profit under conditions of the operation of a system of prices of the optimal plan, the enterprises independently, without superflous tutelage by the higher organs, decide the most important question of their economic activity, simultaneously putting into practice the optimal plan for the development of the whole economy and making their contribution to the national economic criterion . . . .

PAYMENT FOR RESOURCES

The norms of payment for assets, natural resources (rent) and also for the utilisation in production of workers with scarce skills, should find expression in prices. For example if a price for water resources had been established in Kazakhstan, which took account of the limited resources of water in that region, the requirements of the population and the costs necessary for increasing water resources, then obviously the location there of chemical plants would have turned out to be objectively inexpedient.

Unfortunately we still often use natural resources irrationally. Take oilfields. There are many cases where wells are abandoned which retain up to 50 % or more of their oil reserves. If, however, we were to approach natural resources from the standpoint of society as a whole and introduce payment for natural resources, then it would be clear in which case it makes sense to abandon deposits not yet exhausted, and in which cases their exploitation should continue.

An important conclusion of the theory of optimal planning is the need to establish a valuation of the labour of a worker which shows what quantity of consumer goods the worker should receive from the point of view of creating the conditions which allow him to make the biggest contribution to the optimality criterion. Consequently, now, when the measurement of labour costs takes place only via wages, only one side is taken account of in prices, the side connected with the direct participation of man in production. The other side, connected with the cost of training cadres, is not taken into account.

Therefore in the same way that prices of the optimal plan will be introduced for material and natural resources, the valuation of workers should be introduced. This will create the possibility, of estimating the real national economic efficiency of various technical variants (for example the choice between capital intensive and labour intensive variants taking into account the expenditure of resources and time on the training of cadres), and of requiring from economic objects payment for the utilisation of workers of various qualifications and thus stimulating them to the best utilisation of workers, on the training of whom large sums and much time have been spent. It may be that then the problem of the utilisation of qualified engineers as workers or technicians and other similar problems would be solved in a different way from now.

4. CAN THE OPTIMAL PLANNERS HELP IMPROVE THE METHODS OF ECONOMIC CALCULATION?

The third objection [to the use of mathematical methods in planning] is that in a number of cases the initial data are doubtful and are known only very approximately . . . and therefore calculations based on these data may turn out to be incorrect.

In this connection it is necessary first of all to say that it is necessary to use these self-same data for any other method of choosing the plan and there is no reason to think that their doubtfulness and lack of precision play a bigger negative role for a plan chosen in the most effective way, than for an arbitrarily chosen plan . . . .

The fourth objection is that the saving resulting from the transition from the usually chosen variant to the best, is comparatively small, in many cases in all 4–5 %.

In this connection it is necessary to say, first, that the use of the best variant does not require any additional cost, besides the quite insignificant cost of the calculations. Secondly, one may expect the application of this method not in one random question but in many, possibly in the majority of branches of the national economy, and in this case not only 1 % but every 1/10 of a per cent is an immense sum.

L. V. Kantorovich (Nemchinov [1959] p. 276.)

The optimal planners have made a large number of contributions to improving the methods of economic calculation used in the USSR, ranging from the use of linear programming to raise the efficiency of attachment planning (by TSEMI), to the calculation and utilisation of the opportunity cost of fuels when calculating which type of electric power station to build (by the Siberian Energy Institute and Energoset'proekt). In order to examine the significance of their work it is proposed to examine four areas in which they have made contributions, variant calculations of the structure of production in medium term planning, production scheduling, investment planning, and the determination of fuel costs in the electricity industry. The first is an application of input–output, and the others are applications of linear programming.

Table 4.1. *Structure of the national income for 1970 (in %)*

Components of the national income	Variants				
	I	II	III	IV	V
Consumption	75.2	73.8	72.4	71.0	69.6
Investment	24.8	26.2	27.6	29.0	30.4
Of which industrial fixed capital formation	9.0	10.5	12.0	13.5	15.0

Table 4.2. *Average growth rate for 1966–70 (in %)*

	Variants				
	I	II	III	IV	V
National income	5.6	6.1	6.6	7.1	7.5
Consumption	6.7	6.8	6.9	7.0	7.0
Investment	2.5	4.1	5.7	7.25	8.7

SOURCE: Efimov [1969a] pp. 109–11.

VARIANT CALCULATIONS OF THE STRUCTURE OF PRODUCTION
IN MEDIUM TERM PLANNING

Because an input–output table can be represented by a simple mathematical model, and because of the assumption of constant coefficients,
an input–output table can be utilised for variant calculations.

$$X = (I-A)^{-1}Y$$

Assuming that A is given, X can be calculated for varying values of Y.
Variant calculations of the structure of production were not undertaken with material balances because of their great labour intensity.
Variant calculations have a useful role to play in medium term planning
because they enable the planners to experiment with numerous
alternative growth paths and pick the best. The first major use of
variant calculations of the structure of production in Soviet national
economic planning was in connection with the 1966–70 five year plan.[1]

[1] The work done by Gosplan's research institute in working out a planning input–output
table for 1970 was similar in many respects to the work done by the Cambridge Growth
Project in working out planning social accounts for the UK for 1970. In both cases the aim
of the work was to produce a range of possibilities between which an informed political
choice could be made, and in both, personal consumption, investment, government
expenditure and the input–output coefficients for 1970 were estimated, and used to calculate variants of the outputs of the main industries in 1970. Interesting features of the Soviet
work were the reliance on estimates by specialist institutes, rather than on extrapolation,
for estimates of the planning input–output coefficients; and the large number of industries
distinguished in the Soviet planning input–output table (130).

Table 4.3. *Output of steel on various assumptions*

	Variants				
	I	II	III	IV	V
Production of steel in 1970 (millions of tons)	109	115	121	128	136

Table 4.4. *Average growth rate of selected industries, 1966–70*

	Variants				
	I	II	III	IV	V
Engineering and metal working	7.1	8.2	9.3	10.4	11.4
Light industry	6.3	6.6	6.8	7.0	7.2
Food industry	7.1	7.3	7.4	7.5	7.6

Gosplan's research institute[1] analysed the results of various possible shares of investment in the national income for 1966–70. It became clear that stepping up the share of investment in the national income would increase the rate of growth of the national income, but that this would have very little effect on the rate of growth of consumption (because almost all of the increased output would be producer goods). The results of the calculations are set out in tables 4.1 and 4.2. A sharp increase in the share of investment in the national income in the five year plan 1966–70 would have led to a sharp fall in the share of consumption in the national income, and only a small increase in the rate of increase of consumption (with a five year plan period).[2] What is very sensitive to the share of investment in the national income is the output of the capital goods industries, as tables 4.3 and 4.4 show. The Director of Gosplan's research institute has observed that 'As a result of this research it was concluded that an increase in the share of investment, speeding up of the growth rate of the economy as a whole, does not provide a marked increase in the growth rate of consumption. This conclusion, clearly, has an important scientific and practical importance.' (Efimov [1969b] p. 6.)

[1] Considerable work on numerical dynamic interindustry models, and their utilisation in planning, particularly for the study of alternative development paths, has also been done at IEOPP, in collaboration with Gosplan. A summary, with references, is in Aganbegyan [1972] pp. 202–13.

[2] A similar result holds in the Feldman model. In both cases it results largely from the time period considered. Where the use of input–output enables one to go beyond macro-economic models is that it enables one to consider the effect of different macro-economic variants not just on macro-economic variables (such as consumption) but also on particular industries, i.e. on the structure of production.

Conclusion

The mathematical economists have enabled a new type of economic calculation to be performed, i.e. variant calculations of the structure of production in medium term planning. Such calculations have a useful role to play in national economic planning.

PRODUCTION SCHEDULING IN THE STEEL INDUSTRY

Linear programming was discovered by Kantorovich in the course of solving the problem, presented to him by the Laboratory of the all-Union Plywood Trust, of allocating productive tasks between machines in such a way as to maximise output given the assortment plan (Kantorovich [1960b] pp. 410–19). From a mathematical point of view the problem of optimal production scheduling for tube mills and rolling mills in the steel industry, which was tackled by Kantorovich in the 1960s, is very similar to the Plywood Trust problem, the difference lying in its huge dimensions.

The problem arises in the following way. As part of the planning of supply, Soyuzglavmetal, after the quotas have been specified, has to work out production schedules and attachment plans in such a way that all the orders are satisfied and none of the producers receive an impossible plan. Traditionally this was done by production schedulers. They received the orders, on each of which was the address of the consumer and the content of the order (the type of rolled metal, the standard, the type of steel, the profile, size and quantity per month). In the order also is the railway code, the code of the territorial supply organ to which the consumer belongs, and some other data. The production scheduler placed on each order the number of the supplier plant and the number of the mill, keeping a file on each mill so as not to overload it. He started work with a preliminary plan of mill loading which took explicit account of constraints ('not more than N tons') respecting certain types and sizes. There was no guarantee that the production schedules and attachment plans drawn up in this way were optimal. Indeed, there was a presumption that they were not. The optimal planners considered that here was a typical case where the application of optimising methods could bring about useful savings, and in the 1960s an extensive research programme was initiated by the department of mathematical economics (which was headed by Academician Kantorovich) of the Institute of Mathematics of the Siberian branch of the Academy of Sciences, to apply optimising methods to this problem. The chief difficulties were the huge dimensions of the problem and the lack of the necessary data. About 1,000,000 orders, involving 60,000 users, more than 500 producers and tens of thousands of products, are issued each year for rolled metal. Formulated as a linear programming problem it had more than a million unknowns and 30,000 constraints. It was possible to solve a problem of this size with the help of a special algorithm developed by V. I. Shmyrevii. Collecting the data took about six years. Optimal production scheduling was first applied to the tube mills producing tubes for gas pipelines (these are a scarce commodity in the Soviet Union). In 1970 this made possible an output of tubes 108,000 tons greater than it would otherwise have been, and a substantial reduction in transport costs was also achieved. The scientific research institute for the tube industry has estimated that in 1973 the application of optimal production scheduling should enable the output of tubes to be 600,000 tons greater than it would otherwise have been. Work is under way on extending optimal production scheduling to other products, such as sheet steel.[1]

The introduction of optimal production scheduling into the work of Soyuzglavmetal is only part of the work initiated in the late 1960s on creating a management information and control system ('Metall') in the steel industry. This is intended to be an integrated computer system which will embrace the determination of requirements, production scheduling, stock control, the distribution of output and accounting. This corresponds to the aspirations of Western business firms, where operational researchers recognise the need to 'design a system for computer operations which will accept customers' orders, carry out the initial planning calculations, produce schedules for each of ten processes, allocate steel to orders, progress the orders and initiate appropriate action when there are departures from the plan'. (Acton [1964] p. 322.)[2] Research work in this direction began in the late 1960s. (The leading research organisation in this field is IPU.) In December 1971 the general outline of the project was approved by the scientific-economic council of Gossnab, and work on implementing it is under

---

[1] The use of linear programming for production scheduling is a classic example of linear programming, of which there are many examples in the capitalist countries. In BISRA terminology the Soviet work would be described as 'forward loading' rather than 'production scheduling', because it is concerned with quarterly rather than daily production planning. (BISRA is the British Iron and Steel Research Association.)

What distinguishes the Soviet work from that in Western firms is that in the USSR optimal production schedules are being worked out and implemented for all the output of particular products. *Ceteris paribus*, the decentralisation of production scheduling is bound to be less efficient than centralised production scheduling, in exactly the same way that in a classical international trade model free trade is bound to ensure greater world welfare than autarchy.

[2] Such a system was advocated for British steel firms by Cartwright [1961]. For a description of a hypothetical system of this type see Hodge [1969] chapter 14. For a description of the analogous system at the Park Gate plant of the BSC see Wadsworth [1969].

way. The extent to which, in Metall, attachment planning should be decentralised, and the role of the local supply organs, are unclear (Aven [1968], Greshnev [1969]).

Evaluation

It is important not to confuse the optimal plans drawn up in real situations with the optimal solutions to simple examples in textbooks. It is clear that the former are 'optimal' only in a conventional sense. To deal with the huge size of the problem, much of the information is aggregated, many important factors are neglected (for example the cost of transporting the billets from which the required production is rolled is often not taken into account) and a large proportion of orders are changed between the submission of orders and receipt of the metal.[1] As a result of such simplifications, the actual saving in 1970 was only 108,000 tons, although the calculated saving was 200,000 tons. The difference was accounted for by the non-availability of the billets that would have been required to roll the additional tubes. Similarly, the calculations assume an unlimited market for all types of product, which in many cases is an invalid assumption. They also assume that the indents of consumers reflect their real needs, which is often not so, as explained in chapter 1. The production schedulers do have detailed knowledge of the real needs of consumers and the real possibilities of producers, which may well be more reliable than the information available to the compilers of 'optimal' plans. For example in practice there is some substitutability in requirements and for some scarce products the production schedulers can suggest alternatives to the consumer in a way not open to the compilers of 'optimal' plans. In addition, if a shortage does arise, the production schedulers know the relative priority of the specified quotas. They also know the quality of the output produced by various enterprises and required by various users, and the long term contacts which exist between producers and consumers.

Because of the substantial divergences between the problem of production scheduling and attachment planning facing Soyuzglavmetal and its representation by a linear programming model, several writers have suggested that the most useful approach to improving the traditional methods of production scheduling and attachment planning is a heuristic one (Lerner [1969]). Some experimental calculations have been performed in which heuristic programming has been applied to the work of Ukrglavmetal (the Ukrainian section of Soyuzglavmetal), and they showed a useful increase in efficiency compared with the

[1] This is a serious problem. A major reason for it is that, as explained in chapter 1, orders for inputs have to be sent in before the production plan is known.

plans drawn up by Ukrglavmetal using the traditional methods (Mikhno [1971]).

It is important to bear in mind that improving the efficiency of production scheduling does not eliminate the wastes explained in chapters 1 and 2. For example in October 1971 it was still necessary for a writer in *Pravda* to deplore the fact that the assortment of rolled metal products and their weight were substantially different from that required by the national economy because they were planned in tons.

The metal workers produce about 1500 varieties of rolled metal, but we must have an assortment at least twice that large. Items that are especially scarce include thin rod and sheet and thin walled pipe – i.e. the types of products whose manufacture entails considerable labour but yields little in terms of weight. Under the present 'tonnage' system of accounting for the metal-workers' work, the production of these items is always linked with a 'deterioration' of the metalworkers' indices. (Parfenev [1971].)[1]

It turned out, however, that the use of computers in planning the steel industry had a major advantage in addition to enlarging output by making better use of productive capacity. It enabled the degree of aggregation of requirements during the planning process to be reduced, and hence reduced the divergence between output and requirements.

Conclusion

An improvement in the efficiency of production scheduling is the contribution which the mathematical economists have made to the introduction of a management information and control system in the steel industry.

INVESTMENT PLANNING

Yushkov's paper was primarily concerned with what are now known as investment criteria. It was concerned with emphasising that there is generally a choice between alternative ways of meeting a given output target and that it is desirable to choose the most efficient one. Referring to Yushkov's paper, Kantorovich has written that 'Already in the 1920s the problem of "the efficiency of investment" was posed with sufficient precision.' (Kantorovich [1970b] p. 811.) Novozhilov, Lur'e and Kantorovich devoted great efforts to developing the theory and working out practical policy proposals designed to ensure the selection of the most efficient way of meeting given output targets. Neither the methods actually used in planning practice from the 1920s to the 1960s, nor the 1960 official method, nor the 1969 second edition, meet the requirements of the optimal planners, because they do not ensure the choice of the

---

[1] At the enterprise level this appears as a criterion problem, and at the national level as an aggregation problem.

most efficient investment variants. It seems likely that under the influence of the optimal planners and of Western theory and practice, the Soviet official method will gradually make the transition from the recoupment period to discounting methods, as has already happened in Czechoslovakia and Poland. (Nuti [1970], [1971].) Already the 1969 edition recommends a uniform coefficient of investment efficiency (with exceptions in special cases) rather than one differentiated by sectors.

The practical importance of the non-optimality of the official investment criterion depends on the extent to which any criterion, once promulgated, is actually used, and the sensitivity of the efficiency of investment to the criterion, rather than, say, to the data available or the economic mechanism. The use of a criterion to rank possible investment projects is only a small part of the investment process.

The optimal planners have not just confined themselves to making suggestions for improving the official method, but have themselves worked out and implemented on a large scale an entirely new method for calculating investment plans, the calculation of optimal plans for the development and location of industries.

The classic problem to which this new method has been applied is that of minimising the cost of meeting given output targets. This is an application of the open transport problem (first suggested by Yudin and Gol'shtein in 1960) to a future date. The demand for the product concerned is taken as given, and it is sought to satisfy this demand at the lowest cost (transportation, production and capital), the variables being the existing enterprises which should carry on producing as in the base year, the existing enterprises which should be closed down, the places where new enterprises should be constructed and their capacity, and the shipment scheme. Another problem to which this new method has been applied is that of using given output, and given resources for expanding output, in the most efficient way.

The easiest way of explaining what has been done in this field is by summarising two such studies which have actually been applied in planning practice: first, the calculation of an optimal plan for the development and location of the cement industry, which is an example of the first problem;[1] secondly, the calculation of an optimal plan for the structure of production of plastics, which is an example of the second one.

[1] For an analogous study of the Brazilian steel industry see Kendrick [1967a], [1967b]. Whereas the Soviet calculations have been used in planning, Kendrick's calculations have remained purely paper calculations. For an analogous study of the Hungarian cotton industry see Kornai [1967] pp. 51–73. The Hungarian study concentrated on the development side of the problem and neglected the location aspect (which is very important in a huge country such as the USSR, but much less so in Hungary).

Optimisation of the development and location of the cement industry

Economic background. The cement industry is growing fast. In 1965 output was $12\frac{1}{2}$ times greater than in 1940. The cost of production of cement shows a wide dispersion by regions, ranging from 78 % of the all-Union mean in the Ukraine to 136 % in Central Asia. (These and subsequent data refer to 1965.) The efficiency of fixed capital, measured in terms of output per thousand roubles of fixed capital, shows a wide dispersion by size of enterprise. 46 % of output is produced in plants with an output greater than 50 tons p.a. per thousand roubles of fixed capital, and 12 % is produced in plants with an output of less than 30 tons p.a. per thousand roubles of fixed capital. Seven regions which in 1960 produced 47 % of the cement are cement surplus regions, nine regions with 31 % of production are deficit regions, and the remaining regions have a surplus in some years and a deficit in others.

At present transportation of cement is non-optimal. For example some cement is sent from Central Asia to the Urals and even to the Volga, which themselves are surplus regions and export cement to Kazakhstan and Central Asia. In 1964 transport from producers to consumers was 29.75 milliard ton kms. The optimal transport scheme, calculated on the computer Ural 2 using the closed transport model, reduced this by 8.95 milliard ton km, i.e. about 30 %. The calculated saving in railway charges was 20 million roubles.

The poor organisation of the running in of new plants increases costs. For example, the average cost of cement in 1965 at 10 factories brought into operation in 1959–65 was 24 % higher than the all-Union mean.

When siting cement plants the basic need is deposits of carbonaceous rocks (such as limestone), which can be worked by open cast methods not more than 20–30 kms from a railway.

Initial data. For the calculation it is necessary first of all to determine:

a the perspective requirements for cement in each region of the country,
b the points where it would be possible to construct cement plants,
c the current cost, the quality of production and the investment cost of each plant and each variant of capacity,
d the distance and cost of transporting cement from production points to consumption points.

The totality of these indices forms the initial data which are fed into the computer. The reliability of the results depends on how correctly these indices are determined and it is precisely in the calculation of the initial data that the greatest difficulties exist.   Loginov [1968] pp. 28–9.

The perspective requirement for cement will be determined by the volume of building work, with allowance for technical progress. The volume of building work over the next ten years is not known. What is known is only that the demand for cement will continue to increase. Therefore the optimal plan was calculated not for any definite future year, but for certain volumes of cement requirements at some unknown dates in the future. The 1965 output was 72 million tons, and the optimal plans were worked out for requirements of 100, 125 and 150 million tons p.a.

In the calculations it was assumed that 42 existing plants producing c 30 million tons of cement p.a. could not be expanded further (e.g. because of a shortage of raw materials); 45 plants with a capacity of c 57 million tons could be expanded with varying degrees of efficiency, and by the end of 10–12 years could be expanded by 75 million tons to 132 million tons. In addition 34 possible new plants, with a capacity of 76 million tons, were considered. Total productive capacity was more than twice the estimated requirements in 1970, and about 60 % greater than the 150 million ton requirements figure, which gave substantial opportunities for optimisation.

Estimates of future current costs were made.

The basis for calculating anticipated investment costs was the data of typical designs corrected to allow for local conditions, especially for the expansion of existing enterprises where the savings from the utilisation of existing infrastructure is often insufficiently taken into account. In order to make capital and current costs comparable a norm of investment efficiency of 0.17 (which corresponds to a recoupment period of 6 years) was used.

There are several ways of calculating transport costs, and variant calculations were undertaken.

Mathematical formulation of problem. Knowns:

    a capacity and location of existing enterprises, possible variants of construction of new plants, for each variant cost/ton of cement and/ ton of cement of standard quality,

    b consumption points and requirements at each one,

    c the cost of transporting 1 ton of cement from each factory to each consumption point.

Required to find:

    a existing factories which are efficient and which should be used at their existing and perspective capacities,

    b location of new plants,

    c output of cement at each plant, and

    d transportation scheme.

which minimise total costs.

Included in the calculations were 121 productive enterprises, embracing 166 positions (45 factories had two variants considered) with a total capacity of 243 million tons of standard cement; 149 consumption points; and three variants of requirements, 100 million tons, 125 million tons and 150 million tons.

Introduce the following notation:

i is an index signifying a production point ($i = 1 \ldots m$)
j is an index signifying a consumption point ($j = 1 \ldots n$)
n is the number of consumption points
r_i is an index signifying a variant of capacity at the ith production point ($r_i = 1 \ldots k_i$)
k_i is the number of capacity variants at the ith production point
$a_i^{r_i}$ is the quantity of cement which can be produced at the ith point using the r_ith capacity variant
b_j is the requirement for cement at the jth consumption point
$C_i^{r_i}$ is the current cost per unit of cement produced at the ith production point using the r_ith capacity variant
T_{ij} is the cost of transporting a unit of cement from the ith production point to the jth consumption point
E is the coefficient of investment efficiency (the reciprocal of the recoupment period)
X_{ij} is the unknown quantity of cement to be delivered to the jth consumption point from the ith production point
X_i is the unknown capacity of the ith production point.

The problem is to find values of X_{ij} and X_i such that total costs

$$\sum_{i=1}^{m} \sum_{j=1}^{n} X_{ij} T_{ij} + \sum_{i=1}^{m} (C_i + E K_i)$$ (where C_i and K_i are the current and

capital costs corresponding to the chosen capacity variant X_i) are minimised, subject to the conditions

$$\sum_{j=1}^{n} X_{ij} \leqslant X_i \qquad i = 1 \ldots m \qquad (1)$$

(i.e. the total quantity of cement delivered to all the consumption points from the ith production point cannot exceed the capacity of the ith production point)

$$\sum_{i=1}^{m} X_{ij} = b_j \qquad j = 1 \ldots n \qquad (2)$$

(i.e. the total quantity of cement received by the jth consumption point from all the production points equals the given requirements at that point)

$$X_{ij} \geqslant 0 \qquad i = 1 \ldots m; j = 1 \ldots n \qquad (3)$$

(i.e. the deliveries must be non-negative)

$$X_i = \text{one of the values } a_i^{r_i}.\qquad(4)$$

For the results to be interesting it is necessary that there should be values of $a_i^{r_i}$ for which

$$\sum_{i=1}^{m} a_i^{r_i} > \sum_{j=1}^{n} b_j$$

(i.e. the quantity of production which it is possible to produce must exceed requirements – preferably substantially).

Results. The results of the calculations were a list of enterprises which should be closed down, a list of enterprises which should be maintained at their existing capacity, a list of enterprises which should be expanded, and a list of places where new enterprises should be built, in order to meet the specified output targets. Important features of the results were that it was shown that it is desirable to concentrate the production of cement in a small number of large factories, rather than treating it as a local material the production of which should be scattered all over the country (despite an influential opinion to the contrary in cement industry circles); that the development of the cement industry should proceed mainly by means of expanding existing plants rather than building completely new ones; and that some cement factories built within the last 10–15 years have such high current costs that they should be closed down. (Some existing cement plants are so inefficient that the investment required to replace them by well-sited modern plants would be recouped in two years.)

Analysis of results. A feature of these calculations was the great use made of sensitivity analysis. Calculations made in 1963 showed that the decision to build new plants (as opposed to the expansion of existing ones or maintaining existing inefficient plants) was very sensitive to the norm of investment efficiency used. On the other hand the results were not very sensitive to different ways of calculating transport costs, and different regional breakdowns of requirements for cement.

Unless a constraint was introduced that all the existing enterprises should remain open, a number of them were closed down in the optimal plan. In some variants this condition was introduced, in some it was not.

Optimisation of the structure of production and utilisation of plastics

The problem. In the late 1950s, especially at the May (1958) Plenum of the CC, a campaign was launched for the rapid expansion of the chemical industry in general and of the plastics industry in particular.

It was clear that there are many fields in which the use of plastics is more efficient than the use of traditional materials. There are many types of plastic, and the planners had to determine what was the best structure of production (i.e. the relative quantities of the different types) as a basis for investment planning. It was also clear that for many years to come the quantity of plastics available would be insufficient to use them in all the applications where they would be cheaper than traditional materials. Hence the planners were faced with the additional problem of deciding in which fields plastics should be used.

The optimal planners suggested that here was a problem where the application of optimal planning could bring about substantial savings, and in the 1960s extensive research was undertaken to calculate optimal plans for the production and utilisation of plastics for 1970 and 1975 (Val'tukh [1965], *Osnovnye* [1969] pp. 194–206, Ioffe [1971]).

Analysis of requirements for plastics showed that some needs (type I requirements) could only be met by plastics, while others (type II requirements) could be met either by plastics or by traditional materials, the substitution of the former bringing about a reduction in costs. The problem was to use the capacity of the plants currently in operation or under construction, and the resources available for investment, in such a way as to maximise the saving from the substitution of plastics for traditional materials in the planned year. Assuming that all type I requirements will be met, which plastics should be allocated to which type II uses?

Notation

i type of plastic ($i = 1 \ldots m$). The assortment considered was determined in accordance with the Chief Administration for plastics of the Ministry of the Chemical Industry.

j possible use for plastics ($j = 1 \ldots n$). The list of uses was determined in accordance with the Chief Administration for plastics of the Ministry of the Chemical Industry.

X_{ij} unknown volume of type II consumption of the ith plastic in the jth use.

a_{ij} economic efficiency of the ith plastic in the jth use. This is defined as the difference between the cost of producing a unit of the jth output using the ith plastic and using the traditional material.

P_{ij} full requirement (i.e. type I + type II) of the jth use for the ith plastic.

d_{ij} the type I requirements of the jth use for the ith plastic.

Q_i the volume of production of the ith plastic.

r_{ki} amount of the kth scarce resources (e.g. a scarce material) needed for the production of a unit of the ith plastic ($k = 1 \ldots K$).

R_k quantity of the kth scarce resource available for the production of plastics.

c_i investment required for the production of one ton of the ith plastic.

C total investment resources available for the development of the plastics industry.

b_i the volume of production of the ith plastic at existing enterprises and enterprises which are already under construction.

$\beta_{ii'j}$ the rate of substitution between the plastic which is cheapest in the jth use (i), and one unit of another type (i'), which enables the same output to be produced. For example, suppose that a certain quantity of cold water pipe requires 30,000 tons of polyethylene pipe (this is the cheapest material), or 40,000 tons of pvc pipe. Then

$$\beta_{ii'j} = 30{,}000/40{,}000 = 0.75$$

$\gamma_{ii'j}$ coefficient which measures the extent to which it is possible to substitute an alternative plastic (i') for the ith plastic in the jth use. For example, suppose that the jth use is electric power station equipment. The cheapest material for this use is phenolplastic. Some kinds of electric power station equipment can use polystyrene. Assume that it is possible to substitute polystyrene for up to 80 % of the requirement of phenolplastic. Then

$$\gamma_{ii'j} = 0.8.$$

Mathematical formulation. To find the values of X_{ij} (i.e. the volumes of type II requirements that will be satisfied) in such a way as to maximise the gains from using plastics

$$\sum_{i=1}^{m} \sum_{j=1}^{n} a_{ij} X_{ij}. \tag{1}$$

Subject to the constraints that
A

X_{ij} falls between an upper limit determined by the possibilities of efficiently using the ith plastic in the jth use

$$X_{ij} \leqslant P_{ij} - d_{ij} \tag{2}$$

and a lower limit determined by the output of plants already in operation or under construction

$$\sum_{j=1}^{n} X_{ij} \geqslant b_i - \sum_{j=1}^{n} d_{ij}, \qquad b_i \geqslant \sum_{j=1}^{n} d_{ij} \tag{3}$$

B

the investment required be less than or equal to the investment available,

$$\sum_{i=1}^{m} c_i(Q_i - b_i) \leqslant C \tag{4}$$

$$\left(Q_i = \sum_{j=1}^{n} d_{ij} + \sum_{j=1}^{n} X_{ij} \right)$$

C

the scarce resources used should be less than or equal to the scarce resources available

$$\sum_{i=1}^{m} r_{ki} \sum_{j=1}^{n} Q_{ij} \leqslant R_k \tag{5}$$

D

the output of each kind of plastic should grow or remain stationary (but not decline)

$$Q_i \geqslant b_i. \tag{6}$$

If it is possible to substitute some other plastic (i') for the ith plastic in the jth use, condition (2) takes the form

$$X_{ij} + \sum_{i'=1}^{m} \beta_{ii'j} X_{ii'j} \leqslant P_{ij} - d_{ij} \tag{2a}$$

$$\beta_{ii'j} X_{i'j} \leqslant \gamma_{ii'j}(P_{ij} - d_{ij}); \qquad (i, i' = 1 \dots m, j = 1 \dots n) \tag{2b}$$

(2a) and (2b) can be illustrated as follows.

Assume that in the production of the jth article one could use 100 tons of plastic 1 ($P_1^j = 100$), which is the most efficient plastic in this use. The minimum level of requirements for this plastic is 10 tons, i.e. $d_{1j} = 10$. 30 % of the requirement for plastic 1 in the jth use can be met by the (less efficient) plastic 2, 25 % by plastic 3. In other words, $\gamma_{12j} = 0.3$, $\gamma_{13j} = 0.25$. Let $\beta_{12j} = 0.7$ and $\beta_{13j} = 0.5$. The type II requirement of the jth use ($P_{1j} - d_{1j}$) = $(100 - 10)$ can be met by three types of plastic, X_{1j} tons of plastic 1, X_{2j} tons of plastic 2, and X_{3j} tons of plastic 3. Expressed in terms of tons of plastic 1 equivalent, the constraint on the upper level of requirement for plastic in the jth use is

$$X_{1j} + 0.7\, X_{2j} + 0.5\, X_{3j} \leqslant (100 - 10).$$

(This corresponds to (2a).)
The quantity of plastic 1 for which plastics 2 and 3 can be substituted is constrained by the coefficient γ.

$$0.7\, X_{2j} \leqslant 0.3\,(100 - 10)$$

$$0.5\, X_{3j} \leqslant 0.25\,(100 - 10).$$

(This corresponds to (2b).)

Table 4.5. *Optimal output of plastics for varying volumes of investment* (*as % of output with minimum investment variant*)

	600	900	1200	1500	1700
			(millions of roubles)		
Block polystyrene	102	130	143	174	174
Shock resistant polystyrene	100	100	143	219	223
Polystyrene for foam	102	116	224	224	233
Low density polyethylene	108	116	162	163	177
High density polyethylene	100	101	107	110	144
Polyvinylchloride	188	265	265	265	265
Phenol resins	103	106	106	106	106
Phenol extrusions	149	149	149	149	149
Carbamide resins	100	106	106	106	106

Table 4.6. *Optimal utilisation of glass plastics* (*as % of full requirements* $-P_{ij}$)

Consumer	Efficiency (a_{ij}) roubles/ ton	Minimum requirement (d_{ij})	Variants of production				
			1	2	3	4	5
Heavy, energy and transport engineering	760	14.4	14.4	14.4	100.0	100.0	100.0
Agricultural machinery	5,300	14.6	100.0	100.0	100.0	100.0	100.0
Electrotechnical industry	410	15.0	15.0	15.0	15.0	66.7	100.0
Shipbuilding	600	14.9	14.9	14.9	15.6	100.0	100.0
Railway carriage building	120	14.8	14.8	14.8	14.8	14.8	100.0
Construction	3,840	100.0	100.0	100.0	100.0	100.0	100.0
Other uses	900	31.5	34.8	89.1	100.0	100.0	100.0

Results. The results of the calculations were figures for the optimal output and use of the different kinds of plastic, and shadow prices for the resources and the plastics. Some results are set out in tables 4.5, 4.6 and 4.7.

Given the optimal production figures, the research workers at TSEMI went on to determine the location and capacity of the plants necessary to produce the optimal production programmes (this was analogous to the calculations for the cement industry described above) and the order in which they should be constructed.

Analysis of results. The opportunity costs data provided by the optimal plan calculations are useful as a guide to chemical engineers, technologists and designers as to where particular plastics should or should not be used. For example, given that the efficiency of using plastics derived

Table 4.7. *Opportunity cost of plastics (roubles/ton)*

| Type of plastic | Variant of investment | | | |
| | 950 | 1150 | 1310 | 1550 |
		(millions of roubles)		
Phenol resins	470	350	312	255
Low density polyethylene	1,240	940	830	670
High density polyethylene	2,800	2,150	1,920	1,560
Polyvinylchloride	1,060	790	705	560
Polyvinyl spirit	6,350	4,750	4,250	3,450
Plastics derived from cellulose oils	8,400	6,300	5,600	4,550

SOURCE: Ioffe [1971] pp. 75–83.

from cellulose oils is generally 1000–1200 roubles per ton, it is clear that most possible uses for them are inefficient. These opportunity costs are also useful as guides to where effort should be devoted to improving the initial data. Suppose that in most uses the efficiency of using low density polyethylene is 1800–2400 roubles/ton, and the investment variant chosen is 1150. The large gap between the opportunity cost (940 roubles/ton) and the efficiency of utilising the plastic (1800–2400) suggests that even a substantial error in determining the efficiency of utilising low density polyethylene would not affect the optimal plan. On the other hand, if the efficiency of utilising a particular plastic is 650 roubles/ton, and its opportunity cost in the optimal plan is 640 roubles/ ton, then a small change in the initial data might affect the optimal plan, and efforts to improve the data on the efficiency of using that particular plastic would be useful.

Utilisation of the results in planning

The cement calculations were done in stages in 1962–9 and served as a basis for the plans of the cement industry in the five year plans 1966–70 and 1971–5. The plastics calculations were embodied in a joint report of TSEMI and the Chief Administration for plastics which was presented to the Ministry of the Chemical Industry. It was examined and approved by the Ministry and utilised in the 1971–5 plan for the chemical industry.

This new method of compiling investment plans worked out by the optimal planners quickly became an integral part of planning practice. As a result of the favourable evaluation of the experimental work of the early 1960s, in the spring of 1966 Gosplan issued a special order requiring the compilation of optimal plans for the development and location of the industry in several tens of industries, and at the beginning of 1968, when work on the 1971–5 five year plan was being organised, it was envisaged that the plans for 74 branches of industry accounting for three quarters of the capital stock in industry would be compiled only by optimal methods. In 1970 Chernyavsky stated that in the near future all investment projects would be based on optimal plans (Chernyavsky [1970]).

Evaluation

The six main issues which have arisen in the course of this work are: the availability of data, the extent to which the models of the optimal planners reflect reality, the relationship between the optimal plans of the separate industries, the size of the savings resulting from this new method, the influence of the calculations on the decisions actually taken and the relationship between the calculation of optimal plans and the expansion of *khozraschet*.

In the section concerned with the use of mathematical models of a book on improving planning written by some officials of Gosplan it is stated that:

the information required for models, optimising the utilisation of resources, is not readily available, and it is necessary to gather it separately. It is this work which occupies at the present time not less than 80 % of all the work involved in solving such problems, and for complicated problems – 90 %.

At first sight this situation may arouse surprise, because for the working out of plans, it would seem, all the necessary information is available. For the efficient utilisation of models, however, for example for planning production, the nomenclature must be substantially wider than that confirmed in the plan. This results from the necessity to exclude the influence of possible assortment changes on the decision taken. The following examples may clarify this. In the national economic plan there are two figures for the production of leather shoes and children's shoes. The calculations underlying the plan are based on 7 aggregated groups of shoes and 4 small groups. For the problem which enables the maximum production of shoes subject to the structure of demand and the given resources to be calculated, shoes are divided into 257 types, and the full nomenclature of shoes and related items runs to about 36,000 items. These types are chosen in such a way that an alteration in the assortment inside each of them would have a much smaller influence on the plan than changes in the assortment between types.

(Drogichinsky [1971] p. 184.)

The data required are not purely physical, but have to be made comparable by means of prices and a rate of interest. The prices and recoupment period used in many of the calculations were unsatisfactory in a number of respects. The optimal planners have devoted great efforts to overcoming the problems caused by the inadequacy of the data. Indeed, a leading research worker in this field has observed that: 'It is necessary once more to underline the fact that the basic practical results of the work were achieved not only and not so much thanks to the new methods of calculation and electronic technology as to the strict adherence to the principle of the single criterion of optimality, the commensurability of current and capital costs, the correct (within the limits of the possible) determination of the initial indices and so on.' (I. Birman [1970] p. 327.) In other words, Birman argues, the main reason for the savings resulting from the optimal plans compared with the plans drawn up by the traditional methods is that the former are drawn up by research teams headed by distinguished economists such as A. G. Aganbegyan, I. Ya. Birman and N. P. Fedorenko, who pay more attention to the economic aspects of investment planning than did the people who drew up plans by the traditional methods. This is a very plausible argument. Numerous alternative ways of calculating transport costs existed before the optimal planners came on the scene. They, however, were concerned about this, and devoted considerable efforts to working out the 'right' way of calculating transport costs, and there now exist the figures for calculating transport costs worked out by the Institute of Complex Transport Problems, which meet the requirements of perspective planning. Similarly, in the plastics calculations the recoupment period was adjusted to take account of the time pattern of costs and benefits.

It is clear that in a number of respects the models used do not correspond to reality. For example, in the plastics calculations the use of fixed coefficients (c_i) to determine investment requirements implies constant returns to scale. The optimal planners are well aware of the existence and importance of increasing returns to scale. They estimated the relationship between investment per unit of output and the scale of production, and calculated the optimal plan for varying values of c_i. One of the advantages of computerised model building is that it enables alternative values of the parameters to be used and the effect on the optimal plan noted.

It is clearly unsatisfactory to optimise the investment plan of each industry taken in isolation, just as it is unsatisfactory to balance the current plan for each commodity taken in isolation. If the calculations show that it is possible to reduce the inputs into a particular industry below those originally envisaged, then it is desirable to reduce planned outputs in other industries, or increase the planned output of the industry in question, or adopt some combination of these strategies. From this point of view the Soviet work lagged behind similar work in Hungary, where the calculation of optimal plans for particular industries in the late 1950s led to the construction of multi-level plans linking the optimal plans of the separate industries to each other and to the macro economic plan variables. These were used in working out the 1966–70 five year plan and have now been incorporated into normal planning practice (Kornai [1967], [1969]). Soviet research

workers and planning officials are aware of this problem, and experimental work on multi-level planning models had begun in this period
(Baranov [1970], [1971]).

How much cheaper is the output resulting from an optimal plan than
the same output produced by a non-optimal plan? Although the optimal
planners cite figures for the savings (which are always substantial) it is
difficult to see how this question can be answered. It is not possible to
implement two alternative plans simultaneously, and the usual comparison between the indices of the optimal plan and those of a traditional plan, showing that the former achieves the same output as the
latter for a cost 10–15 % lower, implies the very strong assumption that
the degree of divergence between the plan and the outcome is the same
for the optimal plan as for the traditional plan. (Retrospective calculations using actual rather than assumed values of the initial data
would be more useful.) Data on the magnitude of the savings brought
about by this new planning method, relative to the savings that could
be obtained by improving the functioning of the economy (e.g. a
reduction in the construction and running in periods for new plants) or
the savings resulting from technical progress, are not available.

A prominent specialist in this field has stated that in his experience
there is an 'optimal range' for the figure for the savings resulting from
the use of optimal rather than traditional planning methods, of 5–10 %.
If the figure is less than 5 % the officials think that the optimal plan
calculations are scarcely worth doing, and if they are more than 10 %
it is thought that there must be something wrong with the calculations,
because the people who do the calculations by the traditional methods
could not be all that stupid. This suggests that all the published figures
produced in the socialist countries for the savings resulting from using
optimising methods are worthless from the scientific point of view. He
also stated that in his opinion the main gains from the calculation of
optimal perspective plans were that it ensured that the plan adopted
was feasible (the plans drawn up by the traditional methods are often
not feasible, which is one of the explanations of the chronic long
construction periods) and also that it gave the possibility of doing
variant calculations.[1] This is analogous to the fact that an investigation
of the gains by American firms from the use of computers showed that
not only cost reductions, but also better administration and better
service to customers, were achieved with the help of computers (ECE
[1969] pp. 4–5).

The results of the optimal planning calculations have not automatically replaced the plans drawn up by the traditional methods, but

[1] These observations were made in private conversation with the author. Cf. Kornai [1967]
pp. 335–6 and 109–13.

have served as a basis for investment decisions taken by the responsible officials. The fact that the 'optimal plans' are not simply accepted and implemented, but are regarded merely as material useful for the planning officials when they come to make decisions, is regarded as unsatisfactory by some of the research workers who do the calculations.

Even many specialists picture the situation this way: a calculation is a calculation, but the plan must be based on something or other else, in addition to this. It is recommended that first a calculation be undertaken, then the results analysed, and then a decision be made in the light of various circumstances. In other words it is advised that the decisions be made after the calculations, but at the same time it is assumed that the decisions may deviate from the results of the calculations. In essence, this is a variant of the well known proposition that a calculation should give 'material' for competent administrators, who are the ones who should 'decide the question'.

The basic idea, however, of the application of economic-mathematical methods is that 'questions should be decided' by calculations, and not represent a wilful act.
(I. Birman [1970] p. 306.)

This line of argument is understandable, but quite unacceptable. The variables which the 'optimal plans' optimise are only a small subset of the variables whose values are of interest to policy makers. I. Ya. Birman has regretted the fact that 'The imprecisions, conventionalities and debateability of many aspects of the work, not to speak of the fact that some people are unaccustomed to the new methods, provided a basis for the directing organs to reject some of the results (for example the conclusion about the need to liquidate some enterprises).' (I. Birman [1970] p. 327.) The directing organs are concerned not just with cost minimisation but also with maintaining full employment. Academician Fedorenko has recognised that in many cases cost minimisation is an inadequate criterion, and has argued that one of the advantages of optimal planning is that it enables a price tag to be attached to the extra economic factors in decision making.

It would be a mistake to suppose that the compilation of optimal plans is an alternative to the expansion of *khozraschet*. In a report on a conference on optimal plans for the development and location of industries, I. Ya. Birman asked:

Why have the new methods and tools not yet become basic in industrial planning? What prevents this? Mention was made at the conference of certain imperfections in the mathematical apparatus, the limited potential of the electronic machines available, the complexity of obtaining authentic calculations of the initial indices and the debatability (as a result of incomplete elaboration) of many methodological propositions. And yet none of this is the main trouble.

The main trouble consists in the fact that the solution to this economic problem is being pursued not by economic but by administrative methods. For example, the USSR Ministry of the Building Materials Industry is supporting work on optimal perspective planning. It is probable that more practical computations have been made for the branches of this industry than for any other. But under the existing situation, the Ministry has little stake in whether or not the results of these computations are implemented in economic practice.

Of course, everyone must be concerned for the welfare of the state. However, if the optimal computations result in a reduction, by tens of millions of roubles, in the requirements for capital investments, the Ministry's allocation quota will simply be lowered by this sum. There will be no immediate benefit for those who did the calculations and who introduced the optimal plan. For the Ministry, the savings on the haulage of building materials effected through improvements in the siting of enterprises are no more substantial. It is another department – Gossnab – that obtains these savings.

Is it for this reason, perhaps, that the ministry is delaying the creation of a computer centre and is contributing little to the further development of research and the introduction of its results?

Orders and circulars will correct nothing here: the USSR Ministry of Ferrous Metallurgy, for example, despite a special order from Gosplan, is doing nothing at all about optimal planning. It is necessary to create economic conditions in which both the ministries and the planning agencies will have an interest in the optimisation of industrial plans.

(I. Birman [1968a].)

Conclusion

The contribution of the optimal planners to investment planning has taken the form of both suggestions for a criterion of investment efficiency before such a criterion was adopted, followed by suggestions for improving it after it had been adopted, and the calculation of optimal plans for the development and location of industries. Examination of the latter work suggests that it is a useful addition to the techniques available to the planners, the significance of which should be neither exaggerated nor belittled.

THE DETERMINATION OF FUEL COSTS IN THE ELECTRICITY INDUSTRY

An important aspect of investment planning in the electricity industry is the choice between alternative fuels. This is largely determined by the cost of various fuels. An important result of the work of the optimal planners has been an improvement in determining fuel costs when choosing between fuels in the electricity industry. This came about in the following way.

A basic tool of Soviet investment planning is the fuel-energy balance. This is a system of material balances for the fuel and power sector of the economy. It is based on estimates of future requirements and the availability and cost of various fuels, and is used at a preliminary stage of investment planning.[1] One of the first results of the discussion of

[1] For a fuel–energy balance for the UK see Wigley [1968].

mathematical methods in economics was the calculation in 1961, at the Institute of electronic control machines, of an experimental optimal fuel-energy balance for the USSR (Chernyavsky [1962]). Subsequently considerable work was done, largely at SOPS and the Siberian Energy Institute, in calculating optimal fuel-energy balances for the USSR (A. Makarov [1964], Melent'ev [1966], Albegov [1968], Albegov [1969]). The results of these calculations were both physical indices (the optimal output for some future date of coal, oil and natural gas at various locations) and value indices (the shadow prices of the fuels at each location).

The value indices which are relevant for allocation decisions are the opportunity costs. The importance of allocation decisions in the fuel sector results from the technical substitutability of alternative fuels (e.g. coal, oil, natural gas, uranium, running water). The use of marginal rather than average costs is particularly important because of the wide dispersion of production costs.[1] The use of opportunity costs rather than production costs is important because, even at the optimum, the former, but not the latter, take account of the different cost (over and above the purchase price) to the user of alternative fuels and any saving in transport of the intra marginal fuel as in the example below. (For the country as a whole and for each region the opportunity cost of fuel would be the marginal production and transport cost of the marginal fuel, if all fuels had the same cost (over the purchase price) to the user and if the saving in transport of the intra marginal fuel could be neglected.) The shadow prices calculated in the optimal fuel–energy balance are the opportunity costs if the last two factors are taken into account in the calculations and if all the cost figures that enter the optimisation calculations are themselves opportunity costs. The opportunity costs of fuels were computed in the optimal fuel-energy balance calculations for the country as a whole and for each region for various dates. They were used to analyse a number of decisions in which fuel costs played an important part, for example the fate of the Nurek hydro electric station.

In 1958–60 when the efficiency of the projected Nurek hydro electric station (Tadjikstan) was under consideration, a comparison was made between the cost of power produced by hydro stations and by thermal stations run on natural gas (the main local fossil fuel). In these calculations the cost of the natural gas was taken to be 1–2 roubles per ton of standard fuel,[2] the cost of extraction and transport. On this basis the hydro station seemed advantageous, and the go ahead was given for the

---

[1] This has been pointed out by many writers. See for example Dobb [1969] chapter 11.
[2] 1 kg of standard fuel yields 7 mega-calories when burned in a calorimeter. The comparison of fuels in terms of standard fuel is analogous to their comparison in terms of coal equivalent.

project. In 1963–4 it became clear that the actual construction costs of the Nurek station would be 3 times greater than had been planned. It was proposed to abandon construction, because with this level of capital costs the natural gas fired station would be indubitably more efficient. The optimal planners pointed out, however, that this decision would be based on a faulty calculation of the cost of natural gas. Although the extraction and transport cost was only 1–2 roubles per ton of standard fuel, the shadow price of Central Asian natural gas in the optimal fuel-energy balance (i.e. its opportunity cost) was 10–13 roubles per ton of standard fuel (Andreev [1967] p. 73, Albegov [1969] pp. 100–1). The reason for this is that Central Asian natural gas is extensively exported to the European part of the USSR. For given energy requirements in the European part of the USSR and given gas output in Central Asia, the cost to the national economy of each additional ton of standard fuel equivalent of natural gas used in Central Asia is the production and distribution cost of the additional unit of Donbass coal which will be used in the European part of the country to replace natural gas, plus the additional cost to the user of coal rather than natural gas, less the saving on the distribution of Central Asian natural gas to Europe. Hence it was rational to proceed with the Nurek station despite the escalation in its construction costs.[1]

The work done by SOPS and the Siberian Energy Institute in the early 1960s was developed further, with special reference to the electricity industry, by the Siberian Energy Institute and Energoset'proekt (the design institute for the electricity industry). After the calculation of the opportunity cost of fuel at points throughout the country (Andreev [1967]) and widespread discussion of their significance (Andreev [1966], Levental' [1970] pp. 210–17), in the design of electric power stations from 1969 onwards the cost figures used in the comparison of alternative fuels were the opportunity costs. A substantial volume of research has been devoted to examining the stability of these cost figures, for example with respect to errors in the initial data.[2]

---

[1] The use of shadow prices derived from a sector wide optimal planning model to help in the solution of a partial problem, as in this example, is very much in the spirit of Kantorovich's work and its practical usefulness is a tribute to his insight.

[2] The electricity industry is not the only one to have taken advantage of the possibilities created by optimal planning to improve its cost data. Already in 1965 the Scientific Research Institute for Technical-Economic Research of the Ministry of the Chemical Industry calculated the opportunity cost of fuels in various parts of the country as a tool of investment planning in the chemical industry (Shokin [1971]), and these figures have been widely used.

Evaluation

It is clearly desirable that the cost data used in allocation decisions be opportunity costs.[1] The figures currently being used in the USSR, however, are only an approximation to opportunity costs. They are relative to the data used in the calculations, so that, for example, they vary with the assumptions made about future investment decisions, wage rates and rates of growth of labour productivity, and assume that the cost data used are themselves opportunity costs. For example, if it were a fact that Central Asian gas output could easily be expanded, or that wages in the Donbass were much above the opportunity cost of labour there, or that the opportunity cost of investment resources was much above that implied by the recoupment period used in the Nurek calculations, then it might be that continuing with the Nurek station was not so rational after all.

Conclusion

An important result of the work of the optimal planners has been the use of cost figures for alternative fuels in electricity generation which are a better reflection of the national economic cost of alternative fuels than the figures formerly used.

SUMMARY

The optimal planners have made a number of important contributions to improving the methods of economic calculation used in the USSR. Their work has

1 enabled entirely new types of calculations to be performed (e.g. variant calculations of the structure of production in medium term planning),
2 led to an increase in the efficiency of production scheduling and attachment planning in the steel industry,
3 raised the efficiency of investment planning, and
4 improved the calculation of fuel costs in the electricity industry.

Their work is continuing, and is likely to make further contributions to improving the techniques used by the planners.

[1] The fact that the costs relevant for allocation decisions are opportunity costs was argued in 1962 by Vaag and Zakharov (Vaag [1962]). What the optimal planners have added is a method which enables opportunity costs to be calculated and hence incorporated into planning practice.

5. WHAT ARE THE IMPLICATIONS FOR THE ECONOMIC MECHANISM OF LINEAR PROGRAMMING?

It is one of the chief merits of proofs that they instil a certain scepticism as to the result proved. Bertrand Russell (Russell [1903] p. 360.)

Commenting on Soviet writing on optimal planning, Wiles has argued that Kantorovich 'must thus be described as an advocate of perfect computation' (Wiles [1962] p. 203). Elsewhere (Ellman [1971] chapter 4) I have argued that this interpretation is an erroneous assessment of Kantorovich's position, and I described how in fact a number of economists in the socialist countries have used linear programming to derive policy conclusions which are strikingly at variance with the traditional teachings of Marxism–Leninism and which provide a 'scientific' basis for economic reform. The purpose of this chapter is to consider the validity of these policy conclusions.[1]

Kantorovich was the first person to draw the attention of economists to the usefulness for economic calculations of shadow prices. Since then, the latter have been widely used in economic calculations, at the level of the national economy, the industry and the enterprise. Some examples were given in the previous chapter. This chapter will not consider the general question of their usefulness in this role, but will analyse the specific question of their usefulness for calculations of the type for which Kantorovich has advocated using them, and the more general question of their theoretical interpretation.

Kantorovich's variation on the familiar theme of the allocative function of prices is the idea that in an economy where production targets are determined by the planners at intervals, the shadow prices associated with the optimal plan enable the rationality of small changes in the production programme, resulting from changes in the conditions, to be assessed, without the need for recalculating the entire plan. This idea is not valid in general, does not appear to have been applied in the

---

[1] The standard Western discussions of the economic significance of linear programming are Koopmans [1951a], [1951c], [1957], DOSSO [1958], and Hicks [1960].

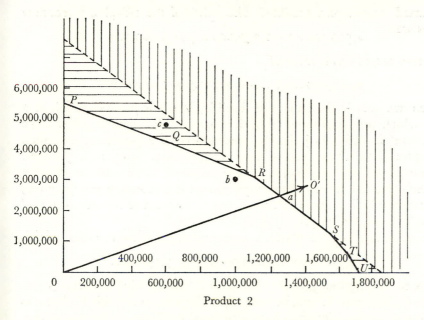

Figure 5.1.   Kantorovich's method for evaluating alternative plans.

USSR, and as far as I know has not been applied elsewhere. The restricted domain of validity of Kantorovich's idea can easily be seen by setting his example out diagrammatically, as is done in figure 5.1.

The production possibility area is *OPU* and the assortment plan is represented by the line *OO'*. The optimal plan is *a*. The slope of the facet on which the optimal plan lies is the rate of transformation of one output into another, or the opportunity cost of each output. In the example, the rate of transformation is 4:1. This ratio can be regarded as the relative valuation of the two outputs in the optimal plan. Taking one product as the numéraire, Kantorovich refers to these relative valuations as objectively determined valuations (a terminology explained in the glossary). They play an important part in Kantorovich's algorithm for solving linear programming problems. (This is an important difference between Kantorovich's algorithm and the simplex algorithm. In Kantorovich's resolving multiplier algorithm the shadow prices are used to enable the optimal solution to be found, whereas in the simplex algorithm the shadow prices and the optimal quantities are found simultaneously.) Kantorovich has argued that they can be used to evaluate the feasibility and efficiency of alternative plans. Suppose that the assortment plan is altered, and the alternative plan *b* is suggested. Is this plan feasible? The value of the old plan in shadow prices was

$$2{,}500{,}000 \times 1 + 1{,}250{,}000 \times 4 = 7{,}500{,}000.$$

The new target has a value of

$$3{,}000{,}000 \times 1 + 1{,}000{,}000 \times 4 = 7{,}000{,}000.$$

Hence not only is the new plan feasible, but it is possible to adopt a plan which produces more of both outputs. The shadow prices have been used in order to judge the rationality of a possible plan. Such examples show 'that prices are indispensable also in a planned economy'. In the particular case examined there was no private ownership of the means of production and the economy was planned, nevertheless 'prices arose naturally and turned out to be necessary and useful'. (Kantorovich [1968] p. 25.)

Consider however the plan c. Using the same method the value of this plan is

$$4{,}750{,}000 \times 1 + 600{,}000 \times 4 = 7{,}150{,}000.$$

Hence the method suggests that the plan is feasible when in fact it is not. From the diagram it can be seen that the reason for this is that c is dominated by a point that would be feasible if the entire production possibility area had the same slope as the facet on which the original optimal plan lies. (This is why Kantorovich states that the shadow prices are stable for 'small' variations in the initial data.) The diagram can be divided into three areas, an area in which Kantorovich's method can be used to check the feasibility and efficiency of alternative plans (the production possibility area), an area in which the non-feasibility of possible plans can be determined by evaluating them in shadow prices (the area above the facet on which the original optimal plan lies) and an area in which the method will give misleading results (the area which has horizontal shading in the diagram). Kantorovich's method for evaluating alternative plans is a special case. Diagrammatically speaking, its usefulness in principle depends on the proportion of the diagram which is horizontally shaded, and on the original optimal plan not being on a vertex (when there is both a left-hand and a right-hand shadow price).[1]

As Samuelson long ago pointed out (Samuelson [1949]), the idea of using shadow prices as guides to rational decision making can be regarded as a generalisation of the classical economists' idea of using

---

[1] Similarly, the economic interpretation of the decomposition method in terms of indirect centralisation is not in general valid. See for example Baumol [1964].

It is well known that some of the criticism of marginal theory on the grounds that 'businessmen know neither marginal cost nor marginal revenue' ignores the distinction between optimality conditions and procedures for finding the optimum. The same applies to some of the proposals for using shadow prices.

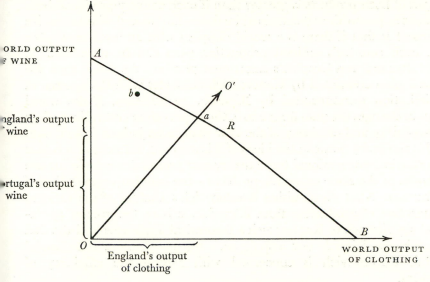

WORLD OUTPUT
OF WINE

ngland's output
' wine

rtugal's output
wine

England's output
of clothing

WORLD OUTPUT
OF CLOTHING

Fig. 5.2. World efficiency problem

comparative costs as a guide to rational decision making in the field of international trade. In a two-country, two-commodity, classical international trade model, comparative costs determine the rationality of specialisation and participation in the international division of labour. A simple example can be set out diagrammatically, as in figure 5.2.

There are two countries, England and Portugal. Portugal's production possibilities are such that the opportunity cost of 1 unit of wine is 80/90 units of clothing. (It is well known that although Ricardo's theory is formulated in terms of comparative costs it can be reformulated in terms of opportunity costs.) This determines the slope of *RB*. England's production possibilities are such that the opportunity cost of 1 unit of wine is 120/100 units of clothing. This determines the slope of *AR*. Ricardo's argument, that trade can be mutually beneficial, is equivalent to the proposition that world efficiency requires Portugal to specialise in the production of wine, and to obtain clothing by trade with England. (The use of this argument to sanctify the division of the world into rich manufacturing countries and poor primary producing ones is, of course, wholly unacceptable to Listian or Marxist poor primary producing countries, which argue that the aim of policy should be to alter the opportunity cost ratio by developing manufacturing industry, and not to accept it as a datum.) England should mainly produce clothing, and obtain most of its wine from Portugal. (The extent of specialisation, as Mill pointed out, depends on demand.)

Output of both products is greater than if each country produced both products in proportions determined by domestic demand. Kantorovich's argument is that if there is a world Gosplan with an assortment plan OO', each country's optimal production plan can be calculated. If world demand and Gosplan's assortment plan are the same, then the optimal plan computed by Kantorovich coincides with the pattern of specialisation recommended by Ricardo. In addition, if the world Gosplan changes the plan from a to b, the opportunity cost ratio enables the feasibility and efficiency of the new plan to be judged. The reason for this similarity between the ideas of Ricardo and Kantorovich is that both classical international trade theory and production scheduling are examples of the same economic problem – the rational organisation of production. What distinguishes Kantorovich's analysis of the rational organisation of production from Ricardo's is both the greater operational significance of Kantorovich's theoretical apparatus and the fact that, whereas Ricardo was a spokesman for mercantile and industrial capital, Kantorovich is concerned with raising the efficiency of socialism.

This argument, that prices have an important role to play as guides to the rational organisation of production, does not play a central role in Ricardian economics. Ricardo was primarily concerned with the distribution of income, as a key to understanding the dynamics of a capitalist society. Similarly, although Marxists are aware of the existence of a question of the rational organisation of the productive forces, this question is less important for them than the question of the development of the productive forces, and both questions are less important than the question of the productive relations, the relations between social groups. In post classical economic theory the role of the rational organisation of production, and of prices as guides to efficiency, hypertrophied. Robbins, following in the footsteps of a number of other writers, explicitly defined economics as the subject concerned with the rational organisation of production. When the theorists of the optimally functioning socialist economy extended their interpretation of the linear programming problem from some problems of the rational organisation of production to national economic planning, both current and perspective, they implicitly endorsed this definition. The reason for this definition, so much at variance with the concerns of economists as various as Smith, Ricardo, Marx and Keynes, was to provide a 'scientific' basis for the doctrine of 'the price mechanism'. The latter doctrine is derived by defining economics as the subject concerned solely with the rational organisation of production, and then focussing attention on the value dual rather than the planning primal. I consider that the hypertrophy of the problem of the rational organisation of production and of value relations as guides to efficiency is undesirable for both practical and theoretical reasons.

From a practical point of view a major problem with drawing policy conclusions from the theorem of the characteristics of an optimal plan is that they throw no light on such central problems of economic policy as how to maintain rapid economic growth at full employment. Instead, they largely consist of proposals designed to raise efficiency by introducing optimal payments for (land, capital and labour) resources and using profit as a local optimality criterion. A number of such proposals are analysed from a practical point of view in the following chapter. Here I wish only to advance the general theses that such proposals may be impracticable, ineffective or irrelevant, and ignore other ways of increasing efficiency.

Optimal payments for resources may be impracticable because in practice it is difficult to distinguish between differences in efficiency which result from the intrinsic properties of the resource in question (a particular piece of land, a particular machine, a particular worker) and those which are due to other factors. Hence in practice those responsible for calculating such payments tend to use some rule of thumb, e.g. to equalise rates of profit between enterprises. Payments calculated in this way are not pure rent payments, but are a mixture of a rent payment and an income tax. The introduction of an income tax element into the payments can have two adverse effects. First, it can create a situation in which the easiest way for an enterprise to improve its financial situation is to convince its superiors that part of the payment is an income tax rather than rent and should be reduced or eliminated. A measure designed to stimulate increases in efficiency has turned into one providing a powerful incentive to secure favours from an administrative superior. Secondly, if the norms are unstable, that is if they fluctuate from year to year in accordance with results, this has the adverse effect on effort of a very high marginal rate of tax.

Policy proposals aimed at raising efficiency by the use of value relations may not be a very effective way of attaining the desired objectives. The example of shift working indicates that the use of payment for capital goods may not be the only, or indeed the best, way of attaining the desired objectives.[1]

Proposals aimed at raising efficiency by the use of value relations may be irrelevant because they assume an institutional milieu which does not in fact exist. In Ellman [1971] chapter 8 I argued that the proposals put forward in 1966–7 for a greater role for profit were scarcely relevant to a reform of the incentive system consisting of the transition

---

[1] In the USSR shift working is substantially more extensive than in the UK and efforts to find an optimal pattern of shift working are of long standing (Kabaj [1968]).

from incentives for plan fulfilment and overfulfilment to incentives for adopting a taut plan, and to an economic environment characterised by administrative price determination. Similarly, in chapter 6 it will be argued that the use of payments for labour resources as an instrument of regional policy is irrelevant in the economic environment which exists in the USSR.

Policies aimed at raising efficiency by the use of value relations ignore the possibility of raising efficiency by increasing the quantity of resources utilised (e.g. by increasing effective demand,[1] or by providing nurseries and kindergartens to enable married women to work) or by technical progress.[2]

From a theoretical point of view a major problem with the hypertrophy of the problem of the rational organisation of production and of value relations as guides to efficiency is that it can lead to a one-sided treatment of the role of value relations in the economy.

One function of prices is the allocative one. Others are discussed in chapter 7. Another is to provide a value reflection of the process of production and growth. The latter role, which was studied by the classical economists and by Marshall in his analysis of the long period, is essential for the understanding of the long run evolution of the relative prices of produced goods. In pure exchange models prices are indices of relative scarcity. Goods available in excess of demand are free goods, and the prices of those goods which have positive prices depend on their scarcity relative to demand. In pure production models prices are a value reflection of the process of production and growth, and relative prices reflect the relative efforts society has to make to obtain the goods.

A number of writers, such as Dobb ([1964] p. 81), Zauberman ([1962] p. 276) and Treml ([1967] p. 115), have argued that Kantorovich's 'objectively determined valuations' are pure scarcity prices; that is that they belong to the same economic category as the prices of Ricardo's scarce goods, prices in pure exchange models and the prices of goods in the Marshallian short period, and to an entirely different category from the produced goods whose pricing is analysed by classical economics and by Marshall in his analysis of the long period.

This is not so. Shadow prices or equivalent concepts (Lagrange multipliers, adjoint or costate variables) exist in many types of extremal problems. Their economic interpretation, however, differs depending on whether the economic problem which is being considered as an

---

[1] This, of course, is the Keynesian criticism of the Lausanne school.
[2] The fact that efficiency can be raised not only by reallocating resources between existing technologies, but also by technical progress, was pointed out by Kantorovich in his 1939 paper.

extremal problem is a model of the organisation of production or of the growth of production.

In the elementary production scheduling example discussed above, the most natural economic interpretation of the shadow prices of the outputs is as opportunity costs, as rates of transformation of one output into another. They are determined both by demand and by technology. The shadow price of each input is its marginal product, the amount by which the value of the objective function would increase if the optimal plan were recalculated to take account of the availability of an additional unit of that input.[1] If a market for inputs exists, local decision makers can use these shadow prices to achieve the efficient allocation of resources (for example to hire out resources where the shadow price is below the market price, or to hire additional units of the resource where the shadow price is above the market price). If the market price of an input equals its shadow price, then the shadow price indicates the opportunity cost of using that input. The liberal idea of the market economy as a device for securing the efficient allocation of resources has been formalised by identifying the prices resulting from market processes with the shadow prices of a linear problem of the organisation of production.

In a closed linear model of the growth of production with constant relative prices, such as von Neumann's growth model, the shadow prices of the optimal plan are determined by the technical conditions of production and the uniform rate of profit as in classical economics and in the Marshallian long period. Price formation in von Neumann's growth model is similar to that in the Sraffa system, with the exception that in the Sraffa system there is one degree of freedom (the division of the surplus between wages and profits). Kantorovich himself has drawn attention to the fact that in the von Neumann model shadow prices coincide with the Marxist concept of the price of production (Kantorovich [1965a] pp. 44–8). The same point has been made by other Soviet mathematical economists, such as Volkonsky ([1967a] pp. 123–6). The Marxist identification of the prices actually observed

---

[1] When the objective function is to minimise the cost of attaining a given output, the shadow prices of the inputs are their marginal costs.

As Amey [1968] has pointed out, there is a slight difference between the concepts of 'marginal product' in the calculus and programming formulations. In the former, where infinite substitutability is assumed, the marginal product of any input is the additional output generated by the new technique employing the additional unit of that input, compared with the output generated by the old technique without the additional input. In the latter, where strict complementarity is assumed, the marginal product of an input is the increase in output (resulting from changes in the activity levels) caused by adding one unit of the input and also utilising available resources which formerly were free goods. (Ijiri [1965] p. 121 refers to this as the difference between the *ceteris paribus* and *mutatis mutandis* assumptions.)

in capitalist industry with the theoretical category of the price of production is based on the idea that equilibrium in capitalist industry can best be represented by a model in which goods are produced under conditions of a uniform rate of profit. The empirical investigations of pricing in capitalist industry which emphasise the importance of costs as a price forming factor treat a fall in demand as a price increasing factor and a rise as a price reducing factor, seem odd to economists brought up on the pure exchange model, but natural to those brought up on the pure production model.

That mathematical apparatus, in this case the dual variables of linear programming, is neutral as between different economic theories should be no surprise. As Novozhilov ([1970] p. 333) has pointed out, it is the assumptions of a theory, and not its mathematical apparatus, which determine its theoretical content. Similarly, what is controversial about the marginal productivity theory of distribution is not the existence and properties of partial derivatives, but their relevance for explaining why property ownership is a source of income under capitalism and what determines the size of this income and its evolution over time.

Kantorovich's theoretical derivation of the rate of interest for investment planning (Kantorovich [1965b] pp. 284–7) is non-operational, except on the two special assumptions that the relative shadow prices remain constant through time and that the shadow prices of the first year are known. In general these two assumptions are not valid, and therefore the conception can not be applied. This can be demonstrated as follows. Kantorovich considers an economy where production can be represented by activities which are proportional (i.e. constant returns to scale prevail) and additive (i.e. there are no externalities). Consider the jth activity, which when operated at the unit level is defined by the numbers $a_{1j}, a_{2j} \ldots a_{mj}$, where $a_{ij} > 0$ signifies that the ith commodity is an output, and $a_{ij} < 0$ signifies that the ith commodity is an input. The test of the efficiency of an activity is the sign of the expression

$$\sum_{i=1}^{m} c_i \, a_{ij} \qquad (1)$$

where c_i is the shadow price of the ith commodity. For efficient activities (1) is non-negative, for inefficient activities (1) is negative.

Now extend the analysis to embrace activities which relate not just to one period but to several periods. Each investment activity is defined by a matrix $||a_{it}||$, where a_{it} is an output (if $a_{it} < 0$) or input (if $a_{it} < 0$) of the project in the tth year. The test of the efficiency of an investment project is the sign of the expression

$$\sum_{i,t} c_{it} \, a_{it} \qquad (2)$$

where c_{it} is the shadow price of the ith good in the tth year.

Criterion (2) can be written slightly differently. Let

$$c_{it} = r_t c'_{it}$$

where r_t is chosen so that

$$c'_{1t} + c'_{2t} + \ldots + c'_{mt} = 1 \qquad t = 1 \ldots T.$$

Define $[r_t/r_{t+1} - 1]$ as 'the normal efficiency of investment' (it is a conversion coefficient which relates the price of a set of goods in one period to the price of the same set in the following period) from period t to period $t+1$.[1] Criterion (2) can now be written in the equivalent form

$$\sum_t r_t \sum_i c'_{it} \, a_{it}. \tag{3}$$

The efficiency of an investment project can now be tested by inspecting the sign either of (2) or of (3).

Assume that the relative shadow prices are constant through time. Then (3) is equivalent to

$$\sum_t r_t \sum_i c'_{i1} \, a_{it}. \tag{4}$$

To test the efficiency of an investment project it is sufficient to calculate (4) and look at its sign. $[r_t/r_{t+1} - 1]$ is a conversion coefficient which relates the price of each good to its price in the following period, and may accordingly be defined as the rate of interest for that period.

For this result to be operational it is necessary that $c_{i1}, i = 1 \ldots m$, be known. (It is also necessary that $||a_{it}|| \, i = 1 \ldots m, t = 1 \ldots T$, be known.) Furthermore, the argument depends crucially on the assumption that relative shadow prices are constant through time. Kantorovich himself provides no reason why this should be so. In general one would expect relative prices to vary over time. In this case, associated with the optimal plan would be, not a vector of interest rates, $[r_t/r_{t+1} - 1]$, $t = 1 \ldots T$, but a matrix of own rates of return $[c_{it}/c_{it+1} - 1]$, $i = 1 \ldots m, t = 1 \ldots T$. (Kantorovich has recognised that relative shadow prices may vary over time, but attaches little importance to it – Kantorovich [1970b] pp. 817–18. His position on this issue is analogous to his assertion that shadow prices have 'a certain stability'.) Accordingly this argument does not provide a way of deriving a single interest rate, uniform for the whole economy, for use in investment planning.

Kantorovich himself has implicitly recognised that his theoretical method of deriving the rate of interest for investment planning has no operational significance, by using an entirely different approach in empirical work. Here he identifies the rate of interest to be used in

---

[1] In von Neumann's model prices remain constant over time, so that $[r_t/r_{t+1} - 1]$ would be zero. In Kantorovich's model prices fall over time as labour productivity rises. Hence $[r_t/r_{t+1} - 1]$ is a small positive number.

investment planning with the marginal product of capital in an aggregate production function (Kantorovich [1967b]). The significance to be attached to the number arrived at in this way, and its relevance for investment planning, have been much discussed in recent years. In the Soviet institutional context, where the share of investment in the national income is a politically determined parameter, the main drawback of this procedure is that there is no guarantee that the rate of interest derived in this way will absorb the given share of investment in the national income. There is an alternative approach which has been advocated by Dobb ([1960] p. 27), Fiszel ([1966] pp. 35–41) and Lur'e ([1969]), and which would seem to be a reasonable rule of thumb in an uncertain world. Given the politically chosen share of investment in the national income, there is normally a unique value for the rate of interest which enables these investment resources to be absorbed in the most efficient projects. The determination of the rate of interest for investment planning in a socialist economy is a sub-optimisation problem. On this line of argument the rate of interest depends partly on technology, is inversely proportional to the share of investment in the national income and can be used as a lever to regulate the share of investment in the national income.[1]

Some writers have argued that Kantorovich's arguments for the introduction of a system of quasi rents into economic practice provide a theoretical basis for the payments for capital that were introduced as part of the reform. For example, in a booklet devoted to explaining the economic significance of shadow prices Terekhov has stated that 'Hire valuations [quasi rents] correspond to the principle of payment for capital which is being put into practice at the present time as part of the new system of planning and management of the national economy.' (Terekhov [1967] p. 58.) This is not so. What does correspond more to the theory are the fixed payments which have been introduced into the economy to take account of especially favourable circumstances facing some enterprises. The question of payments for assets is considered further in chapter 6.

Kantorovich's ideas about payments for labour resources concentrate on their allocative function and ignore their redistributive function. If, as part of an economic reform, there was a major reorganisation of the financial relations between enterprises and the state budget, there would be a case for introducing a substantial pay roll tax, the magnitude of which would mainly depend on macro economic balance considerations (such as the share of personal consumption in the national income).

Many of the theorists of the optimally functioning socialist economy consider that profit has a major role to play in such an economic system

---

[1] A rigorous analysis of this question would require an independent investigation.

as a guide to efficient resource allocation. This idea is not new in economic thought. It is an integral part of the doctrines of the liberals in general and of the Lausanne school in particular. This conception of the role of profit in an economy is entirely different from the role that profit has traditionally played in the Soviet economy (and in neo-Keynesian models). Traditionally in the Soviet economy the sum of profit and turnover tax was the financial reflection of the share of non-private consumption activities (e.g. investment, defence and social consumption), less savings, in the national income. Profit and profitability had nothing to do with efficiency (except in the special case in which profits were increased by cost reductions). Kantorovich's own ideas on how to calculate prices and quasi rents in such a way as to turn profit into a guide to efficiency have been clearly explained in connection with the work which he has done for Soyuzlavmetal in calculating optimal production schedules in the steel industry, and are considered in chapter 6.

To apply to the national economy the Kantorovich conception of profit as a guide to efficiency, if an optimal system of prices and payments for resources existed, would require a comprehensive reorganisation of the financial and price systems. Such a reform has been described by Joan Robinson (Robinson [1964] pp. 514–16), and was advocated in 1966 by TSEMI (Fedorenko [1967] p. 14), whose Director criticised the enterprise incentive fund system actually adopted by the September (1965) Plenum and argued that:

In our opinion the following scheme for evaluating the work of enterprises would be more correct. Every enterprise receives norms of payment for resources (productive capital, natural-transport conditions, labour resources) and also output prices. The norms of payment for resources are established at that level which balances supply and demand for them on the scale of the national economy for the planned period. On the same principle output prices are calculated; essentially they characterise the marginal limits of socially necessary costs on this or that product and themselves determine those enterprises which should produce the given type of product.

Comparing income with costs (including payment for capital goods, rent and so on) the enterprise works out its final profit. At those enterprises where costs are very high, there will be a loss. They will have to diversify, reconstruct or close down (depending on which is the more desirable). In an extreme case there will be left only those enterprises which cover current costs, including payments to the state (including payments for land and natural resources).

If the profit of an enterprise is sufficient to pay for capital and labour resources, and rent payments, then they will cover all costs. (We do not exclude some modification of this scheme, in which part of the social payments are retained by the enterprise as its own source of finance for development and premia, received even on condition of plan fulfilment.)

If the enterprise collective works better than envisaged by the norms, then it will receive above the plan profits. From this one could establish norms for payment into incentive funds, and the remainder pay into the budget. Alternatively, one could introduce a tax on above the plan profit and the remainder pay into the incentive funds. The losses of productive units should be met out of these funds and from credits. Obviously the transition to a system of economically well founded payments for resources requires considerable time in connection with the necessity for detailed elaboration of the method for calculating them. But it is possible already now to begin the preparations for an experiment.

What this appears to describe is a system in which the authorities fix payments for the use of resources (capital goods, natural resources and labour) and prices for outputs at levels which balance supply and demand. The enterprises then determine their own production plans, guided by profit. Net profit (after meeting all costs) would only arise for those enterprises which did better than the norms.

This policy suggestion follows logically from the conception of profit as a guide to efficiency if an optimal system of prices and payments for resources exists. It is, however, vulnerable to criticism.

The existence of optimal payments for resources and of marginal cost prices are not sufficient conditions for reconciling profit maximisation with social optimality. 100 % X efficiency is another necessary condition. In addition, it was long ago known to Marshall and Pigou that in the presence of increasing returns, externalities and consumers' surplus the theory that the price mechanism can ensure social optimality is not valid.[1] They and their followers saved it by resorting to a conventionalist strategy. Each time a counter-example was discovered they suggested modifications to the price mechanism so as to overcome it. The familiar argument about the need for subsidies in diminishing cost industries has been repeated by leading optimal planners such as Novozhilov ([1965] pp. 651–2) and Lur'e ([1968] p. 130). The danger of the conventionalist strategy is that it risks diverting attention from the economic problems which the rational kernel of the theory could be used to solve, to the puzzles created by the need to elaborate the epicycles. At the time when Novozhilov and Lur'e were repeating Pigou, the problem of improving the enterprise incentive fund system involved such questions as whether incentives should be related to adopting a taut plan or to actual high results, the division of the net income between profit and turnover tax, the stability of the norms and the system of incentives for managerial personnel. (This is explained in Ellman [1971] chapter 8.)

In addition such policy suggestions, and the theory underlying them, lead to a misunderstanding of why it is desirable to increase the role of profit in guiding and evaluating the work of enterprises. In the administrative economy, where enterprises receive plans for current production, the appropriate criterion for guiding and evaluating the work of enterprises is plan fulfilment. In the *khozraschet* economy, on the other hand,

---

[1] Uncertainty also raises problems for the theory.

where current planning has been abolished and whose central conception is that for purposes of simple reproduction the economy is based on the *khozraschet* enterprise or association, some value index which sums up the contribution of the enterprise to the national economy is required to guide its work. What is important is not the proof that in some allocation models the absence of profit is a sign of efficiency, but the following two points. First, some value index which measures the difference between the costs incurred by an enterprise and the results of its work should be regarded as the criterion for guiding its work in an economy where value relations are important. Secondly, a convenient source of finance for material incentives, socio-cultural and housing expenditures, and decentralised investment, is required. One such index is value added. Another is profit. The question of which of these two is the most appropriate criterion for guiding and evaluating the work of enterprises has given rise to a lively discussion in recent years in the socialist countries. The latter seems the most suitable, as the most synthetic. As Khanin [1970] has argued, it is the logic of the economic mechanism (rather than the conditions for the efficient allocation of resources) which is decisive for understanding the role of this or that of its parts (such as profit or prices). To express the same thought in another way, to understand the role of this or that value relation, or this or that institution, it is necessary to know which ownership and allocation model it forms part of. What gives profit its importance under capitalism is not that in some allocation models its absence is a sign of efficiency, but partly that it is a source of finance for investment and partly that it forms the income of the owners of the means of production. Similarly in the labour managed market economy (Vanek [1970]) the natural criterion for guiding enterprises is value added per head, a criterion inappropriate in the *khozraschet* economy where wages are a first charge on the income of the enterprises and where profit is divided between the state and the enterprise funds in accordance with specified rules.

CONCLUSION

Kantorovich's theorem of the characteristics of an optimal plan has played a useful role in Soviet economic thought, both with respect to the methods of economic calculation and with respect to the economic mechanism. In both fields it has introduced the idea that prices have a role to play as guides to efficient resource allocation which is both permanent and important. In the former field it has introduced into Soviet economic thought the idea that planning calculations should take account of opportunity costs and that investment planning should use a rate of interest uniform for the whole economy, and has emphasised the importance of economic-mathematical analysis of the results of plan calculations. It has provided a theoretical basis for the recognition of capital intensity, the use of scarce natural resources and demand as price forming factors. In the latter field it has provided a theoretical basis for price flexibility, rent payments, payments for the use of capital goods and labour resources, the use of profit as a criterion and the devolution of decision making. More generally, it has provided a theoretical basis for the use of value relations which carries more weight with many people (because of its mathematical basis) than the arguments put forward by Yushkov (in 1928) or in the discussion of the law of value in the late 1950s.

Kantorovich's ideas on how shadow prices can be used are not valid in general. To regard shadow prices as pure scarcity prices, as is often done, is wrong. Kantorovich's theoretical derivation of the rate of interest for investment planning is non-operational, and his empirical derivation not very helpful. The identification of quasi rents with uniform interest payments for capital is mistaken. Kantorovich's ideas about payments for resources raise a number of practical difficulties and concentrate on their allocative function at the expense of their redistributive function. Kantorovich's conception of the role of profit in an economy leads to a misunderstanding of the reasons for expanding the role of this index in guiding and evaluating the work of enterprises or associations.

The concrete policy proposals to which Kantorovich's work has given rise are analysed in the following chapter.

6. CAN THE OPTIMAL PLANNERS HELP IMPROVE THE ECONOMIC MECHANISM?

In chapter 4 of Ellman [1971] I described how the study of linear programming leads to suggestions for improving the economic mechanism, and in the previous chapter I have analysed the validity of these suggestions. I concluded that the optimal planners provided a theoretical basis for the use of value relations. In the following chapter I outline the economic reform which in my opinion the USSR needs, and draw attention to a number of points of contact between my ideas and those of the optimal planners. The purpose of this chapter is to examine some specific policy suggestions which have been put forward by the optimal planners and which follow from the theory of the optimally functioning socialist economy, in order to consider the usefulness of this theory as a source of ideas for improving the economic mechanism.

The optimal planners have made a large number of suggestions for improving the economic mechanism. These suggestions derive from the theory of the optimally functioning socialist economy (which is outlined in chapter 3), from Kantorovich's theorem of the characteristics of an optimal plan (the economic implications of which were described in Ellman [1971] chapter 4 and analysed in chapter 5 of this study) and from the concrete policy problems for whose solution the authorities look to scientific research institutes. These policy suggestions include: the recognition of capital intensity as a factor in price formation; the introduction of rent payments for the use of land and other natural resources and quasi rent payments for the use of capital goods; the development of wholesale trade; marginal cost pricing and greater flexibility in price formation. In order to consider the usefulness of the policy suggestions put forward by the optimal planners, six of their proposals will be analysed in detail. They are: the introduction of rent payments in agriculture and extractive industries, the introduction of payments for assets, the introduction of payments for labour resources, the use of profit as a local optimality criterion, the introduction of optimal functioning into the steel industry and the transformation of the economy as a whole into an optimally functioning economic system.

RENT PAYMENTS[1]

The additional income derived from the best pieces of land as a result of their natural fertility and also as a result of their more advantageous location with respect to markets, will be devoted to social needs in accordance with the instructions of the organs of state power.   Article 17 of the law 'On the socialisation of the land' (1918)

The desirability of rent payments follows directly from Kantorovich's theorem of the characteristics of an optimal plan (as explained in Ellman [1971] pp. 35–7) and is an integral part of the theory of the optimally functioning socialist economy. The purpose of introducing rent payments is to reconcile *khozraschet* with the interests of the national economy, by stimulating the more efficient utilisation of natural resources, preventing differences in natural conditions affecting the distribution of income and turning profit into a measure of efficiency.

In agriculture rent payments *per se* do not exist, although there are regionally differentiated procurement prices, an income tax on the collective farms and deductions from the profits of the state farms, which can be regarded as crude ways of collecting differential rent. The fact

---

[1] For an English language discussion of this topic see Wilczynski [1969]. This suffers from a number of weaknesses:

a 'Today, agricultural land is subject to differential rent ranging from 0.4 to 1.8 kopecks per square metre according to the six Regions into which the USSR has been divided' (p. 542). This is incorrect. Careful reading of the Soviet source which is referred to shows that it relates to ground rent on urban land and on non-agricultural land in the countryside.
b 'Proposals for the valuation of land under socialism go back to the 1920s, but the real impetus to the new approach has come from the three Soviet economists, L. V. Kantorovich, V. S. Nemchinov and V. V. Novozhilov, founders of the mathematical concept of differential rent' (p. 543). Is this really so? The general recognition of the existence of differential rent under socialism, at any rate in agriculture, goes back to the debate of the 1950s on the Law of Value. The compilation of a cadastre as a basis for rent payments was suggested in this debate. The introduction of payments for land taken from agriculture by non-agricultural organisations follows East European practice. Evidence for the thesis of the influence of the mathematical economists on practice in this area (other than in the natural gas industry) is lacking. The proposal for the general introduction of differential rent in agriculture and the extractive industries, which they have persistently advocated, has not been accepted. The increased differentiation of procurement prices announced at the March (1965) Plenum and the changes in the taxation of collective farms implemented in recent years, are alien to their position.

What is 'the mathematical concept of differential rent' which Kantorovich *et al* 'founded'? What Kantorovich has done in this area is, first, to repeat the Barone argument that the existence of differential rent is necessary for the efficient allocation of resources, and secondly, to provide a new method for calculating it.
c As far as the determination of land rent is concerned, 'Two schools of thought can be distinguished – one advocating a decentralised empirical approach and the other a centralised mathematical model' (p. 545). This is a complete travesty.
d It ignores the lengthy debate as to how differential rent should be allowed for (i.e. whether it should be extracted directly or via differentiated procurement prices).

that differential rent is formed, but is only collected in a crude way, leads to unjustified income inequalities, distorts the allocation of invest-ment, hinders rational specialisation and opens up a wide field for subjective decision making.

According to some calculations by Turchins for the 24 collective farms of the Talsinsky region of Latvia, the introduction of rent pay-ments and their redistribution by alterations in procurement prices would have altered average wages on the farms by amounts ranging from an increase of 48 % on one farm to a decrease on another by 28 % (Turchins [1969] pp. 32–3). This exaggerates the effect, because implicit in the calculations is the assumption that labour productivity is inde-pendent of wages, but nevertheless it does suggest that the absence of rent payments leads to major violations of the socialist principle of payment according to work performed. For the country as a whole the changes in relative wages brought about by introducing rent payments would probably be much greater than within one region of a small republic.

The absence of rent payments (and their equivalent, the value of land) distorts the pattern of investment by artificially cheapening land-intensive investment projects relative to non-land-intensive ones. An important example of this is the choice between hydro electric power stations and thermal stations, where the value of land lost to the economy by flooding should be taken into account.

The rational specialisation of argiculture depends on data about production costs in different regions. From a national economic point of view these costs include differential rent. Without reliable cost data, rational specialisation is impossible.

The fact that the absence of rent payments can give rise to subjective decision making has been emphasised by the Estonian economist Bronshtein.

Unfortunately the differentiation between regions and collective farms is often explained in a simplified way. Only recently differences in the level of economic development of the collective farms were explained mainly by differences in the level of management. This ignored the important differences in the natural economic conditions. The latter were assumed to be equal or approximately equal. The absence of sufficient data on the economic evaluation of land opened up substantial possibilities for a subjective approach to the problem of differentiation in collective farm produc-tion. As a result the correct idea about the need to strengthen the management of agriculture was discredited.

The one sided treatment of the reasons for the existing differentiation led to an unnecessary enthusiasm for various reorganisations in the field of the management of agriculture, to excessive reshufflings of managerial personnel, to attempts at foisting identical solutions to questions of the development of agricultural production on different regions of the country. At the same time economic levers for creating more equal opportunities for growth for the collective farms were clearly used insufficiently.

(Bronshtein [1967] p. 287.)

The existence of differential rent was recognised, and various proposals put forward for collecting it, prior to 1929. Stalin's speech at the conference of agricultural economists, with its stress on the gain to the peasantry from the free use of land, was understood as a denial of the existence of rent under socialism, and in 1936 the USSR adopted a Constitution which treated the free use of land by the collective farms as one of the advantages of socialism. The existence of differential rent under socialism was subsequently recognised (Laptev [1944], *Zemel'naya* [1952]) but was not universally accepted, and no concern was expressed at the misallocation of resources resulting from the absence of the direct calculation and payment of differential rent. The general recognition of the existence of differential rent under socialism (at least in agriculture) was one of the fruits of the discussion of the law of value which took place in the late 1950s (*Zemel'naya* [1959]).[1] A number of steps have been taken in the direction of giving effect to it.

A feature of the agricultural reform programme announced at the March (1965) Plenum was an increase in the extent of the regional differentiation of procurement prices. This, however, is a very rough and ready way of collecting differential rent. Not all procurement prices are differentiated by regions, a number of important products having uniform procurement prices for the whole country. Furthermore, the use of differentiated procurement prices distorts calculation of the relative efficiency of different uses of materials and of alternative investments. For example, the use of fertilisers in grain growing brings approximately the same increase in yields in the Volga-Vyatka and North Caucusus regions. In calculations of the efficiency of using fertilisers carried out in value terms, however, it appears that the return in the Volga-Vyatka region is much higher than in the North Caucusus because procurement prices are much higher in the former region than in the latter.[2] In addition within each price region there are great differences in the quality of land, and it often happens that farms with identical production costs receive different prices because they are in different regions.

To overcome this difficulty would require that prices be differentiated not by location but by cost of production, so that farms with the same

[1] The argument that the absence of rent in the USSR was a major advantage of socialism for the peasants was understandable at a time when the advantages of socialism to the peasantry were notoriously hard to find. It facilitated the misallocation of resources, but had an important ideological function. Once the leaders implemented measures to raise rural living standards (in 1953–8), spurious arguments ceased to be necessary, while the misallocation which they facilitated remained.

[2] This type of problem is an important reason why the planners often use physical units in their calculations rather than values, a practice often criticised by the optimal planners. The physical units used by the planners are no doubt imperfect, but they may well be less imperfect than the value units which exist in the Soviet economy.

costs received the same price. Such a system was implemented in Lithuania towards the end of this period. It aimed at equalising the economic conditions of farms with varying quality of land, location of land and capital equipment. Differences in the supply of labour and materials between farms were also taken into account. Compared to the calculation and payment of differential rent this system has both advantages and disadvantages. On the one hand, it reduces or eliminates income differentials caused not just by rent, but also by non-rent factors such as differences in capital equipment between farms. On the other hand, by taxing the income created by greater effort and/or efficiency it may have an adverse effect on incentives (particularly if the classification of farms is reconsidered at frequent intervals), and it fails to generate comparable cost data for use in specialisation decisions. It is only possible when all the land has received an economic evaluation (i.e. when the cadastral work has been completed). This is the case in Lithuania, but not for the rest of the country.

In addition a decree of the Presidium of the USSR Supreme Soviet of 2 February 1970 replaced the former proportional income tax on the collective farms by a progressive one. (The basis for the tax on the collective farms was changed from gross income to net income by the March (1965) Plenum.) This will have the effect of increasing the retained income of the collective farms in unfavourable natural conditions and reducing it for farms in favourable conditions.

Furthermore article 19 of the law 'Foundations of the land law of the USSR and the union republics' adopted by the Supreme Soviet in December 1968 provided that enterprises, organisations and institutions which take land for construction and other non-agricultural purposes should compensate the agricultural enterprises for the income which they have lost, a system which had earlier been introduced in the DDR. The purpose of this is to ensure that the opportunity cost of land enters into investment calculations, and thus to eliminate one of the wastes, pointed out above, which result from the absence of rent payments. The form and size of this compensation are still being discussed.

This law also envisaged the introduction of an all-Union land register (cadastre). At the present time work is proceeding in a large number of institutes on the economic evaluation of land in this connection. How to provide an economic evaluation of land is a controversial question, and different methods are being used in practice and debated in the specialist literature.[1] One of the uses of this cadastre is to enable the size of the payments by non-agricultural enterprises for land which they have taken from agricultural purposes to be calculated (Medvedev [1971] pp. 144–8). It could readily be used for the calculation of rent

---

[1] For a survey of the various methods see A. Mints [1972] pp. 157–81.

payments, as the Estonian economist Bronshtein and the Latvian economist Turchins have shown. In fact, the compilation of a cadastre, in order to enable the calculation of rent payments to be undertaken, was advocated by Levshtein at the September 1958 conference which led to the general recognition of the existence of differential rent under socialism (*Zemel'naya* [1959] pp. 158–66).

A tax on the cadastral value of land, would correspond to the introduction of differential rent if the cadastral value of the land represented the capitalised value of the rent stream, if the tax rate was the reciprocal of the coefficient used for capitalising the rent and if decisions were made on a post tax basis. Were such a tax to be introduced, it is doubtful whether any of these conditions would be met. The most influential methodology in cadastral work seems to be that of Professor Cheremushkin of VNIESKh, which has been approved by the Ministry of Agriculture and VASKhNIL[1]. This suffers, from the standpoint of the optimal planners, from two weaknesses. First, it uses the existing regionally differentiated procurement prices and hence cannot form a basis for the comparable evaluation of land throughout the country. Secondly it is concerned with capitalising not just rent but the sum of rent and profit, i.e. rent (of land), quasi rents (of capital goods used in agriculture) and rent of (managerial) ability. This follows traditional cadastral practice (e.g. the Nizhegorod type of cadastre in Tsarist Russia).[2]

The idea of introducing rent payments into economic practice has not been accepted. The reasons for this appear to be that it is a very radical measure, which raises a number of practical difficulties, and which if it were introduced would not make a significant contribution to attaining the policy objectives of the party.

That the introduction of differential rent payments would be a very radical measure can be seen from the fact that the free use of land which is granted to the collective farms in the Constitution of the USSR is 'one of the important economic and political conquests of the Great October Socialist Revolution which should remain firm and inviolable' (Udachin [1970] p. 135) and has international implications (Romanchenko [1969]).

[1] In 1967 the Bureau of the Economics Section of the Academy of Sciences recognised the Institute of Economics and VNIESKh as the chief organisations concerned with the specific problem of the economic evaluation of land. Although it simultaneously recognised the Institute of Economics and TSEMI as the chief organisations for research on the economic evaluation of natural resources in general, VNIESKh, which is a departmental rather than an academic institution, appears to be more influenced by the traditions of Russian land economy than by the ideas of TSEMI.

[2] The Cheremushkin method is opposed not only by mathematical economists but also by geographers such as Lebedev and Zvorykin.

It is often said to be impracticable because of the radical reform of the agricultural pricing system that it would entail and the lack of a generally accepted method of calculating it. The first problem arises because the logic of the proposal to introduce rent payments is to base prices on the costs of the marginal producer, which means a very substantial increase in prices for farms on the marginal land and a substantial increase in retail prices. This problem, however, could easily be dealt with by introducing a dual price system, with prices based on marginal costs to the producers, the present prices for consumers, and the resulting subsidy self-financed out of rent payments. Experimental calculations on these lines have been made by a number of economists, but the suggestion is not favourably regarded in the Ministry of Agriculture, where it is said to be too complicated. I agree with the optimal planners that the latter argument is an example of bureaucratic conservatism, because it would be no more complicated than the use of settlement prices in the extractive industries or differentiated procurement prices in agriculture, and the suggested reform would enable the differentiated procurement prices to be replaced by uniform ones.

The direct calculation of rent payments is possible by comparing the costs of different farms. The collective farms are obliged to record their costs in their accounts, and a number of economists have used these cost figures for the calculation of rent. The main difficulty with this method is that of distinguishing between differential rent, quasi rents and differences in income resulting from varying degrees of managerial and labour efficiency. Another method of calculating rent payments is from the dual prices of a linear programming problem for the most efficient use of agricultural land, and some experimental calculations in this direction have been undertaken.

One important practical difficulty in the calculation of rent payments is raised by the frequent alterations in the sizes and specialisation of farms. In practice rent calculations are normally per farm, and the frequent changes in the boundaries of farms mean that once and for all calculations would be grossly inadequate. The frequent changes in the specialisation of farms mean that a substantial part of the differences in costs between farms are a result of differences in efficiency (resulting from greater or lesser periods of learning by doing) rather than differences in the 'original and indestructible powers' of the land. This is a most important practical objection to the use of rent payments, and one often deployed by Academician (of VASKhNIL) Udachin.

The main policy objectives of the party in agriculture are to expand output, raise labour productivity, develop socialist productive relations and raise rural living standards. In 1965–70 there was a sharp increase in agricultural output. This resulted from relaxing the restrictions on private plots, increasing state procurement prices and investing heavily in agriculture. It remains to be demonstrated that the gains which would follow the general introduction of differential rent payments would be substantial relative to those which party policy has brought about. (The introduction of stumpage payments in the lumber industry in 1949 did not bring about substantial gains in efficiency.) In addition to increasing efficiency, a major objective of the introduction of rent payments is to make possible the elimination of procurement plans for each crop and their replacement by a situation in which each farm, guided by profitability, would itself choose a socially rational output programme. This can scarcely be regarded as a major objective of the party.

It seems that the solution to which the USSR is moving is a tax on the cadastral value of land, a progressive profits tax on the collective farms, zonally or qualitatively differentiated procurement prices and payment by non-agricultural organisations for land which they have taken from agricultural purposes. The second, third and fourth already exist and the first will probably be introduced when the cadastral work is complete (which will also enable the zonally differentiated procurement prices to be replaced by qualitatively differentiated procurement prices, as in Lithuania). This would not be a perfect guide to the efficient allocation of resources, but it would be practicable, would eliminate the grosser misallocations of the traditional system and would represent a substantial improvement over it.

I agree with the optimal planners that the direct calculation and payment of rent could help raise efficiency, but I have two reservations about this policy proposal. The first concerns the practical difficulties of implementing it, which were mentioned above. The second concerns the importance of the gains resulting from introducing rent payments relative to those resulting from other possible policies (such as the replacement of the supply of materials and machinery by wholesale trade, the development of the *zveno*, investing in facilities for processing and distributing agricultural products, making the chairman of the collective farm responsible to the members rather than to the secretary of the local party committee, the development of improved varieties and the development of rural transport).

The optimal planners have had slightly more influence in the extractive industries. Prior to the reform the only rent type payments were the stumpage payments introduced in the lumber industry in 1949. As part of the reform rent payments were introduced in the oil, natural gas and asbestos industries, and in some mining enterprises in ferrous metallurgy. Not only did the optimal planners provide a theoretical basis for rent payments, but TSEMI performed some calculations for determining the numerical magnitudes of the rent payments in the natural gas industry.

At the present time rent payments have not been universally adopted in the extractive industries. This hinders the smooth working of *khozraschet*, both for consumers and producers. For example, for the coal industry it is preferable to achieve any given quantitative increase in output in high cost rather than low cost enterprises (because this contributes more to sales) and for consumers the inappropriate pricing of substitutable fuels leads to a clash between their interests and those of the supply organisations. Similarly, the same product produced in regions with different costs may have different prices. This may explain a substantial part of the cost differences between two plants producing the same product. Thus the idea of profit as a sign of efficiency and of net profit as a fund forming index are undermined.

The method of calculating the rent payments is unsatisfactory because it is charged per ton of output rather than for the use of particular deposits (and it is paid out of profits rather than treated as a cost item) and hence provides no economic incentive to end such wastes as the burning off of natural gas produced as a by product at oilfields. The reason for this is the way rent payments were introduced into the pricing system. The traditional way of dealing with the cost differences that exist in the extractive industries between regions was by means of settlement prices. These are individual cost plus prices and they provide no incentive for the efficient use of inputs. These settlement prices are, naturally, per physical unit of the commodity, and the rent payments introduced as part of the 1967 price reform simply enabled the dispersion of these settlement prices to be reduced. The fact that, in order to provide an incentive for the efficient use of natural resources, rent payments per deposit are required is widely recognised, and may be incorporated into planning practice in due course.

The reason why rent payments have not been introduced on a wider scale in the extractive industries appear to be both that this would be impracticable, and that their introduction would not make a significant contribution to attaining the policy objectives of the party.

The reason why they were not introduced in the coal industry was partly that the calculation of rent payments for individual mines is a difficult business. In particular it is not easy to distinguish between differences in costs that are due to different natural conditions, and differences that are due to differences in efficiency. There is a grave danger that rent payments, designed to eliminate objective differences in conditions between mines, will turn out in practice to be yet another example of individual norms with their well known adverse consequences (Ellman [1971] pp. 146–8). It is for this reason that a progressive profits tax, rather than individually calculated rent payments, has been suggested to absorb the differential rent created by differences in natural conditions. In addition it was desired to avoid both a general increase in prices and the redistribution of rent within the industry.

The main objectives of the 1967 price reform were to reduce the percentage of loss making enterprises, to bring prices nearer to real national economic costs (for example by recognising capital intensity as a factor in price formation) and to reduce the dispersion of profitability rates. The calculation of rent payments would be necessary in order to turn profit into a measure of efficiency and hence make it socially rational to devolve decision making to enterprises or associations, which is scarcely a major objective of the party.

Conclusion

The optimal planners have persistently argued for the introduction of rent payments in agriculture and the extractive industries. Up till now the ideas of the optimal planners appear to have had no influence in agriculture and only a limited influence in the extractive industries. The reasons for this appear to be:

  a the radical nature of the proposals and the inertia and conservatism of the responsible officials,
  b the practical problems connected with their implementation, and
  c the existence of other policies which promise to make a greater contribution to achieving the policy objectives of the party.

Nevertheless, there have been a number of steps in the direction of taking account of differential rent (the introduction of stumpage payments in the lumber industry in 1949, the increase in the extent of the regional differentiation of procurement prices in 1965, the introduction of rent payments in a number of extractive industries as part of the 1967 price reform, the introduction of payment by non-agricultural organisations for land taken from agricultural purposes by the 1968 law, the changes in the taxation of the collective farms in 1965 and 1970) and further steps in this direction (such as the introduction of a tax on the cadastral value of land) both in agriculture and the extractive industries seem probable.

PAYMENTS FOR ASSETS

It follows from the theorem of the characteristics of an optimal plan that payments for the use of capital goods should be introduced into economic practice to act as a guide to efficient decision making and in particular to turn (the absence of) profit into a guide to efficiency. The economic interpretation of these payments, as I pointed out in Ellman [1971] p. 39, is as quasi rents.

The introduction of payments for assets was advocated by Narkomfin at the time of the transition to NEP, but was rejected on the ground of the low profitability of heavy industry. They were introduced in Yugoslavia in 1950–4 and in the other European socialist countries including the USSR in the middle 1960s as part of the reform. A variety of reasons have been put forward for their introduction. The most important seem to have been to prevent enterprises applying for investment goods and investment funds when the prospective return is below their opportunity cost, and to prevent enterprises hoarding fixed and circulating capital when the return on them is below their opportunity cost.[1] The first problem arose from the fact that investment was largely financed out of grants from the budget, and the second arose from the absence of wholesale trade (and takeover bids). 'Prior to the reform the rights of enterprises in the sale of superfluous and unnecessary equipment were extremely limited: the sale of equipment and machines, as a rule, was forbidden, and the sums received by the enterprises for the sale of equipment, in the cases where it received permission for this, were paid into the budget.' (Rybalkin [1969] p. 83.) To the extent that investment is financed out of bank loans which have to be repaid at a substantial interest rate, or self-financed by enterprises or associations which can receive a substantial return on funds left with the banking system, and wholesale trade is well developed, as is advocated in chapter 7, this allocative case for payment for assets will disappear. It is interesting to note that in Yugoslavia, which was the first of the European socialist states to introduce such payments, they have become less and less significant. (The rate was 6 % when this lever was introduced in the early 1950s, and was reduced to 4 % in 1964, with a reduction to 2 % in some cases, and to 3.5 % with a reduction to 1.7 % in some cases, from 1967. The payment was abolished altogether as from 1971.) On the other hand, giving the enterprises a greater role in the initiation of

---

[1] For example in 1965 a state farm on the virgin lands sent in an application for 10 tractors, although it already had 40 'unemployed' tractors (Lisichkin [1966] p. 60). This is analogous to the fact that in United States defence contracting there is a tendency by firms to hoard

'engineers, technicians, skilled production workers, and administrative personnel not required on current contracts but useful for winning and executing future contracts.... Performing work 'in house' which could be done more efficiently by specialist vendors is another means ... of building up new capabilities for future business. Engaging in technical tasks and buying equipment essentially unrelated to an ongoing development effort also enhances an organisation's ability to compete in fields for profitable future contracts.' (Scherer [1964] p. 183.)

Such phenomena arise whenever the accounting cost of an activity is less than the user cost of not engaging in it.

investment, combined with the absence of payment for assets, can lead to the misallocation of investment (there is no reason why high quasi rents should be a good indicator of investment needs), and the transition from social property to group property, as Yugoslav experience has shown. Accordingly, I suggest that this lever be retained, even when wholesale trade has been developed and the banking system plays a more active role in the provision of finance for investment. The main controversial issues arising from the introduction of payments for fixed and circulating capital were the valuation of capital, which goods should be among those on which the charge is made, whether it should be at a uniform rate, what the rate should be, the relationship between the rate and the rate of interest on bank loans, and the effectiveness of this measure in stimulating the more efficient use of capital goods.

In the USSR, for the purpose of calculating the magnitudes of these payments (and also for calculating profitability) capital goods are valued at their original cost and not at their written down value. The purpose of this was to prevent these payments becoming an impediment to technical progress by providing an incentive to continue using depreciated machines and a disincentive to use new ones. I consider that, as in Poland and Czechoslovakia, the values used in the calculations should be the depreciated values, because the allocative function of these payments is to remind enterprises of the opportunity cost of these machines, and historical costs are irrelevant for this. This is also the position of TSEMI. By the end of the period it was already the case in some industries, such as the oil industry.

In the USSR these payments are levied on both fixed and circulating capital (as is also the case in Bulgaria, Hungary and the DDR) with certain exceptions, such as the first two years of the life of fixed assets financed out of the PDF, and purification equipment designed to prevent noxious wastes being discharged into the air or water.

In principle there is a uniform rate (6 %), but in practice some low profitability industries (such as the coal industry) pay a reduced rate of 3 %, and in some special cases the rate is zero. TSEMI has suggested that there should be a uniform rate, which should equal the rate of interest on bank loans (which should be raised from its present low level) and the national economic norm of investment efficiency (12 %). The reasons for this are that the allocative function of these payments is to ensure that enterprises should take account of the opportunity cost of capital in an economy without a capital market and that the norm of investment efficiency can be regarded as the opportunity cost of capital, and the general disadvantages of individual norms. Kantorovich has argued against a uniform rate and in favour of differentiated rates. The reason for this is that he conceives of these payments as quasi rents.

The existing system of payments for assets clearly can not be regarded as a system for collecting quasi rents, because they are not charged per capital good at a level equal to the marginal product of each capital good. What corresponds more to quasi rents are the fixed payments which have been introduced to take account of the especially favourable circumstances facing some enterprises, because these are calculated per enterprise and are designed to reduce the (excess) profit to zero. They are similar to the rent payments which Joan Robinson recommends for her Utopia (Robinson [1960] pp. 227–30). The fixed payments are often calculated in such a way as to provide a disincentive for efficiency. What tends to happen is that 'The basis for determining the fixed payments is not the additional profit, associated with better technical-economic conditions of production, but that part of the profit of an enterprise which is in excess of the average profit for the industry.' (Yegiazaryan [1970] pp. 5–6.) Hence I consider that there is a good case for a more or less uniform rate for payments for capital (possibly combined with *stable* fixed payments in some cases), based on the desire to encourage the efficient use of capital, the absence of a capital market, the difficulty of calculating quasi rents without providing a disincentive for efficiency, the desire to avoid a transition from social property to group property, and the needs of the state budget. In order to prevent the general absence of quasi rent payments from having undesirable effects on the distribution of income, the allocation of investment and the usefulness of profit as a criterion, one could introduce a regressive system of payments from profit into the funds available to an enterprise for incentive payments, welfare expenditures and investments, or a progressive profit tax (if an enterprise were allowed to keep all the profit remaining to it after it had met its obligations to the state). This is advocated in chapter 7 and has been suggested by TSEMI.

The question of the relationship between the payments by enterprises for assets and the rate of interest on bank loans has been much discussed in recent years. At present the rate of interest on loans to finance centralised investment is $\frac{1}{2}$% p.a., a rate which TSEMI considers to be too low; this is a view which I share.

The introduction of payments for assets, combined with the use of profitability as a fund forming index and the creation of the PDF did lead to the widespread selling, or giving away, of superfluous equipment. In general, however, the evidence supports the view that 'The practice of utilising payments for capital both in the USSR and in the other socialist countries does not yet allow us to answer the question what role it has played in improving their utilisation.' (Rybalkin [1969] p. 31.)

Conclusion

As part of the reform, payments for fixed and circulating capital were introduced into the Soviet economy. The introduction of these payments was an attempt to overcome some of the problems caused by financing investment by grants and loans at nominal interest rates, and the absence of wholesale trade (and takeover bids). A similar measure had been introduced a decade and a half earlier in Yugoslavia as part of the first steps in economic reform in that country. The optimal planners supported this measure, although the system introduced does not correspond to their theory and their influence appears to have been negligible. I consider that the introduction of these payments was a progressive move. What corresponds more to the theory of optimal functioning are quasi rents for particular capital goods. I consider (and so does TSEMI) that to attempt the general calculation of quasi rents is undesirable, because it would be very difficult and would lead to the emergence in this field of the well known problems of individual norms, as has already happened with fixed payments. Kantorovich considers that the regular calculation of quasi rents is both feasible and desirable as part of an optimally functioning economic system and has done some work aimed at demonstrating this in the steel industry. This is considered in a subsequent section of this chapter.

PAYMENTS FOR LABOUR

In Ellman [1971] I explained that it followed from the theorem of the characteristics of an optimal plan that payments for labour resources ought to be introduced into the economy as guides to efficient resource allocation, and that if such payments were to be introduced for purposes of regional planning they would correspond to the Regional Employment Premium introduced in the UK as part of the Selective Employment tax. Such payments have not been introduced into the USSR for the very good reason that although they are relevant in a market economy they are not relevant in the administrative economy. Kantorovich's proposal is relevant for market economies in which the location of industry is decided on economic grounds and it is desired to guide industry to areas where wages are above opportunity costs. In the USSR the reverse situation exists. The location of industry is administratively determined and the problem is to use indirect central-isation to fit the regional location of the labour force to the desired regional location of industry. Hence the authorities have introduced such measures as regional differentiation of wage rates, regional differences in holiday entitlement and regional differences in the number of years of work required to qualify for a pension. Similarly, in his classic study of regional labour problems (Perevedentsev [1966]) Perevedentsev discussed a large number of measures for improving living conditions in areas suffering from a labour shortage (such as improved housing and shopping), but regional wage subsidies were not even mentioned. Kantorovich's proposal is relevant in the administrative economy as a suggestion for location planning, i.e. that when calculating optimal (least cost) locations the planners should use not actual wages but opportunity costs. In the NEM payments for labour have been introduced, not in the form of regionally differentiated pay roll taxes (or subsidies) to equate actual wages with the shadow wages necessary for indirect centralisation, but in the form of a uniform pay-roll tax whose purpose is to redistribute the national income. In the USSR even in the *khozraschet* economy the case for introducing payments for labour for allocative purposes would be limited, as administrative methods would remain very important in location decisions.

Conclusion

The optimal planners have advocated the introduction of payments for labour resources. Such payments have not been introduced and are irrelevant for solving regional problems in the administrative economy. In the NEM there are payments for labour, but they have a different theoretical basis, distributive not allocative. The case for introducing payments for labour into the economic mechanism for allocative purposes (as opposed to using them in plan calculations) would be stronger were location decisions left to market forces, which is scarcely conceivable in the USSR.

PROFIT

Marxists have traditionally regarded profit under capitalism as a measure of the exploitation of the workers by the capitalists, and have ignored the liberal contention that profit is really an essential index in any economy as a guide to the efficient allocation of resources. In an interview with the first American workers' delegation (1927) Stalin stated that 'the extraction of profit is neither an aim nor a motive force of our socialist industry'. (Stalin [1950] p. 119.)

It follows from the theorem of the characteristics of an optimal plan that in the absence of externalities and increasing returns to scale, and in the presence of optimal payments for natural resources, capital goods and labour resources (the absence of) profit is a sign of efficiency. It is this which has led some of the optimal planners to advocate the use of profit as a local optimality criterion, a position strikingly at variance with that advocated in *Economic problems of socialism in the USSR*. In that work Stalin explained that in a socialist planned economy profitability must be considered 'not from the standpoint of individual plants or industries, and not over a period of one year, but from the standpoint of the entire national economy and over a period of, say, ten or fifteen years'.

It is widely believed that an important part of the reform was an increase in the role of profit as a criterion to guide the work of enterprises, as a source of finance for material incentives, and as a source of finance for investment. In fact the main criterion for guiding the work of enterprises continues to be plan fulfilment and overfulfilment. The difference made to this by the reform was that whereas formerly the most important plan indices were gross output and cost (reduction), now the chief synthetic indices are profitability and incremental sales (or incremental profit). The main source of material incentives for the workers continues to be the wages fund. Whereas formerly the engineering-technical personnel and employees received bonuses both from the wages fund and from the enterprise fund, now all their bonuses come from the MIF, i.e. are related to the fund forming indices and paid out of profit. As part of the reform a substantial proportion of investment in existing enterprises is now financed out of the PDF, i.e. largely out of depreciation.

The optimal planners considered that the system of incentive funds introduced as part of the reform was undesirable for the following reasons:

a the use of profitability as a fund forming index can have an adverse effect on investment efficiency,[1]

b incremental sales are an inadequate guide to efficient decision making,[2]

c the use of incentives for adopting a taut plan is ineffective,

d incentives should be for high results,

e free remainder is very important, but has no efficiency encouraging significance,

f profit has an insignificant role as a source of finance for increasing fixed and circulating capital.

I agree with this, and concrete proposals aimed at overcoming these difficulties are put forward in chapter 7. In connection with the evident need to improve the system of incentive funds and the creation of associations, at the end of this period a number of experiments concerned with reorganising the distribution of the profit of an enterprise

---

[1] For an explanation of how this can happen see Ellman [1971] p. 141, point (4).

[2] This is largely a result of the present price system and the permanent sellers' market.

were proceeding. Amongst other experiments, there was one in Minpribor, and another at Glavmosavtotrans (the Chief Administration of automobile transport of Moscow City Council), on which TSEMI's ideas had had considerable impact.

The system of distribution of profit in these experiments differs from the normal one in the following respects. Whereas under the existing system enterprises are only interested in increasing profit to the extent to which their incentive funds are increased (which may be easier via an alteration in the fund forming norms), under the experiments an increase in actual profit over the planned level automatically increases the funds available to an enterprise for its own purposes. In addition the planned payments into the budget are minimum guaranteed payments. If actual profits are below planned profits the budget does not suffer, although under the existing system it would, via a reduction in free remainder. Moreover in the experiments the enterprise incentive funds are related directly to profit, which means that the principle of incentives for high results has been incorporated into the experimental system. Furthermore, the role of self-finance for investment in fixed and circulating capital has been increased. TSEMI's ideas go further than the experiments actually implemented.

OPTIMAL FUNCTIONING IN THE STEEL INDUSTRY

Kantorovich's ideas about how to establish an optimally functioning steel industry are an application of his general theoretical ideas, which were described in Ellman [1971] chapter 4 and are analysed in chapter 5 of this study. In chapter 4 I briefly described the work which Kantorovich has done to introduce optimal production scheduling into the work of the steel industry. In connection with this work Kantorovich has provided a clear theoretical analysis and simple numerical example to explain not only that the use of linear programming can enable optimal production schedules to be calculated, but also that the theorem of the characteristics of an optimal plan can be used to establish an optimally functioning economic system in the steel industry (Kantorovich [1968] pp. 48–53). I have translated this argument in Ellman [1971] pp. 165–70.

Kantorovich's argument is unconvincing, for both logical and planning reasons.

The logical basis of his conception of optimal functioning is a modification of the theory that the price mechanism can lead to the efficient allocation of resources. It is well known that this theory (as formulated for example in the basic theorem of welfare economics) is false, or as it is usually put, suffers from 'exceptions' (such as increasing returns to scale and externalities).[1] In Ellman [1966] I have given some counter-examples on the preferences side. As far as the production half of the theory is concerned, in the previous chapter it was argued that even under conditions of constant returns to scale, no externalities and certainty, it is not general possible to use shadow prices in the way Kantorovich has advocated. In addition reference was made to Baumol's analogous critique of the interpretation of the decomposition method in terms of indirect centralisation, and to the distinction between optimality conditions and search procedures. It is easy to extend this general argument to the specific example offered by Kantorovich and Gorstko. The increase in the output of both products depends on enterprise *B* switching some capacity from 2 to 1, and *B* has no *khozraschet* reason for this. Moreover, suppose that engineers at *C* discover a way of producing an additional output of 2 for a cost of manufacture of 20. Using the shadow prices it would seem that the additional output should not be produced (20 > 18), although if the object is to maximise output given the assortment plan, then it would be socially rational to use this method, and there would be a clash between *khozraschet* and the plan, in which it would be socially rational to ignore *khozraschet*.[2]

The main planning objection to Kantorovich's scheme is that it represents a hypertrophy of one side of a mathematical representation of one part of the process of planning in the steel industry. As explained in chapter 4, at the present time the work done by Kantorovich in introducing optimal production scheduling and attachment planning into the steel industry is being incorporated into the management information and control system Metall. That shadow prices will have a useful role to play in Metall is possible, but evidence in favour of the gains to be had from using shadow prices to enable enterprises themselves to make socially rational decisions in the light of information which comes to hand between the calculation of optimal plans, is lacking at the present time. By the end of 1971 experience of optimal production scheduling had indeed shown that there was an additional gain over and above the extra tubes planned. It was not, however, the result of using shadow prices, but of using computers. The introduction of computers into planning steel tubes enabled the degree of aggregation of requirements to be reduced, and hence reduced aggregation errors.

The adoption of Kantorovich's ideas would amount to a major change in the status of plans. At present plans are obligatory for enterprises, which are provided with incentives for adopting taut plans and

---

[1] For a methodological discussion of how it is possible to prove theorems for which there are 'exceptions' see Lakatos [1966].
[2] Similarly, Barron [1972] has shown that Solomons' ideas about the use of shadow prices as internal prices for decentralised firms are not very helpful.

are liable to penalties for underfulfilling them. If Kantorovich's ideas were adopted, plans would have the character of suggestions by an enterprise's OR department, and an enterprise would be free to ignore them if it could do better than they envisaged. This would be a major change in the significance of plans, which I. Ya. Birman has referred to as the transition from 'plan-directive' to 'plan-consultant' (I. Birman [1968b] p. 225). It would amount to the replacement of *planirovanie* by *planirovka*[1]. It is scarcely surprising that responsible officials are doubtful about the need for such a radical change in planning procedures when the gains in efficiency which it promises are limited to taking into account changes in conditions since the original optimal plan was computed. How big are these likely to be, given the small increase in efficiency which the transition from traditional to optimal production scheduling usually brings about, the short period since the computation of the original optimal plan, and the limited domain of validity of the theoretical basis of the scheme?

Kantorovich's scheme is not an isolated aberration. It is simply a typical attempt, by a mathematical economist, to give an operational economic content to the separating hyperplane theorem, and is analogous to Koopmans' game between a helmsman, custodian and managers (Koopmans [1951] pp. 93–4), Samuelson's rules for the market determination of optimal prices and quantities (Samuelson [1966] pp. 436–8 and 469–71) and Lancaster's decentralisation theorem (Lancaster [1968] p. 108). I am doubtful about the usefulness of these studies for raising efficiency, for the reasons given above, although I recognise their interest for those who wish 'to elucidate the theory of linear programming and to see whether economic intuition suggests any computational methods for the solution of purely mathematical problems of linear programming'[2]

Conclusion

Kantorovich's ideas about how to establish an optimally functioning steel industry have not been applied, although his work on calculating optimal production schedules has been implemented. His ideas about an optimally functioning steel industry are unconvincing, and their non-implementation seems to be a result more of their exaggeration of one aspect of a mathematical representation of one part of the planning process, than of the 'bureaucratic conservatism' of the responsible officials of Soyuzglavmetal.

---

[1] Both of these words are usually translated by the English word 'planning', but they describe two very different concepts. *Planirovka* means plan compilation, and *planirovanie* implementing the plan by means of directives.
[2] This is Samuelson's description of his own aim. See Samuelson [1966] p. 438.

THE OPTIMALLY PLANNED AND FUNCTIONING ECONOMY

TSEMI's ideas about how to transform the economy as a whole into an optimally planned and functioning economic system were outlined by Fedorenko in the 1966 debate (*Diskussiya* [1968] pp. 13–15 – I have translated this passage in the appendix to chapter 3), in an article published by Fedorenko in 1967 (Fedorenko [1967a] p. 14 – I have translated the relevant passage in Ellman [1971] pp. 158–9), and in a book edited by Fedorenko (Fedorenko [1969a] pp. 499–500 – I have translated the relevant passage in Ellman [1971] pp. 160–1). From these publications it would appear that what TSEMI has in mind is the formulation of an optimal plan by means of a multi-level tâtonnement process, followed by its implementation by enterprises guided by the profit maximisation rule in an environment characterised by wholesale trade, flexible prices and optimal payments for resources. The introduction of rent payments in agriculture and the extractive industries, payments for fixed and circulating capital and for labour resources, the use of profit as a local optimality criterion and optimal functioning in the steel industry, are simply specific applications of TSEMI's general theoretical ideas.

In connection with TSEMI's position the following observations are relevant.

1 The schema outlined is an application of general equilibrium theory to a socialist planned economy. The purpose of analysing the general equilibrium model, according to leading researchers in this field, is to establish the assumptions under which Adam Smith's assertion about the hidden hand is valid (Arrow [1971] p. vii). The result of the analysis is to emphasise how very strong are these assumptions. The model focusses attention on trade rather than production; ignores the central role of labour; treats prices as guides to efficient allocation rather than as a reflection of the mode of production, the distribution of the national income and the methods of production; treats competition as a socially rational process for ensuring efficient allocation rather than as a mechanism for fostering technical progress or as a cost increasing factor; emphasises the equilibrating role of markets and neglects the disequilibrating role of markets; ignores information other than price information; approaches all decision making from the standpoint of maximisation; focusses attention on the combination of individually rational choices into socially rational choices while neglecting the possibility of individually rational choices combining into socially irrational choices; neglects the role of increasing returns in manufacturing; concentrates on auction markets; treats the quantity of resources and the effectiveness with which they are

used, rather than the level of effective demand, as the determinants of the level of output; considers an economy without a past and with a certain future; plays down the difference between a barter and a monetary economy .... Why should the planning and functioning of a socialist planned economy be patterned on a model which simply shows how strong are the assumptions it is necessary to make in order to construct a model in which hidden hand doctrines are valid?[1]

2 The writings of the optimal planners often fail to distinguish clearly between a description of algorithms and a description of the operation of economies. Walras 'confused the matter by not being altogether clear as to whether he was talking about an iterative solution or about an actual temporal process' (Goodwin [1951] p. 4) and this confusion has persisted in the literature. Some examples may clarify the point.

The economic interpretation of the decomposition algorithm is well known and has been used by some Soviet economists to provide a basis for decentralisation.[2] In many cases, however, it turns out that decomposition algorithms are inefficient, and that the direct solution of the problem is quicker. Does this mean that decentralisation is undesirable?[3]

In the planning scheme espoused by TSEMI, which is translated in the appendix to chapter 3, the process of compiling the optimal plan is treated as an iterative process to be repeated as many times as necessary to attain the required level of accuracy. Assuming that the algorithm has the required properties, a computer can iterate many times till the required level of accuracy has been reached. As Kornai has observed, however, there is no reason to suppose that a ministry could very many times in a year estimate what its reaction would be if plan x were submitted to it.

Kantorovich considers that the natural development after optimal production scheduling has been introduced is to complement it by using shadow prices in the functioning of the steel industry. The reason for this is that, quite naturally as a mathematician, he approaches the question of the organisation of the steel industry from the point of view of the properties of the mathematical model which represents that part of it which he has studied. In the previous section of this chapter I argued that this approach was not a useful source of policy ideas.

3 The planning process outlined by TSEMI is based on a misunderstanding of the nature of the planning process and may not be feasible; if it were feasible it would lead to the compilation of a plan which was 'optimal' only in a conventional sense.

---

[1] For a brief discussion of the logic of this approach see Bliss [1972] especially pp. 99–100.
[2] For example in the passage quoted on p. 47 of Ellman [1971].
[3] This example, and the following one, were used by Kornai in a lecture in Cambridge in November 1971.

a TSEMI's scheme for calculating the national economic optimal plan is conceived of as an algorithm for maximising the national economic objective function. It assumes that such a function exists and that national economic planning is concerned with its maximisation. As Kornai has argued, however, this is an unsatisfactory way of thinking about the planning process. It is not often that before the planning work begins the decision maker has a well defined preference ordering over all the possibilities. A more usual situation is one in which the goals of development are subject to conflict, and the wishes of decision makers take the form of aspirations (Kornai [1970]). Hence the planning process is not concerned with calculating one optimal plan, which is then implemented, but is a process of mutual adjustment between the set of explored plans and the set of acceptable plans, leading to the adoption of a plan which is acceptable, feasible, and optimal relative to the assumptions on which it is based.

b It remains to be demonstrated that the planning process outlined by TSEMI would converge to the optimum in a reasonable time, given the size of the problem, the information that is available and the technology that exists. The time taken to solve the much smaller problem of introducing optimal production scheduling into the work of the steel industry, the difficulties in obtaining reliable data both for current planning and for optimal planning of the development and location of industries, and the arbitrary technological assumptions made in many theoretical analyses of the problem, testify to the importance of these problems. The problem of drawing up consistent, let alone optimal, current plans remains unsolved, as I explained in chapter 1. The main reason for this is the difficulty of collecting and processing the necessary data.

c In chapter 4 some specific areas in which TSEMI's ideas about the calculation of optimal plans have been applied were considered. It was shown that this work leads, not to the calculation of a single plan, the unique optimal plan, but rather to the calculation of numerous plans, each of which is optimal relative to the assumptions made. This is a useful process, which ensures that the plan adopted is feasible and that a useful gain in efficiency is made, but the plan adopted is only 'optimal' relative to the assumptions made in calculating it.

4 TSEMI's proposals about the implementation of the optimal plan, i.e. about the establishment of an optimally functioning economic system, raise a number of difficulties.

a In the previous chapter I pointed out that profit maximisation, optimal payments for resources and optimal prices were not sufficient conditions for the efficient allocation of resources.

b The views about the role of value relations in the economy from which TSEMI's proposals are derived were analysed in the previous chapter. There it was argued that TSEMI's treatment of payment for resources is one sided and raises important practical difficulties. In earlier sections of this chapter some of the concrete proposals of the optimal planners for improving the functioning of the economy were analysed from a practical point of view. Even in the case of differential rent in agriculture, where the *a priori* case for the position of the optimal planners seems very strong, it turned out that there existed an alternative to the policy which they recommend, which is practicable and overcomes some of the problems caused by the absence of rent.

c In the following chapter it will be argued that the important questions in economic reform concern such issues as the elimination of current planning, the creation of a buyers' market, the role of the association and the position of the white collar intelligentsia, rather than the questions on which the work of the optimal planners has focussed.

Conclusion

TSEMI's ideas about how to organise the national economy as a whole in an optimally planned and functioning way were put forward in a number of works in the late 1960s. The suggested method for national economic optimal planning and functioning was similar to ideas widely discussed in the international economics literature (Robinson [1964], Malinvaud [1967], Kornai [1965], Novozhilov [1969]) and whose ultimate source is *The elements of pure economics*[1]. The main result of one hundred years analysis of the model in that book is the strict demonstration of the extremely restrictive nature of the assumptions which are necessary to demonstrate the existence, economic meaningfulness, uniqueness and stability of a solution. The relevance of the model either as a descriptive model of industrial capitalism or as a normative model of a socialist planned economy remains to be demonstrated. The suggested way of drawing up the plan is based on an understanding of the planning process which is of doubtful validity. Its feasibility remains to be demonstrated. The plan resulting from such a process would be 'optimal' only in a conventional sense. The suggested way of imple-

---

[1] A clear textbook exposition of this line of approach is Meade [1965] chapter 14. For critiques of this line of approach see Mikhalevsky [1971], Kornai [1971], Georgescu-Roegen [1971]. The classic critiques, of course, are those of Marx, Veblen and Schumpeter.

menting it has a number of positive features (such as wholesale trade). In the following chapter I outline the economic reform which, in my opinion, the Soviet Union requires, in order to establish that the work of the optimal planners focusses attention on less important issues (such as the need for rent payments) at the expense of more important ones (such as the social basis of reform).

CONCLUSION

In order to examine the usefulness of the ideas of the optimal planners for improving the economic mechanism, six topics were analysed in detail. The first five were specific proposals and the sixth was the general theoretical framework within which the specific proposals are being put forward.

By the end of 1971 the impact of these proposals had been extremely limited, being confined to such things as the introduction of rent payments in some extractive industries (where they were calculated in a way which TSEMI opposed) and the experiment in reorganising the financial relations between Glavmosavtotrans and the state budget. The reasons for the extremely limited impact of these proposals throughout the period appear to have been threefold. First, it was only in the late 1960s that the optimal planners began putting forward their ideas in a form suitable for incorporation into the economic mechanism. The importance of *khozraschet* was emphasised by Yushkov in 1928, but it was only in the Glavmosavtotrans experiment that the optimal planners put forward a practical scheme which could fit into the existing Soviet planning and financial system. Secondly, they were extremely radical. The introduction of differential rent payments in agriculture and of payments for labour resources would have been major innovations. Thirdly, the objectives of the optimal planners were at variance with the policy objectives of the party. The purpose of introducing rent payments, payments for capital goods and labour resources, and the use of profit as a local optimality criterion, which the optimal planners have been advocating since 1928, is to create an economic mechanism in which enterprises, guided by value relations, would make decisions that were socially rational, and hence to reduce the role of administrative methods. This objective is ultimately based on a certain idea of what constitutes the good society. In essence the optimal planners subscribe to the view that a society in which some decisions are made in accordance with value relations is more desirable than one in which all decisions are made in accordance with instructions. This is a view which I share. It is not however one that appealed to the Tsarist government, that appeals to the Soviet government, or that fits in with the traditions of the party. It was indeed specifically attacked, during War Communism, with special reference to labour, by Trotsky (in a famous speech at the Third All-Russian Congress of Trade Unions) and by Bukharin (in *The economics of the transition period*). At the present time many of the ideas of the optimal planners about the economic mechanism are unacceptable because of their similarity to 'market socialism'. The latter, an official of Gosplan has explained, is unacceptable because 'in practice it means a weakening of the role of the socialist state and the party of the working class in the management of the economy' (Krylov [1969]).

I consider that the specific proposals of the optimal planners fall into three groups. First, those that are undoubtedly helpful. Examples are the proposal to replace the present system of incentives for adopting a taut plan and the present system of the division of the profit of an enterprise by incentives for high results and the use of net profit as a fund forming index. TSEMI has not confined itself to making proposals, but calculated rent payments for the natural gas industry as part of the 1967 price reform and played an important role in the Glavmosavtotrans experiment. Secondly, there are those which are sensible but not very important, such as the proposal to base the charge for fixed assets on depreciated values rather than historical costs. Thirdly, there are those which are not useful contributions to overcoming existing economic problems, such as the proposal to introduce regionally differentiated payroll taxes in an economy where the location of plants is administratively determined but the movement of workers is (more or less) free.

I consider that the general theoretical approach of the optimal planners does not provide a satisfactory approach to the question of economic reform.

7. WHAT KIND OF ECONOMIC REFORM DOES THE SOVIET UNION NEED?

If one may resort to an anachronism, [Adam] Smith can be termed a progressive intellectual. The most odious social types for Smith were the politicians, struggling for power and the *chinovniki*-bureaucrats, executors of their will, who as he said are inclined to a blind nationalism and a dangerous narrowness of opinion, which limit natural freedom, which is the only thing that allows a society to flourish.

A Soviet writer[1]

The 'thoroughly thought out, centrally coordinated series of reforms' which is required in order to overcome the problems described in chapters 1 and 2 would amount to a major change in the productive relations of socialism comparable to the transition from War Communism to NEP, a comparison made by writers such as Blyakhman [1969] pp. 3–7 and Rakitsky [1969] p. 10.

In the whole history of the USSR there have been only two such reforms, the transition from War Communism to NEP in 1921–3, and the transition from NEP to the administrative economy in 1928–31. Both were put through in a short space of time by the political leadership. In the period 1962–7, that is in the period between the 22nd Congress and the 1968 events in Czechoslovakia, it seemed as if a third major change in the productive relations of socialism might be put through from above. At the present time it is clear that the political will for this is lacking, although this situation may not last indefinitely.

The social basis of the transition to NEP is clear. It was the decision to reach a compromise between the party and the peasants. The social basis of the transition to the administrative economy is equally clear. It was the decision to liquidate the kulaks as a class. What would be the social basis of a major change in the productive relations of socialism at the present time comparable to the transition from War Communism to NEP? To answer this question an economist naturally turns for guidance to the work of sociologists.

[1] *Novyi Mir* 1969 No. 8 p. 280.

Sociologists tend to approach the question of economic reform from the standpoint of social stratification theory. From this standpoint economic reform is seen as simply one front of a struggle between two social groups, the white-collar intelligentsia, i.e. those who hold 'professional, managerial and administrative positions' (Parkin [1971] p. 147),[1] whose training and knowledge are indispensable to the running of any industrialised society, and the *apparatchiki*, the officials occupying the leading positions within the party and the state security organs, who at the moment hold power by virtue of the doctrine of the leading role of the party of the working class armed with a knowledge of Marxism–Leninism, and of the political institutions in which this doctrine is embodied but who are not essential for the running of a modern industrial state. Parkin has suggested that these two groups should not be regarded as separate classes but should rather be seen as two groups within a single dominant class. According to this interpretation, the white collar intelligentsia is struggling to replace the *apparatchiki* as the dominant group in society and to increase its material position vis-à-vis the manual workers. To achieve the first objective it emphasises technical competence (as opposed to political reliability) as the main criterion in appointments and promotions, and the need to replace 'arbitrary' political decisions (which are made by the *apparatchiki*) by 'rational' economic decisions (which are made by the white collar intelligentsia). To achieve the second objective it advocates the transition from the administrative economy to a market economy, because 'differentiation on the basis of thorough application of the principles of performance ... is naturally linked with the extension of commodity and value relations' (Machonin [1969] p. 159). 'Although the issue is a confused and complex one, it is not too simplistic to suggest that much of the impetus for economic reform did in fact come from certain groups in the white collar intelligentsia who felt relatively disprivileged in an egalitarian system. This seems particularly to have been the case in Czechoslovakia in 1968.' (Parkin [1971] p. 175.)

The Parkin–Lane analysis of the role of the *apparatchiki* seems to me rather superficial, for four reasons. First, it completely fails to distinguish between different groups within the broad category of full time party officials. As Hough has noted,

if we are to treat the party apparatus as a unified interest group in the political process, let us be fully aware of the assumptions that we must accept. We must assume that the agricultural department and the defence industry department of the Central Committee (with their leaders of quite different backgrounds) have greater community of views and interests than do the agricultural department of the Central Committee

---

[1] In previous writings I referred to this group as the 'specialists'. It consists of those with a completed higher education and corresponds to the British professional middle class.

and the Ministry of Agriculture. We must assume that the specialized local secretaries who have spent their lives in industrial, agricultural, and cultural-educational work respectively, and who in the future will probably return to governmental work in their branch, function more as allies than as competitors in the policy sphere. We must assume that the former coal industry administrator who is *obkom* first secretary in the iron and coal *oblast* of Kemerovo has much the same set of perspectives on important political issues as the former agricultural administrator who is the *obkom* first secretary in the flax *oblast* of Smolensk. We must assume that the construction engineer whose party and Soviet work in urban areas apparently warranted his appointment as Minister of Industrial Construction has a set of interests and outlooks which are basically in common with the agronomist whose party and Soviet work in rural regions earned him appointment as Minister of Agriculture.

(Skilling [1971] p. 59.)

The extent to which the holders of full time party posts really do form an 'objective' social stratum (in the sense of forming an homogeneous group with similar interests and career patterns) and a 'subjective' one (in the sense of having a group consciousness), and the type of decisions on which they have a common position, are important areas for further research.

Secondly, the idea that the leading role of the party and its officials in economic matters is dysfunctional is both very old and clearly invalid. The question was raised at the 12th Congress (1923), where Krasin's 'Answer to com. Martynov' precipitated a lively discussion. It described the members of the Central Committee as being little more than a group of 'journalists, literateurs and professional politicians' and called for the election of 'production leaders and economic executives' to the party's leading organs. Many managers were reported to have told the provincial party committees, 'Comrades, you are not competent in economic matters.' Subsequently these same 'economic incompetents' carried out the industrialisation of the USSR and now maintain full employment, stable prices and steady 'economic growth (and have defended the country from aggressors and maintained internal order). The allegedly dysfunctional *apparatchiki* can surely more reasonably be regarded as that stratum of the white collar intelligentsia which administers society as a whole and thus has to place the requirements of society as a whole above its own sectional interest. For example, although some members of the white collar intelligentsia advocate both an increase in the dispersion of earnings and equilibrium prices for meat, and could expect to find shopping easier were these policies to be adopted, those responsible for public order are bound to have a different attitude.

Thirdly, as Hough has pointed out, a major reason for the opposition to reform by many *apparatchiki* is not that they hold party posts but that they are part of 'the engineering-managerial personnel who have dominated Soviet industrial administration and much of the political system in recent decades – men whose training has not accustomed them to the idea of an 'invisible hand' and whose position might be severely shaken in an economic system in which different skills (e.g. those of the economist) became more vital'. (Skilling [1971] p. 70.)

Fourthly, a major weakness of the Parkin–Lane analysis is that it ignores the historical and political aspects of economic reform.

The formative experience of the Soviet state was the Civil War. A major result of this for the management of the society and the economy was the prevalence of the practice known in Russian as *administrirovanie*. This term has no exact English equivalent, and is variously translated as 'a system of management based on coercive measures, used by the bureaucracy' (Lewin) or 'rule by fiat' (Joravsky). This style of leadership was used by the bosses (*nachal'stvo*) who emerged from the Civil War in the leading positions. As Kalinin[1] noted at the time: 'The Civil War has created cadres of people for whom the only law is expediency, ordering, power. To govern, as far as they are concerned, means to issue orders in complete independence, without submitting to the regulating articles of the law.'[2]

The social basis of the power of these people was the political power of the party in a society characterised by the virtual absence of an independent working class (resulting from its small size, its links with the peasantry and the absorption of many of its members into administration), the hostility which existed between the party and the peasants, the suspicion with which the party regarded the specialists and the precarious position in Soviet society of the Nepmen.

The transition to the administrative economy in 1929–30 represented a triumph of *administrirovanie* and the bosses who exercised it, over the peasants, the specialists, the workers and the Nepmen. It was no accident that in December 1929, a few days before Stalin's speech to the agricultural economists, *Pravda* reprinted a telegram Stalin sent Lenin during the Civil War which exalted *administrirovanie* and disregard for the advice of specialists.

The naval specialists declare that taking [the fortress] by sea subverts naval science. All I can do is bemoan so-called science. The swift taking [of the fortress] is explained by the roughest interference on my part .....

I consider it my duty to declare that in the future too I will act in this way, in spite of all my reverence for science. (Stalin [1929c].)

This transition was accompanied by the liquidation of the bourgeois specialists as a class.

---

[1] Kalinin was a prominent party member who for many years was Head of State.
[2] Quoted from Medvedev [1972] p. 397.

The tolerant compromise that Lenin had arranged was cancelled. Henceforth all specialists were to be, like Vavilov, Tulaikov and Serebrovskii [three prominent biologists] active participants in the renewed revolution. Any critical comment, any silence that could be interpreted as criticism or mental reservation, became grounds for dismissal, or jailing, or even shooting . . . . At the very end of 1929 Stalin went further. He erased the fundamental distinction on which that compromise rested, the distinction between the political views of specialists and their professional work. Stalin told a conference of agricultural economists that their studies were being proved useless by practical party workers in the countryside, who were pushing collectivisation much faster than any economists had believed possible. Henceforth such practical achievements were to be the test of scientific truth. The implications for agricultural economics [and not only agricultural economics] were very clear; it was immediately transformed from autonomous scholarly enquiry into sycophantic commentary on the snap judgement of political bosses.[1]

Shortly afterwards numerous specialists were arrested, and many were tried, *pour encourager les autres*.

A feature of the period since Stalin's denunciation (in *Marxism and linguistics* published in *Pravda* in 1950) of Arakcheev regimes[2] in science has been the reemergence of autonomous groups of specialists in control of their own specialisms. The most dramatic example, of course, is genetics, where the quack Lysenko has lost his authority and science has been reestablished. It might seem that the reemergence of mathematical economics after the 20th Congress is an analogous phenomenon. In part it is. The theoretical and practical work which has been done by the mathematical economists in improving the methods of economic calculation is an example of what economists can contribute to improving economic decision making and the gains in efficiency which it has brought about are examples of the losses which *administrirovanie* has caused the Soviet economy. In part, however, it is very different, reflecting the difference between the natural and social sciences.

Consider, for example, the thesis that the study of optimal planning models

yields two conclusions of importance for the management system:
1 under certain conditions the market can be an instrument for achieving economic optimum. Consequently, there is precise mathematical proof that the market is capable of operating as a leading factor in the national economy under socialism;
2 conditions can be provided under which the participants of the economic process – guided by the logic of the market – act in accordance with the optimal economic plan (without the need to apply administrative compulsion). From this angle the plan appears as a model of the futures market. It should be emphasised that this quality belongs to an optimum plan only. A non-optimum plan has to be put through by administrative methods if it is not to remain a document of little significance.

[1] Joravsky [1970] pp. 36–7. Two footnotes omitted.
[2] Arakcheev was a reactionary minister in Tsarist Russia. An Arakcheev regime is one in which an infallible leader suppresses all criticism of his ideas.

Consequently, our criticism of command plans will carry little weight until it is aimed at the root of the matter, i.e. against the absence of optimal planning.

(Kouba [1969] pp. 37–8 quoting Rendek.)

A similar position was upheld in 1966–7 by Volkonsky, who declared for example that 'The most important achievement of world economic-mathematical science is the strict proof that, on fairly wide assumptions, such a system of prices [i.e. equilibrium prices] exists, and that it is possible to establish a system of decentralised optimal control on the basis of market relationships.' (Volkonsky [1967a] p. 10.)

How are we to interpret such statements? Considered from a scientific point of view they are simply out of date. As Bliss has noted 'It has been shown that it is not correct to claim that there is any necessary connection between the price system, here taken to mean a system where decisions are guided by the principle of profit maximisation, and efficient resource allocation.' (Bliss [1972] p. 100.) I suggest that the Rendek–Volkonsky use of the theorem of the characteristics of an optimal plan to provide a scientific basis for economic reform should be understood as an ideological expression on the economic front of what turned out, in the USSR and Czechoslovakia in the 1960s, to be an abortive process of social change, a change with four aspects, economic, social, political and historical.

Economically, it would have represented the transition from one allocation model to another. There have been two such transitions in Soviet history, in 1921–3 and 1929–30, and two in recent British history (in 1940 and 1948–55). Socially it would have meant a restriction of the power of the bosses and an improved position for the white-collar intelligentsia.[1]

Politically, it would have meant the establishment of civil liberties. The white collar intelligentsia is striving to end the arbitrary powers of the state security organs, to end the all embracing pre-publication censorship, to establish the classic liberal freedoms of the person, of travel (the restrictions on foreign travel are severely felt by the creative intelligentsia) and of opinion. They are struggling to obtain the freedoms which the Government stated its intention to grant in the October (1905) Manifesto, which declared the intention 'To grant to the population the unshakeable foundations of civil liberty on the basis of the principles of inviolability of the person and freedom of conscience,

---

[1] By 'boss' I understand a wielder of power, who may work in the *apparat* of the party, in state security or in a central or republican ministry or department, who wields arbitrary political power subject only to the approval of his superiors. He is distinguished from a 'government official' in states with limited governments by the lack of firm legal constraints on his power and the absence of autonomous public bodies which can stand up to him. ('Boss' and 'government official' are here understood as ideal types. There are 'bosses' in the UK and 'government officials' in the USSR.)

speech, assembly and union.' Every number of the unofficial typewritten periodical *A chronical of current events*, which was the organ of the Soviet civil liberties movement at the end of the period, carried on its front page article 19 of the UN's Universal Declaration of Human Rights:

Everyone has the right to freedom of opinion and expression; this right includes the freedom to hold opinions without interference and to seek, receive and impart information and ideas through any media and regardless of frontiers.

Bearing in mind the role of the Academy of Sciences within the civil liberties movement, and the ideological function of some of the writing on optimal planning and functioning, it was no accident that at the end of this period there were political dismissals from TSEMI of people who were suspected of being members of the movement.

Historically it would have represented a reaction against Stalinism.[1] On the eve of the break-through, in the aftermath of the July (1928) Plenum, a distraught Bukharin told Kamenev[2] about Stalin's 'idiotic-ally illiterate' theory that the further socialism advanced the stronger the opposition to it would become, and hence that the building of socialism required 'firm leadership'. He foresaw that 'we will have a police state as a result'. The validity of this observation was shown by the events of the next few years. Bukharin added that 'The root of the evil is that party and state are so completely merged.'[3]

After the 20th Congress, Lange argued that it had been necessary to create a strong state apparatus to smash capitalism and ensure rapid economic growth, but that this mighty state apparatus and its dominat-ing role vis-à-vis civil society had led to the well known negative features of the Stalinist period. The latter created a

necessity for a retreat from excessive centralisation, for assuring democratic control in the state, Party and economic apparatus; and the need for the direct workers self-government – in the form of Workers' Councils or in other forms – for the autonomy of cooperatives, of agricultural circles; as well as the activisation of the trade unions in the workshops as organs of social control. There arose too the need for

[1] In the Introduction I drew attention to the links, both intellectual and personal, between the discussion of mathematical methods after the 20th Congress and the work of Soviet economists prior to 1929. It was no accident that in the 1960s the mathematical economists received strong support from the literary journal *Novyi Mir* and came under strong attack from Boyarsky. The political perspective of *Novyi Mir* was clear, Marxist–Leninist but anti-Stalinist. As for Boyarsky, his criticism of optimal planning was as natural as Rusanov's apprehension about criticism of the personality cult. (Rusanov is the state security man in Solzhenitsyn's *The Cancer Ward*.) Boyarsky was one of those who backed the break-through and benefited from the personality cult. He published an attack on Groman and Bazarov in 1930 (Boyarsky [1930]) and became a professor in 1934 at the age of 28.
[2] Kamenev was a prominent Soviet politician of the 1920s.
[3] Reports of this conversation are in *Sotsialisticheskii Vestnik* 1929 No. 6 pp. 10–11, and in I. Deutscher, *The prophet unarmed* (1959) pp. 440–3. See also E. H. Carr, *Foundations of a planned economy* 1926–1929 vol. 2 (1971) p. 65.

working out new, less centralised forms of leadership and management of the national economy, resting to a greater extent on the workers, localities, trades and enterprises' initiative in the entire economy. (Lange [1962] p. 52.)

Economic reform, he explained, echoing Bukharin, was concerned with the 'separation of the management of the national economy from the extra-economic activities of the state, that is from the exercise of political power'. (Lange [1962] p. 14.)

In the minds of some of its keenest supporters, such as the writer quoted at the head of this chapter, a major objective of economic reform is to end the combination of all economic and political power in the same irresponsible hands. Economic reform aims to end this concentration of power by transferring much economic power to bodies independent of the political apparatus, such as enterprises, associations, banks, trade unions and workers' councils, and at the same time to make economic decision making responsible by bringing it under democratic control, at both the local and national levels.

From this perspective, the challenge mounted to political economy by the theory of optimal planning in the 1960s, and in particular in the 1966 debate, appears as an ideological expression of this social change. It was an attempt to replace one doctrine, political economy, which provides the ideological legitimation for rule by the bosses, by another doctrine, optimal planning, which legitimises the rule of the white-collar intelligentsia (which both calculates the optimal plans and manages the optimally functioning socialist economy), as the theoretical basis of the economic policy of the Soviet state. The recognition by the optimal planners in the late 1960s of the primacy of political economy, and the withdrawal of the more extreme claims which they made for optimal planning at the 1966 debate, appear on this interpretation as a reflection on the theoretical level of the defeat by the bosses of an abortive challenge by the white-collar intelligentsia.

It follows from the Parkin line of argument that, from the standpoint of the working class, economic reform, at any rate as understood by the white-collar intelligentsia, is undesirable. It simply replaces one dominant group by another, while increasing inequality, creating unemployment and raising prices. The position upheld by the Novotnyites in 1967–8, and which is orthodox in the USSR and in the European socialist states other than Yugoslavia and Hungary, has now been given qualified support by sociologists such as Parkin [1969], [1971], and Lane [1971] p. 128. Parkin ([1971] p. 177) has noted that

it would be unrealistic to ignore the fact that those groups which were most enthusiastic in their support for the [abortive Czechoslovak] reforms were the white collar specialists who seemed most likely to gain from the erosion of egalitarianism. There is

Table 7.1. *Income differentials in Yugoslavia*

	1951	1954	1957	1959	1961
White collar	(Wages of unskilled workers = 100)				
Highly qualified ⎱		238	290	316	333
Qualified ⎰	125	155	170	186	190
Unqualified	101	123	119	132	135
Blue collar					
Highly skilled ⎱		205	223	243	249
Skilled ⎰	120	146	149	159	160
Semi-skilled	105	118	117	125	124
Unskilled	100	100	100	100	100

SOURCE: Parkin [1971] p. 173.

little doubt that many of the latter were greatly discontented with a reward system which seemed to them to make insufficient distinction between mental and manual work. This appears to have given rise to an undercurrent of hostility against the working class . . . .

It is not difficult to collect evidence in support of this thesis.

Economic reform in Eastern Europe, for example Czechoslovakia, *was* largely concerned with improving the position of the white-collar intelligentsia relative to that of the workers. In Czechoslovakia in the early 1960s the distribution of income was very equal. As a result, the most important factor determining relative living standards was not differences in earned income between persons, but differences in the ratio of dependents to earners per family. A major objective of the abortive Czechoslovak reform *was* to overcome this situation. The Czechoslovak white-collar intelligentsia used functionalist arguments in support of its redistributive aims. Parkin has suggested that these arguments were purely ideological and has put forward the thesis that the 'need' to increase inequality will become apparent when the children of the white-collar intelligentsia aim to become manual workers (Parkin [1971] pp. 179–80).[1] Similarly, the main distributive effect of the introduction of the MIF in the USSR has been to improve the position of the white-collar intelligentsia relative to that of the workers. Similarly in Yugoslavia the deepening of the economic reform has been accompanied by an increase in the dispersion of earnings, as table 7.1 indicates.

Parkin, as a sociologist, concentrates on occupational stratification. An economist, however, is bound to take account also of the effect of a change in the economic mechanism on regional stratification. In

[1] It is possible that an increase in differentials in the USSR was 'necessary' by 1965 even on the Parkin criterion.

Table 7.2. *Per capita national income in Yugoslavia in 1947 and 1964*

	1947	1964
Yugoslavia	100.0	100.0
Slovenia	162.7	195.1
Croatia	107.9	118.9
Kosmet	50.4	37.1
Bosnia-Herzegovinia	79.8	71.1
Montenegro	71.1	73.2
Macedonia	68.6	69.4

SOURCE: Milenkovitch [1971] p. 181.

Table 7.3. *Unemployment in Yugoslavia in 1965/occupational group*

	As percentage of the work force	As percentage of the unemployed
Unskilled manual	41	78.2
Skilled manual	31	11.7
Lower white collar	14	5.6
Higher white collar	14	4.5

SOURCE: Parkin [1971] p. 174.

Yugoslavia the issue of economic reform has been closely linked with the national question, with the more advanced republics backing the abolition of investment planning and supporting other measures aimed at strengthening the role of market relations. As one would expect, the declining role of planning has led not only to increased occupational differentiation, but also to increased regional differentiation, as table 7.2 shows.

Economic reform in Yugoslavia has led to the emergence of widespread unemployment. This unemployment is not spread evenly over all occupational groups, but bears disproportionately on the manual workers, and in particular on the unskilled manual workers, as table 7.3 indicates.

Similarly in Czechoslovakia in the period January–August 1968 there was much talk of the need to close uneconomic enterprises. In the USSR too some economists argue that some existing enterprises, which are unable to cover their costs, should close down altogether (A. Birman [1967]). This idea has been rejected by the authorities. For example the Chairman of Gosplan has decisively rejected as 'alien to socialism the principles of competition and the inevitability of liquidating enterprises for some reason or another experiencing financial difficulties' (Baibakov [1968] p. 27). This position is entirely understandable in a multinational socialist state and Yugoslav experience has clearly shown the problems which could arise from listening to people such as A. M. Birman.

The rejection by the authorities of economic reform, as that was understood by some people between the 22nd Congress and the 1968 events in Czechoslovakia, reveals itself not only in the extreme slowness of the transition from allocation to wholesale trade and in the rejection of proposals for greater flexibility (in the Hungarian sense) of prices, but also in a number of measures for improving the position of the lower paid workers. A minimum wage of 60 roubles per month was introduced as from 1 January 1968, and is scheduled to be raised to 70 roubles per month by the end of the 1971–5 five year plan. Another feature of the 1971–5 five year plan is the introduction of transfer payments for families where income per head is less than 50 roubles per month. The plan also provides for a sharp increase in minimum pension levels. As from 1 July 1971 the minimum pension for workers and employees was raised from 30 to 45 roubles per month, and for *kolkhozniki* from 12 to 20 roubles. The 1971–5 plan also envisages a substantial increase in the level of grants to students. Similarly from 1969–70 preparatory faculties were introduced in higher educational institutions to give those with a poor educational background a chance of higher education. Whereas advocates of economic reform have argued in favour of expanding the network of paying services (education, medical care and housing) in order to reduce the suppressed inflation and expand the role of the rouble (Rakitsky [1969] p. 118), the authorities have adopted precisely the opposite policy.

While recognising the strength of the arguments outlined above, I reject the thesis that the maintenance of the administrative economy is desirable because economic reform is simply an expression of the self interest of the white-collar intelligentsia (and more advanced regions) and offers the workers (and backward regions) only increased inequality, unemployment and higher prices. I accept that 'the erosion of a command system and the release of market forces can have a detrimental effect on the life chances and the share of rewards of those who lack the kinds of skills which give bargaining power in the marketplace'. (Parkin [1971] p. 174.) One must bear in mind, however, that the waste generated by the administrative economy, and its negative effects on personal consumption, have a severe adverse effect both on working-class living standards and on working-class attitudes to production. Numerous studies have demonstrated the long hours which the economic mechanism forces women to devote to chores such as shopping. Similarly several observers have noted that in the administrative economy, in which an enthusiastic attitude to socialist production is expected, an apathetic and cynical attitude is in fact widespread (Karol [1965] p. 35, Holesovsky [1968] p. 54). Attempting to describe the present attitude of the people a Soviet writer has written:

nobody knows what moods exist among broad layers of the people. It seems to me that these moods can most correctly be called 'passive discontent'. This dissatisfaction is not directed against the regime as a whole – about that the majority of the people do not think, or reckon that no alternative is possible – but against partial features of the regime, which nevertheless are essential conditions of its existence. The workers, for example, are irritated by their lack of rights vis-à-vis the factory management, the collective farmers by their complete dependence on the chairman [of the collective farm] who himself is fully dependent on the regional boss, all by the marked economic inequality, the low wages, the difficult living conditions, the inadequacy or absence of essential commodities, the forcible tying to place of work and so on. Now that this dissatisfaction begins to appear ever louder many people ask themselves who is to blame? The gradual, though slow, increase in the standard of living, mainly thanks to the intensive housing programme, does not reduce this dissatisfaction, but to some extent neutralises it.

(Amalrik [1969] p. 29.)

One can scarcely expect an enthusiastic attitude to production in a factory where the workers are producing something other than that which is really required in order to fulfil the plan, find it impossible because of shortages to obtain numerous desired commodities, and have no more control over their working lives than workers in a capitalist factory.

After the December (1969) Plenum a lot was written and said about the need to tighten up discipline among workers and managers, about bribery, embezzlement, absenteeism and drunkenness. The proposition that successful efforts to raise efficiency require not only the use of economic levers, but also the support and cooperation of workers, engineers, managers and scientists, is undoubtedly correct. I consider, however, that what is required to gain this support and cooperation is not more discipline but an economic reform which improves the position of personal consumption (for example by widening the assortment of consumer goods available and eliminating shortages), is careful to avoid food price increases and strives to maintain approximate stability in the general level of retail prices, maintains full employment, reduces unjustifiable inequalities, expands democracy and establishes civil liberties.

Although economic reform could be accompanied by the emergence of unemployment (and has been in Yugoslavia) and unemployment was rife under NEP, this is not inevitable, as Hungarian experience has shown. In addition one must bear in mind that permanent urban full employment in the USSR since the creation of the administrative economy is partly an illusion created by the passport system. While recognising that from a technocratic point of view unemployment has advantages (it makes it easier for output to adjust to change in demand, and reduces upward pressure on prices), I consider that for social reasons it is unnacceptable, and that an integral feature of the *khozraschet* economy should be an active manpower policy designed both to provide jobs for all who want them and to adapt the flow and stock of skills to the needs of the economy.

The social stratification system in the socialist countries differs markedly from that in the capitalist countries. The minimal income differentials between holders of first degrees and skilled manual workers and the fact that some manual workers, such as coal miners, earn more than nearly all members of the white-collar intelligentsia, are facts familiar to all visitors to the Soviet Union. Distinctive features of the stratification system in socialist countries to which Parkin has drawn attention are: the lack of a sharp manual/non-manual distinction and hence the lack of a working-class/middle-class dichotomy, as a result of the fact that skilled manual workers are better off than lower white-collar workers; the extensive opportunities for promotion within the manual group, resulting from the widespread retraining programmes; and the ease of entry into privileged occupations by the children of those in unprivileged occupations. Associated with these differences in the stratification system are such differences in the value system as the absence of a defensive orientation by the manual workers and of sharp cultural and normative differentiation between those in privileged and unprivileged occupations.

Parkin's conclusions have been queried. Lane, for example, has questioned whether it really is true that the major break in the stratification system in socialist countries lies between skilled and unskilled rather than, as in Western capitalist societies, between manual and non-manual (Lane [1971] p. 78). Analysing the situation in Poland, Lane concluded that

While in the years after the seizure of power by the communists there was much collective mobility by manual workers into the strata of non-manual executive and administrative personnel, with the passing of time and the consolidation of communist power, such features of the system of stratification have faded away to be replaced by more traditional barriers between manual and non-manual workers. The boundaries between manual and non-manual are often diffuse and allow for movement but are demarcated by levels of income, life-styles, access to education and to the employment market. Hence we do not consider that in contemporary Poland there has been a significant merging of manual and non-manual strata and a strengthening of barriers between skilled and unskilled.   (Lane [1973] p. 311.)

The evidence given in support of Parkin's non-crystallisation thesis is unconvincing. To suppose that data on the social origin of admissions to the Sverdlovsk Mining Institute throw any light on the recruitment to leading positions (Parkin [1971] p. 166) ignores the fact that this is a non-prestigious institution which does not provide easy access to the highest positions.

It would be a serious mistake to suppose that the USSR is a society of the worker type, that is one in which 'the organisation of society gives privileges to the direct material producers' (Machonin [1969] p. 154), on the basis of the absence of some of the characteristics of inequality observed in advanced capitalist countries such as Britain, the fact that far reaching economic changes are being advocated by a group which wishes to improve its position relative to that of the workers, and the role of the working class in Marxism–Leninism. This would be to ignore the very substantial inequalities which do exist and have been explored by both sociologists and writers. The former have conducted numerous surveys of the relative esteem in which different occupations are held by the population, which all show that substantial inequality of esteem exists, that non-manual occupations (such as scientific research) have the highest esteem and that there does not seem to be 'any substantial residue of ascriptive dominance of the working class' (Machonin [1970] p. 738). Among the latter a classic account of the existence and importance of inequality is Solzhenitsyn's account in *The Cancer Ward* of a party official discussing his son's marriage:

He was such a naive boy, he might well be led up the garden path by some ordinary weaver girl from the textile factory. Well, perhaps not a weaver, there'd be nowhere for them to meet, they wouldn't frequent the same places . . . . Look at Shenyapin's daughter, how she'd very nearly married a student in her year at teachers' training college. He was only a boy from the country and his mother was an ordinary collective farmer. Just imagine the Shenyapin's flat, their furniture and the influential people they had as guests and suddenly there's this old woman in a white headscarf sitting at their table, their daughter's mother in law, and she didn't even have a passport.[1] What ever next? Thank goodness they'd managed to discredit the fiancé politically and save their daughter.[2]

I do not accept that economic reform *inevitably* entails greater inequality. To maintain rents of ability at zero I advocate the vigorous use of manpower planning. (Preserving equilibrium in the retail market in an egalitarian society would provide a challenge for the perspective planning of consumption.) Preventing a brain drain in an egalitarian society (assuming that the frontiers are opened as part of the reform) would provide a challenge to the party to build a society that is more attractive than capitalist society and a test of its ability to do so. A major source of inequality in the socialist countries is the importance of administrative privilege as a source of consumption benefits. At the

---

[1] In the USSR villagers do not have the (internal) passports which all townspeople have.
[2] Quoted from Lane [1970] p. 410.

present time a network of special shopping facilities, luxury housing, hotels, clinic, hospitals and sanatoria exists. I advocate the elimination of administrative privilege as a source of consumption benefits for top people. The purpose of this would be to improve the attitude of the workers to production, to convince the *narod* that what was being done was part of a progressive policy of social change and not simply a policy representing the class interest of the white-collar intelligentsia, to improve economic policy by ending the isolation of the authorities from the effects of their policies on living standards, and to bring nearer a society in which a person's contribution, rather than the official position he temporarily occupied, was decisive for determining his living standards.

Whenever this question of administrative privilege as a source of consumption benefits is raised, some people always suggest that it is necessary to revert to the position taken by Lenin in the April Theses – 'The salaries of all officials, all of whom are elective and displaceable at any time, not to exceed the average wage of a competent worker.' I do not accept this view, and share the position of Academician Sakharov ([1968] pp. 41–2), who has argued that inequalities can be justified, but that those inequalities that can be justified should be public knowledge and that no inequalities that cannot stand publicity should exist.

To expand democracy requires measures both at the level of the individual enterprise or association (such as elected committees to take major decisions) and at the level of the national economy as a whole (determination by representative organisations of the main policy objectives of each perspective plan before detailed calculations are made, discussion by representative organisations of preliminary versions of the plan). In this connection it is very important to bear in mind Academician Friss's three conditions (quoted in Ellman [1971] p. 19) for the plan to be optimal not just from the point of view of the techniques of planning, but also from the point of view of the development of the society. They are that the organ which takes the major decisions should have the confidence of society, that a wide circle of specialists should take part in working out the plan variants and that the mass of the population should take part in the planning work both directly and via representative organisations.

Under capitalism the worker is treated as a part of the production process, has no control over it and is subordinated to it. Under capitalism, the expansion in the real income of the workers which economic growth brings about mainly takes the form of an increase in consumption during leisure time. Socialists have traditionally regarded this as unsatisfactory, on the ground that a worker should find much of the satisfaction of his life in his work, which requires inter alia that he should be treated not as an animate machine but as someone fulfilling himself in a collective of creators. This aspiration, formulated by intellectuals and often regarded as a reflection of their own position, has flared up at dramatic moments of working-class history, such as Petrograd in 1917, has been officially adopted in Yugoslavia in the form of workers' self management, and has led elsewhere (e.g. in Sweden) to changes in the organisation of production which reduce efficiency but also increase the interest of the worker in his work. In other advanced capitalist countries, such as Norway and Britain, it has led to widespread discussion of fundamental changes in company law. I consider that the idea of fulfilment in work, and of self management as a necessary condition for this, is a valuable one and should be incorporated in economic reform in the USSR. The reality of self management in Yugoslavia has been doubted by many observers, who have pointed to such features of the system as the role of the League of Communists. A sympathetic sociologist who made a study of the system noted the existence of 'three sources of retardation in the development of real workers' self-management within the Yugoslav factory:

1 The extreme complexity of the system of factory organization and income distribution for workers with a low educational level.
2 The existence of large scale dissatisfaction with methods of distribution of income, with income levels, and with differentials.
3 The tendency for members of the workers' council to become assimilated to management perceptions of the problems of the factory in their role as worker-managers.
(Riddell [1968] p. 68.)

Nevertheless Riddell adds that 'It is inconceivable that the system should be replaced; weaknesses or not, alienation or not, in general it has become accepted among Yugoslav workers. One young worker in a Sarajevo factory asked me quite seriously at the end of an interview, " Is it true that in England the workers don't manage the factories?"' (Riddell [1968] pp. 68–9.)[1]

A fundamental feature of the administrative economy is the state ownership of the means of production. Socialists have traditionally advocated the social ownership of the means of production in order to ensure the use of resources for society by society. Considered from this standpoint, Lange ([1962] p. 12) has observed that two types of degeneration of state ownership are possible. First, there is anarchosyndicalist degeneration, which turns state ownership into group ownership. This emphasises one half of the socialist objective (use by society) at the expense of the other half (use for society). The other is

---

[1] Similarly on one occasion a Soviet economist who was explaining to me the need for radical reform in the USSR interrupted his exposition to ask me 'Why do you still have private ownership of the means of production in your country? Don't you understand, private ownership means exploitation.'

bureaucratic degeneration, which emphasises use for society at the expense of use by society. The type of reform which I advocate seeks to avoid both these extremes and to transform state ownership into social ownership by increasing social control over decisions made, both locally and nationally, while not allowing each productive group to become entirely independent.

When the question of self management comes up in Soviet discussion many officials refer to the poor results which it gave during the Revolution and the Civil War. In this connection it is important to note both Rakitsky's distinction (Rakitsky [1968] chapter 5), between technical questions which have to be resolved by experts and major policy questions which could be decided by elected committees, and also the fact that the difficult conditions of the Revolution and Civil War scarcely provide ideal conditions for experiments in self management. A. M. Birman has described how many economic officials regard talk of improving the productive relations of socialism as mere 'philosophy' of no interest to practical men (A. Birman [1968] p. 202). This is a profoundly short sighted view. As Sen has noted (Sen [1970] p. 192), 'The difference between success and failure in planning is often closely related to public enthusiasm and cooperation, and while the so-called "realists" not infrequently seem to pooh-pooh "vague normative considerations" like fairness or justice, these considerations seem eminently relevant to success or failure even in terms of most crude indices.' It is most important that the mass of the population should understand the need for reform and accept that it is in the interests of the further development of the economy and of the society. This requires both measures of the type outlined above and appropriate publicity. A feature of the Hungarian reform was the cartoon character Dr Agy ('agy' means brain in Hungarian) who explained the significance of the reform on Hungarian television for much of 1970.

Economic reform is simply one part of a wider process of social change, of which the establishment of civil liberties is an essential part, and is advocated by its supporters as such. Accordingly I regard it as progressive, even though some aspects of it, taken in isolation, can only be regarded as retrogressive.[1] I consider that its essential features should

---

[1] In some quarters the 'progressive' nature of the type of changes advocated in this chapter has been challenged. I consider that these changes are undoubtedly 'progressive' because they contribute to removing a major obstacle to rapid economic growth (popular indifference), because of Marxist attitude to civil liberties and because of the traditional historical perspective of all factions (including the Bolshevik) of the Russian Social Democratic Workers' Party.

'The point of the socialist critique of "bourgeois freedoms" is not (or should not be) that they are of no consequence, but that they are profoundly inadequate, and need to be extended by the radical transformation of the context, economic, social and political, which condemns them to inadequacy and erosion.' (Miliband [1969] p. 267.)

be: the transition from the determination of current production plans by a process of bargaining between the producing enterprises and their administrative superiors, to their determination, in many cases, on the basis of orders received; the transition from the supply system to wholesale trade; the transition from a sellers' market to a buyers' market; changes in the function of prices, the price formation formula and the price formation method; the transition from incentives for adopting a taut plan to incentives for high results; the use of value indices such as profit to guide and evaluate the work of enterprises; a reorganisation of the financial relations between the state budget and the enterprises; a changed role for the banking system; a change in the initiation and financing of investment; and a change in industrial administration.

CURRENT PRODUCTION PROGRAMMES

Experiments began in 1964 in the replacement of production plans determined from above with production plans determined on the basis of orders received from customers. From 1 July 1964 two clothing plants, the Bolshevichka in Moscow and the Mayak in Gorky, were switched over to production on the basis of orders from the retail trade. The progressive nature of such experiments was clearly shown by the substantial differences which often appeared between production plans imposed from above and production plans based on orders from the retail trade. An example was given in chapter 2.

   The measures which have been taken up till now are far from sufficient to ensure that consumers' requirements determine production plans. A Soviet specialist has observed that 'It would be a mistake to suppose that the introduction of a system of orders automatically provides for the

The strategic problem facing the founders of the RSDWP was the role of the party in the bourgeois revolution. As the Manifesto adopted at the 1st Congress (1898) noted:

   The further east one goes in Europe, the weaker, meaner and more cowardly in the political sense becomes the bourgeoisie, and the greater the cultural and political tasks which fall to the lot of the proletariat. On its strong shoulders the Russian working class must and will carry the work of conquering political liberty. This is an essential step, but only the first step, to the realization of the great historical mission of the proletariat, to the foundation of a social order in which there will be no place for the exploitation of man by man.

The validity of the first part of this diagnosis was strikingly shown in 1917, when it became clear that the Romanov Empire would revert to whichever party would advocate peace and black repartition, neither of which were socialist demands, and only the Bolshevik party supported these demands. (Black repartition was the peasant demand for an egalitarian redivision of the land.)

   It follows from this perspective that a reform which removes a major obstacle to rapid economic growth, brings about the realisation of 'political liberty' and which contributes to the 'foundation of a social order in which there will be no place for the exploitation of man by man' (by establishing self management and democratic control over national decisions) *is* undoubtedly 'progressive'.

establishment of the necessary economic links between trade and industry, directed at the full satisfaction of the demand of purchasers.' (Sarychev [1970] p. 201.) The reasons why consumer goods enterprises are still not producing in accordance with requirements appear to be as follows. First, the system for determining output programmes adopted by the September (1965) Plenum (see the decree of the CC and the Council of Ministers of 4 October 1965 No. 729) was a compromise between 'production for plan' and 'production for use' and was a retreat from the full Bolshevichka–Mayak experiment. The official, reformed, procedure for drawing up production plans for an enterprise is as follows. To begin with, an aggregated output plan is determined for the enterprise. Then, on the basis of this plan and of the orders from customers respecting assortment and other details, the enterprise draws up contracts with its customers, after which the plan must be approved by the higher administrative bodies and issued as obligatory indices to the enterprise. Secondly, manufacturers still have difficulties in obtaining the necessary materials (most producer goods are still rationed). Thirdly, the permanent sellers' market persists. Fourthly, the wholesale price system is such that the assortment pattern required by consumers is often not the most profitable assortment.

TSEMI supports direct contacts, but has endorsed the idea that enterprises should continue to receive obligatory plans for the output of the most important commodities.

I consider that, in general, production programmes should be determined in accordance not with plans imposed from above, but with orders received from customers. The purpose of this is to ensure the adaption of production to requirements. This is particularly important in industries where output is heterogeneous, such as clothing and engineering, and less important in industries where output is homogeneous, such as electricity. I entirely agree with the observation of three strong advocates of economic reform (one of whom is a leading optimal planner) who, in the course of arguing for an expansion of *khozraschet*, stated that: 'We do not want to be misunderstood. We are by no means against centralised management where it is really necessary. Network planning methods are highly effective, in particular, in the management of major construction projects, complex scientific operations and production systems requiring frequent retooling. The need for centralised management of electric power systems and gas pipelines is obvious. Evidently it is necessary to manage the work of railways and fishing fleets centrally. Other examples are also possible.' (Berg [1966].)

WHOLESALE TRADE

The desirability of making the transition from the rationing of producer goods (the planning of supply) to wholesale trade in them was urged in 1964 by the late Academician Nemchinov, and in his speech at the September (1965) Plenum Kosygin declared that it was intended to 'develop wider connections between producer enterprises and consumer enterprises. It is essential gradually to make the transition to wholesale trade in separate types of materials and equipment.' The purpose of this transition is to bring production into line with requirements. As the late Professor Novozhilov observed:

As a rule the consumer knows his needs better than the supply organisations. It is only necessary that he should not be interested in presenting exaggerated claims. Such an interest is unavoidable if demand is larger than supply. Experience also demonstrates that if the demand for a commodity is not covered by its supply, it is difficult to ensure the distribution of the commodity in conformity with actual need. This is obvious in regard to consumer goods. Queues, speculation and other negative phenomena appear in the distribution of goods.

Less evident but still more urgent is the need for equality of supply and demand of means of production.   (Novozhilov [1970] pp. 278–9.)

A number of steps have been taken to develop wholesale trade. Some 'trade only' shops have been set up for the free sale of producer goods. By the spring of 1971 there were almost 1000 such shops. Wholesale trade fairs have been developed. Up till 1971 the possibility of these fairs playing a progressive role in bringing production into line with requirements was limited by the fact that they were held after both the production plans and the indents for supplies of the producer enterprises were drawn up. In addition the Chief Administrations of the USSR Ministry of Trade determined in the plan for inter-republican deliveries both the total of goods to be sold at the inter-republican fairs and their assortment. In October 1971 a decree of the CC and Council of Ministers provided that as from 1972 the wholesale trade fairs for consumer goods should be held before the production plans are compiled.

There have been a number of experiments with trade in, rather than the supply of, producer goods. For example, the free sale of petroleum products was introduced in Voronezh oblast, and was later extended to Estonia, the Minsk, Kursk, Lipetsk and Orlovsky regions, and Dagestan. The free sale of building materials was tried out in Chelyabinsk oblast. In 1969–71 trade (as opposed to allocation) was extended on an all-Union scale to a number of commodities, e.g. certain building materials and certain sorts of engineering products. From 1970–1 the material needs of scientific research and design institutes were met by wholesale trade. In spite of all these measures, the overwhelming bulk of turnover in materials is still allocated rather than traded, with the adverse effects described in chapters 1 and 2.

TSEMI has persistently argued in favour of wholesale trade. I agree with the optimal planners that allocation should be replaced by trade, and am of the opinion that the view often advanced by officials of Gossnab, that first it is necessary to overcome the shortages and only then can the transition of trade take place, is fallacious because it ignores the fact that it is often the allocation system which creates the shortages.

A BUYERS' MARKET

The permanent sellers' market has a serious adverse effect on the adaptation of production to requirements and on technical progress.

A number of administrative measures have been taken in recent years to improve the position of customers relative to producers. For example, in order to raise the low standard of contract discipline (which results from the permanent sellers' market and from the fact that the primary obligation of an enterprise is to satisfy, not its customers, but its administrative superiors), compensation for losses resulting from contract violations has been introduced. This has not been very successful. It was pointed out in chapter 2 that one of the reasons is that in a sellers' market producer enterprises are often prepared to 'amnesty' their suppliers for breaches of contract discipline.

Similarly, the standards of quality control are being raised and zero defect systems introduced. A state mark of quality has been introduced to reward high quality goods. There is a system of standards, norms and technical conditions. As from 1 January 1970 revised standards, incorporating indices of reliability and life, were being introduced. Polish experience, however, suggests that administrative measures alone are inadequate to overcome the problems caused by the permanent sellers' market (Zielinski [1971] pp. 426–8).

I consider that to establish a buyers' market it is necessary to run industry with a reserve of capacity (but not with a reserve army of unemployed, as is done in capitalist countries, because the party's commitment to full employment makes this unacceptable), and to encourage competition between enterprises. The necessary reserve of capacity can be created partly by making the transition to wholesale trade, thus saving the idleness of men and machines caused by the supply system, and partly by expanding capacity faster than output for a period.

For consumer goods one way of strengthening the position of consumers relative to producers would be to encourage the formation of local and national consumer organisations. Representatives of local consumer organisations could be included on the committees which would run the associations. Another way would be to encourage the growth of trade organisations which would represent the interests of consumers and negotiate with producers from a position of strength, i.e. a 'socialist Marks and Spencer'. The giant department stores in Moscow, such as Gum, Tsum, Detskii Mir and Moskva, have established direct contacts with their suppliers and do now have considerable influence on production programmes.

In the administrative economy the emphasis placed on quarterly plan fulfilment (both for incentives and criteria), combined with the permanent sellers' market, provides a powerful disincentive for technical progress. Schumpeter and J. M. Clark emphasised that the importance of competition is not so much in the field of prices and costs, driving prices down to costs and costs to a minimum, but in the field of production, the introduction of new processes and new products. This seems to be a valuable insight, and in the *khozraschet* economy enterprises and trusts or associations should be encouraged to compete against each other in order to stimulate technical progress, so as to contribute to 'the securing of the maximum satisfaction of the constantly rising material and cultural requirements of the whole of society through the continous expansion and perfection of socialist production on the basis of higher techniques'.[1]

PRICES

The function of prices, the price formation formula and the price formation method all depend on the type of economic mechanism. In the administrative economy prices are used to distribute the national income, to maintain equilibrium in the market both for consumer goods as a whole and for particular goods, to control the costs of the enterprise and in planning.

Relative prices play an important part in the distribution of the national income between social groups. This is particularly important in the field of the relative prices of industrial and agricultural commodities, which has always been a crucial political question in the USSR because it simultaneously determines the real incomes of the farmers and the workers.

In an economy in which there is a free market in consumer goods and in which direct taxes on persons are not very important, the prices of consumer goods have to include a tax calculated in such a way that total retail expenditure of the population approximately equals the disposable income of the population (net of savings) and demand and supply for particular goods are approximately equal. If the tax is too

[1] This is Stalin's formulation of the basic economic law of socialism.

low, queues and shortages will appear; if is is too high, unsold stocks will accumulate. In exceptional circumstances goods can be rationed, as in 1928–35 and 1941–7.

In order to control the costs of enterprises it is convenient for prices to be slightly above the costs incurred by enterprises. This enables the authorities to check their progress in cost reduction, and allows some scope for *khozraschet* to operate.

The planners use prices in their calculations, both for highly aggregated current planning (e.g. the calculation of material balances) and for choosing between variants in investment planning (it was in this field that capital intensity was first recognised as a cost factor in Soviet planning practice). For these purposes it is convenient that prices be stable.

In the *khozraschet* economy prices will continue to be used to distribute the national income and in planning. Their role as a device for balancing supply and demand will widen to embrace producer goods (which will no longer be rationed). Moreover, they will have an additional function, to guide associatons and other economic organisations to socially rational decisions.

It is most important to ensure that the prices of agricultural products are such as to provide an incentive for the farmers, while at the same time not generating discontent in the towns. The 'scissors' was a major destabilising factor under NEP and should not be allowed to recur. A feature of the late 1960s was the rapid growth of agricultural subsidies (which by 1971 amounted to about 5% of the national income). These should be retained, because they are preferable to low procurement prices which provide no incentives for the farmers and may necessitate rationing in the towns, or high retail prices which can generate discontent and riots in the towns. Both Khruschev and Gomulka had reason to rue their neglect of this consideration. It is interesting to note that in Hungary three years after the introduction of the NEM the prices of a number of basic products (meat, milk, bread, transport) were still such that their production was loss making – a reflection of the responsiveness of the government to popular feeling.

A feature of planning after the 1967 price reform was the general recognition of the need for current planning to take account of the alterations in the price lists introduced by the State Committee on Prices, and for perspective planning to take account of the alterations likely to be made in the planned period. The attempts to take account of price alterations in current planning have not proved very satisfactory (Komin [1971] chapter 5, section 1) and would be much less needed in an economy where the centre did not issue output and supply plans to the enterprises. The first large-scale work on taking account of price changes in medium term planning was in drawing up the 1971–5 five year plan. This was an important progressive development, but there are still many problems, both practical and theoretical, in the field.

Traditionally Soviet retail prices have been below the supply and demand equilibrium level, generating shortages and queues. A sudden transition from non-equilibrium prices to equilibrium prices would clearly generate a politically unacceptable increase in prices, given the degree of suppressed inflation which exists. One way of reducing the suppressed inflation would be to transfer some commodities (such as housing, education and medical care) from the sphere of social consumption to private consumption. Clearly such measures as cooperative housing can play a major role both in reducing suppressed inflation and in ensuring the reality of cash incentives, but widespread measures in this direction might well have an adverse effect on the distribution of real income. Another way would be to expand the production of commodities which can readily be sold at prices incorporating very high indirect taxes, notably motor cars. This is being done, although its economic advantages are reduced when account is taken of the additional public expenditures which cars require (e.g. on roads). Another way of reducing the suppressed inflation would be to reduce the share of the national income devoted to space, security and 'non-economic' investment projects. (Given the present world political situation, it is unfortunately scarcely possible to reduce the share of defence in the national income.)

In the *khozraschet* economy the role of prices as instruments by which the centre judges the performance of the enterprises in cost reduction will not be significant. To secure cost reductions and increase efficiency, reliance should be placed on the spread of management education and training and the utilisation of modern management techniques, the desire of the enterprises to increase their profits and competition between enterprises.

Traditionally the main area in which the authorities were conscious of the importance of prices as guides to the efficient allocation of resources was agriculture. This was the only area in which this function was recognised in *Economic problems of socialism in the USSR*. At the present time another important area in which the authorities are conscious of the importance of prices as guides to efficient decision making by enterprises is in the field of the pricing of new industrial commodities, where the problem is how to determine prices in such a way that they simultaneously provide an incentive for producers to produce the commodity and for consumers to use it. In 1965 Gosplan USSR confirmed a methodological regulation on the establishment of prices for new products worked out by the Bureau of prices attached to Gosplan together with the Scientific Council on price formation of the

Academy of Sciences. On the basis of the experience gained with this method, and in the light of the new conditions created by the reform, a new method for determining the prices for new industrial products was adopted in 1969. This problem, however, is simply one particular case of the general need to establish prices which will serve to guide enterprises to socially rational decisions. It was pointed out in chapter 2 that the present prices often do not meet this requirement. If giving enterprises more autonomy in determining their production programmes is to have the desired results (to bring production into line with requirements), it is clearly necessary that the price system be such as to guide enterprises to socially rational decisions. To use profit as a criterion to guide the work of enterprises while retaining the price system suitable for the administrative economy immediately gives rise to 'the assortment problem' (as Kornai long ago forecast). This arises because the relative profitability of different products does not reflect their relative social valuations. At present this problem is often dealt with by reducing the MIF if the plan for the more important items of output is underfulfilled and by making the managerial bonuses conditional on fulfilling the assortment plan. For prices to be suitable as guides to efficient resource allocation substantial changes would be needed both in the price formation formula and in the price formation method.

The recognition under the 1967 price reform of capital intensity as a price forming factor was clearly an improvement in the price formation formula. However, the values of the capital goods which were used for this, the rate of profit used and the method of incorporating profitability into the prices of particular goods, all requires further improvement. At the present time the recognition of the use of natural resources as a price forming factor is very topical and the incorporation of this factor into prices should encourage the more rational use of natural resources. At the moment the labour cost which enters into prices is actual wages, plus a mark up for social security which is differentiated by branch of the economy and over the whole economy averages 6.2 % of the wages fund. It is often argued that this method of calculating labour costs understates the real national economic cost of labour, because it ignores such factors as the cost of educating the workers, and that there ought to be a much larger mark up on wages when labour costs are calculated. In general the calculation of costs contains a number of conventionalities and requires further improvement.

The traditional method of price formation was for prices to be fixed at irregular intervals (1949, 1952, 1955 and 1967) by the State Committee on Prices (or its predecessors) and, in general, to remain unchanged until the next price revision. It is now generally accepted that, although the price stability which this provides is very useful, it prevents

Table 7.4. *Types of wholesale price as percentage of turnover in Hungary in 1968*

	(1) Firm	(2) Maxima	(3) Flexible	(4) Free
Raw materials and basic semi-fabricates (e.g. coal and steel)	30	40	2	28
Products of manufacturing industry	1	10	4	85
Agriculture	60	10	20	10
Consumer goods	20	30	27	23

SOURCE: Golubeva [1969].

prices serving as guides to rational resource allocation (because the prices rapidly lose contact both with costs and demand), and that greater flexibility in price formation is required. The purpose of enlarging the flexibility of prices is to enable the rationing of producer goods and shortages and queues in the retail market to be replaced by the smooth flow of goods to those points where there is a demand for them. This can be attained by supply and demand balancing prices, together with the use of profit as a criterion, wholesale trade and the determination of current production programmes in accordance with orders received, but not by administrative methods, as explained in chapters 1 and 2. Greater flexibility in price formation is an integral feature of the NEM. Under the NEM there are four types of prices: those which are firmly fixed by the authorities, those for which the authorities set maxima, those which are free to fluctuate within limits set by the authorities and those which are entirely free to fluctuate in accordance with supply and demand. Table 7.4 shows the relative importance of the different types of prices. In 1969, 1970 and 1971 the proportion of prices in columns (3) and (4) increased. In its first five years the NEM managed to avoid a Yugoslav type chronic inflation.

In the USSR the idea that the flexibility of prices is important is generally accepted, but the view put forward by some economists that the way to achieve the necessary and desirable flexibility is to give enterprises a greater say in price formation has come in for strong criticism. A book produced by officials of the department of Gosplan USSR responsible for implementing the reform has explained that:

In the economic literature the opinion is very widely expressed that the necessary flexibility of prices can and should be created only by considerably expanding the rights of enterprises in the confirmation of prices. This is a deeply mistaken approach. In the practice of our price formation various methods are used for providing flexibility of prices: the differentiation of prices by stage of distribution (enterprise wholesale prices, industry wholesale prices, retail prices), by time period (permanent, step, seasonal, one off), by location, etc. Here are included also the development of the system of additions (or deductions) from prices. The flexibility of prices is helped also by the distribution of the right to establish them between various management organs. It is incorrect to reduce the flexibility of prices to any one form or method.

(Drogichinsky [1971] p. 423.)

Nevertheless the need to provide greater flexibility than at present exists has been recognised by responsible officials of the State Committee on Prices. For example V. K. Sitnin, the chairman of the committee, has suggested that the solution of the problem of combining a unified state price policy with a greater role for the enterprises lies in working out methods for the calculation of prices by the State Committee on Prices which will then be used by the enterprises. (V. K. Sitnin [1969].)

It is clear that the present price system is insufficiently flexible and that it would be desirable to make it more so, while preserving the relative stability of prices that is a feature of the administrative economy. (In this connection one should note that the declining price level shown by the index of state retail prices is not fully representative of the actual movement of retail prices.)[1] To prevent increased flexibility in price formation giving rise to chronic open inflation requires appropriate policies in the fields of agriculture, foreign trade and income distribution, and appropriate price fixing organs. The first three issues require detailed examination, which cannot be given here. As for the last one, it seems reasonable to place price fixing in the hands of wholesale trade organisations 'guided not by considerations of maximising profitability, but by the interests of maximising the satisfaction of the needs of society' (Sukhotin [1970] p. 79), which would be charged simultaneously with ensuring that production is in line with requirements and with preventing open inflation, as has been suggested by Joan Robinson and Sukhotin. These wholesale organisations should ensure that prices of commodities with above-average rates of increase of labour productivity steadily fall, thus defusing a major inflationary mechanism. (This is the function of step prices.)

It would be a mistake to imagine that a perfect price system could be introduced overnight. As an observer of the 1967 price reform noted: 'If the new prices mark an advance over the old ones, that is a considerable achievement. That a great deal more could be done is true not only for Soviet prices but for prices anywhere else in the world for all human affairs in general.' (Chandra [1970] p. 104.)

[1] According to official statistics, state retail prices in 1969 were 75% of the 1950 level (*Narkhoz* 1969 p. 625). This, however, gives a misleading impression of the movement of retail prices. It often happens that goods are replaced by 'new' goods which differ from the old ones only by virtue of their higher prices. Moreover these figures take no account of the substantial increases which have taken place in the prices of food products sold at the collective farm markets in the towns. *Narkhoz* 1968 shows that prices at these markets were 28% higher in 1968 than in 1960 (p. 655). *Narkhoz* 1969 omits this revealing table. By the end of 1972 prices at these markets had risen very substantially over their 1968 levels.

The optimal planners have persistently emphasised the allocative function of prices and have argued for greater flexibility in price formation and for the recognition of capital intensity and the use of natural resources as price forming factors. I agree that the allocative function of prices is very important, but I consider that excessive emphasis on the allocative function of prices at the expense of other functions of prices can lead to untenable policy proposals (such as price increases for basic foods), neglect of the policy implications of changes in relative prices over time and an exaggerated emphasis on the importance of prices relative to other parts of the economic mechanism.

INCENTIVES

At the end of the period incentives were mainly used to motivate enterprises to aim at taut plans. Incentives for plan fulfilment and over-fulfilment were still important, for example in inter-enterprise socialist competition and in the evaluation of enterprise managers by their superiors. The system of incentives for high results was used to form the PDF for some building organisations, and officials of the department of Gosplan USSR which supervises the reform had suggested extending this method of calculating the PDF to the economy as a whole (Drogichinsky [1971] p. 333).

In Ellman [1971] I explained how the system of incentives for plan fulfilment and overfulfilment provides risk averting enterprise management with a strong disincentive for adopting taut plans, and why the system of incentives for adopting a taut plan introduced by the reform had not succeeded. In an economy in which directive output and supply plans have been replaced by orders received from customers and whole-sale trade, incentives for adopting taut plans are irrelevant, and incentives should be aimed at motivating the achievement of high results.

The optimal planners are in favour of the transition from incentives for adopting a taut plan to incentives for high results, a position which I share.

In Hungary the principle of incentives for high results is applied not just to enterprises but also to individuals. I consider that to provide individuals with an incentive to attain high results requires certain social changes, the nature of which was considered above.

CRITERIA

In chapter 2 some of the problems arising from the use of inappropriate criteria for guiding and evaluating the work of enterprises in the administrative economy were described. One of the features of the reform was the replacement of gross output and cost reduction as the chief indices for guiding and evaluating the work of enterprises by two new fund forming indices, profitability and incremental sales. It was hoped that the former would provide an incentive for efficiency and the latter would provide an incentive for meeting the needs of customers. The use of profitability as a criterion can have adverse effects on technical progress and investment efficiency (as explained in Ellman [1971] chapter 8) and already in 1969 experiments began with ways of forming the enterprise incentive funds which do not use it as a fund forming index. Incremental sales often depend neither on efficiency nor on meeting the needs of customers, but on centralised investment or the assortment plan.

The question, what is the appropriate criterion for guiding and evaluating the work of enterprises in a socialist economy with peripheral decision making, has been much discussed by economists in the capitalist countries, both neo-classical and neo-Keynesian, and by economists in the socialist countries.

Lange argued that enterprises should choose that 'combination of factors of production and the scale of output which minimises the average cost of production'. (Lange [1937] p. 62.) Arrow and Hurwicz pointed out that this formulation may not define the behaviour of the firm (if there are constant costs) or may lead to non-optimal decisions (if firms control several processes, each of which is subject to increasing returns). (Arrow [n.d.].) Lerner argued that for each enterprise output should be determined by the Rule:

If the value of the marginal (physical) product of any factor is greater than the price of the factor, increase output. If it is less, decrease output. If it is equal to the price of the factor continue producing at the same rate. (For then the right output has been reached.)   (Lerner [1949] p. 64.)

Under constant returns to scale the private firms would be driven out of business and the publicly owned ones would break even. Under increasing returns the enterprises would make losses. Commenting on Lerner, Meade noted that in the presence of externalities adherance to the Rule would not lead to the optimal allocation of resources (Meade [1945] p. 57). Neither Lange nor Lerner show any interest in the problems of applying their prescriptions to particular sectors of the economy. Joan Robinson [1960], chapter 5, argued that enterprises should maximise their profits, subject to the general calculation and payment of (quasi) rents, wholesaler determined prices and the inapplicability of this rule to public utilities and monopolies.

In recent years an extensive discussion has taken place in the socialist countries about the appropriate criterion to use for guiding and evaluating the work of enterprises in the reformed economic system. It has been widely agreed that what is required is a synthetic value indicator. The indicator should be synthetic because of the problems that arise with the use of partial indices (these were mentioned in chapter 2). It should be a value indicator if the economic mechanism is to be based on the extensive use of value relations. Two indices, in particular, have been widely discussed, profit and value added. The optimal planners are divided over the question of the appropriate local optimality criterion to use in an optimally functioning socialist economy, some supporting profit in general (a position derived from the theorem of the characteristics of an optimal plan, as explained in Ellman [1971] chapter 4), some supporting profit in some cases and others criteria such as the sum of consumers' and producers' surplus.

It seems to me that in general wages should mainly be determined nationally and should not depend on the economic position of particular enterprises.

If demand for a particular commodity is expanding faster than supply, there is no reason why the workers who happen to be already in the industry concerned should receive a bonus. Or if the industry has to lose, say 10 % of its workers, there is no reason why the 90 % who are to remain should be penalised. Labour must be steered from one use to another by the offer of jobs, and the system has to operate in such a way that in each neighbourhood the number of jobs offered is equal to the number of workers available. (Robinson [1960] p. 217.)

In addition profit is a source of finance for investment. Hence I consider that, in an economy with a buyers' market, in many cases profit is a suitable criterion, subject to the neo-Keynesian reservations and to the following points. First, where free or subsidised distribution is a sensible way of redistributing income, or where externalities are significant, or where the cost of revenue collection is significant relative to the misallocation resulting from providing a good or service free, then some other criterion may be appropriate. Secondly, the appropriate criterion depends largely on the level at which a decision is made. At the highest level many decisions must depend on the balance of political forces. At the lowest level, the attainment of a given goal for minimum cost may be appropriate.

THE FINANCIAL SYSTEM

The present financial system does enable resources to be redistributed in accordance with the objectives of the state, but it often fails to stimulate the efficient use of inputs and hinders the adaptation of production to requirements. At the present time the main sources of revenue in the state budget are payments by the enterprises out of their profits (34.3 % of the income of the state budget in 1969) and turnover tax

Table 7.5. *Distribution of profit of enterprises working in new conditions (in %)*

	1968	1969
Profit retained by enterprises	33.0	39.6
Profit paid into the budget	67.0	60.4
of which		
payments for capital	17.0	19.5
fixed payments	5.0	5.1
free remainder	45.0	35.8

SOURCE: Drogichinsky [1971] p. 373.

(31.8% of the gross income of the state budget in 1969). This two-channel financial system has existed since the tax reform of 1930. The main payments by the enterprises out of their profits are payments for fixed and circulating capital, rent or fixed payments and free remainder of profit.

A major feature of the financial system created by the reform is the free remainder of profit. This arises in the following way. Out of its gross profits – *obshchaya pribyl'* – (sales revenue less material and labour costs and depreciation) an enterprise makes payments to the state for its capital, rent or fixed payments (if applicable), and interest on bank loans (if applicable). The net profit (*raschetnaya pribyl'*) remaining is the figure for profit used in calculating profitability (*raschetnaya rentabel'-nost'*). Out of this net profit the enterprise incentive funds are formed (except for that part of the PDF which comes from depreciation or the sale of superfluous equipment). The profit remaining is called 'the free remainder of profit' and is paid into the state budget. The relative importance of payments for capital, fixed payments, and free remainder, is shown in table 7.5. The optimal planners, and other economists, have persistently argued that the existence and importance of free remainder is an undesirable part of the financial system, because it reduces the incentive of an enterprise to increase profits, an opinion which I share.

The turnover tax serves both to redistribute the national income and to influence the relative quantities of commodities consumed (e.g. to discourage the consumption of alcohol and tobacco). Its disadvantage is that to a considerable extent it insulates the production of consumer goods from demand.

An important defect of turnover tax as a way of influencing production is that it is mainly derived from a small number of goods. In actual fact more than half the turnover tax is collected from four groups of goods, textiles, sugar, tobacco and alcoholic drinks. Such a concentration of the income of the state budget is convenient for the local economic and financial organs, but it hinders the development of the production of a mass of other commodities which are no less necessary and useful for society. Having received from one source a large sum of turnover tax and having balanced the local budget, the officials of the local economic and financial organs reckon that their business has been completed. They have lost the incentive to influence production from the point of view of expanding the sources of income and providing for the interests of the state budget not from one large source of income, but from small ones. To balance their budgets the local organs often increase the production of vodka, but less often develop new items or expand the output of old but extremely necessary ones. The needs of the population for those very commodity groups in the increased output of which the local organs could play a decisive role, are often not satisfied.

Only to a limited extent are the requirements of the population for items made out of wood, for domestic chemicals, for metal workers' or joiners' instruments, for shoe polish, for capsules for making fizzy drinks at home, and for many others, satisfied. There are tens of thousands of such items, but the production of many of them is not developing. The degree of satisfaction of the requirements of the population for various kinds of domestic goods, and in the first place for household utensils, does not exceed 25–30 %.

The explanation for this undesirable phenomenon is the same: a more equal distribution of profit in the prices of goods and a more precise determination of the economic efficiency of production is hindered by the existing procedure for collecting turnover tax.

(Kondrashev [1969] pp. 119–20.)

I advocate a financial system in which the income of the state budget comes from a profits tax, payments by the enterprises for the use of resources and a turnover tax. The purpose of reorganising the financial relations between the state budget and the enterprises is simultaneously to permit the redistribution of the national income in accordance with the policies of the state, to encourage the efficient use of inputs, to turn profit into a reasonably good guide as to what is socially desirable and to facilitate the adaptation of production to requirements.

The absence of a profits tax in the post 1965 Yugoslav economic mechanism has had serious adverse effects. Combined with the abolition of payment for assets it creates unwarranted income inequalities and adds to inflationary pressures. In Hungary an enterprise's profits are divided into two parts. Part of the profit, proportional to the capital employed, pays a proportional tax and the remainder of this part is available for financing the expansion of production. The other part, proportional to the wages bill, pays a progressive tax and the remainder is available for bonuses. The reason that this part of profit pays a progressive rather than a proportional tax is to reduce excessive income differentiation. I recommend for the USSR a system under which an enterprise's profit is divided into three parts. One part, proportional to capital employed, should pay a proportional tax and the remainder be used for financing investment. Another part, proportional to the wages bill, should pay a progressive tax and the remainder be used for financing socio-cultural and housing needs. The third part, also proportional to the wages bill, should pay a progressive tax and the remainder be available for paying bonuses. Both the existing system of calculating enterprise incentive funds and the free remainder of profit should be abolished. The desirability of a progressive profits tax has been recognised by Petrakov [1971] p. 43.

A convenient way of redistributing the national income is by a pay-roll tax. Under the NEM enterprises have to pay the state both social security and a wages tax which, in general, together amount to 25 % of wages; I advocate a similar system for Soviet industry as part of the transition to the *khozraschet* economy.

I consider that the present high rates of turnover tax should only be retained on alcohol and tobacco and that in general an attempt should be made to spread the tax more evenly so as to reduce the insulation between production and demand. Alterations in turnover tax rates are a convenient device for influencing prices.

The values of the profits taxes, the payments for resources and the turnover taxes should be derived from the national economic plan for such variables as the volume of personal consumption and the share of decentralised investment in total investment.

BANKS

In the *khozraschet* economy banks will have a major role to play, in particular in the provision of short term credits and long term loans. Banks should extend loans for investment in projects which accord with national economic policy, for measures to raise the quality of production and for the output of new goods for which there is a demand. At present the primary function of Gosbank is to ensure the fulfilment of the financial plan. As some officials of Gosbank have observed, however, it makes little sense to use profitability and incremental sales as fund forming indices while simultaneously providing bank credits for goods which have been produced but which are unsaleable (Chelnokov [1967]). TSEMI supports the idea that banks should play a more active role in the management of the economy.

The replacement of commercial credit by bank loans issued in accordance with the plan was decreed by the Central Executive Committee and the Council of Ministers in the decree 'On the credit reform' of 30 January 1930.

THE INITIATION AND FINANCING OF INVESTMENT

The initiation and completion of uneconomic investment projects, the wasteful spreading of resources over incomplete investment projects, and long construction and running in periods, are characteristic features of the administrative economy. If current planning were abolished, then the enterprises would cease to receive investment plans in their tekh-promfinplans and would themselves have a greater say in the initiation of investment, which would be largely financed out of deductions from profit, from depreciation and by bank loans. State investment would be confined largely to such sectors as fuel and power, transport and other infrastructure and social investment. Social control over investment made by enterprises would be exercised mainly through the banks and by fiscal and monetary levers (e.g. the proportion of profits which may be retained by enterprises for financing investment, the availability of and rate of interest on bank loans). The purpose of reorganising the initiation and financing of investment in this way would be to increase the efficiency with which investment resources contribute to meeting the requirements of society. The introduction of the PDF, and a greater role for the enterprise in the initiation and financing of investment were important features of the reform, but the possibility of enterprises utilising their PDF was limited by the rationing of producer goods. For enterprises or associations to be able to utilise their PDFs in the intended way requires, as Academician Fedorenko has pointed out, the expansion of wholesale trade.

A greater role for the enterprise in the initiation and financing of investment was a feature of the NEM, and is generally regarded as having been a useful and valuable reform. Nevertheless, a number of problems arose. For example it turned out that it was much easier to earn profits in sheltered industries than in industries which faced competition from imports. Hence investment funds accumulated not where they were most needed, but in industries sheltered from international competition. Another problem was that enterprises over-estimated their costs when prices were being fixed. Hence their profits were greater than envisaged, and their funds for financing investment were greater than intended. It was necessary to reduce the proportion of their profit which they retained for investment and increase the share used for financing state investment.

INDUSTRIAL ADMINISTRATION

An important feature of economic reform in the European socialist states has been the development of the association.

Under NEP industry was predominantly organised in trusts, such as Yugostal', the steel concern, and L'noupravlenie, the textile concern. The enterprise, rather than the trust, was established as the basic unit of industrial management by a decree of the CC of 5 December 1929 'On the reorganisation of the management of industry'. Associations began to develop in the early 1960s, an initial experiment being the merging of several shoe enterprises in the Lvov *sovnarkhoz* into the association Progress. The creation of the ministries, a major feature of the reform, often had adverse effects on the associations, because the component enterprises of the associations were often subordinated to different chief administrations, or sometimes even ministries. Well known associations are the Lithuanian computer firm Sigma and the all Union record firm Melodiya.

At the end of this period a commission was working out the Statute of the Association.[1] One of the members of this commission was Academician Fedorenko. The position taken by TSEMI on the role of the association, and its relation to the views of other interested parties, were not public knowledge. Such evidence as there was suggested that TSEMI was arguing for real financial autonomy for the associations, in particular for the self finance of investment, that its model was the Western corporation, and that it was opposing those who simply wished to rename the former administrations without introducing any economic changes. One TSEMI author had drawn attention to the dangers of cartelisation.

An extensive discussion has taken place in the socialist countries about the role of the association in the reformed economic system.[2] Those who support the creation of associations point to the existence and importance of economies of scale and the need to provide common services. The opponents of the associations point to the dangers of monopolistic practices and the impossibility of combining a guided market economy with the cartelisation of industry.

In this connection the following observations are relevant.

1 The abolition of current planning as advocated in this chapter implies a major change in the activities of associations, because at present these are largely concerned with current planning. Experience in Poland, the DDR and Hungary suggests that in an economy where current planning has been abolished, the need for associations with the right to give instructions to their enterprises is much reduced, but that in some cases associations formed on a voluntary basis do have a useful role to play in the provision of common services.

2 Different conditions exist in different industries and it is not sensible to attempt to lay down rules applying to all industries.

3 In the emphasis on the importance of economies of scale there is a danger of overlooking the fact that small enterprises have a useful role to play in the management of the economy. Commenting on the

[1] To work out the Statute of the Association is analogous to working out a Companies Act in the UK.
[2] The Polish literature is conveniently summarised in Zielinski [1970].

initial experience of the NEM, a Hungarian economist has argued that:

> In the past two decades large scale industry has been brought about in Hungary partly by the amalgamation of a network of small and medium sized plants originally destined to satisfy the demands of the population and to cooperate with large scale enterprises. Thus a gap has come about in the pattern of large scale production units. While in this country more than 50 per cent of industrial labour are employed in plants with more than 1000 workers, the corresponding ratio is 40 per cent in the Federal Republic of Germany, 35 in Great Britain and 32 in the USA etc. The process of concentration and centralization has eliminated the small and medium sized plants to a greater degree than justified. The organisational setup of almost every branch is characterized by the insufficient number of small and medium sized plants. International experience points to the fact that a modern and efficient large scale industry can function only together with the complementary small and medium size plants. Only such a harmonious economic pattern is able to secure a pattern of supply that will flexibly adapt itself to demand.   (Csikos-Nagy [1969] pp. 8–9.)

4 A feature of economic reform in Eastern Europe has been the legalisation of small scale private enterprise. It is clear that small scale private enterprise in the field of services can play a useful role in raising living standards. Nevertheless, it would promote inequality and might well encounter popular opposition for this reason. Accordingly I suggest that the material and financial resources placed at the disposal of local authorities to enable them to undertake those activities, from household repairs to motor car repairs, in which private enterprise typically flourishes, be substantially enlarged, and that the relative incomes of workers in services be increased. To some extent this is already happening, and I advocate the expansion of efforts in this direction.

I consider that in the *khozraschet* economy industry should be organised in enterprises, trusts or associations which are independent *khozraschet* entities whose constituent enterprises neither have their own relationship with the state budget nor receive their own plans from the centre, and associations which provide services for their members but do not issue them with obligatory instructions.

THE ROLE OF PLANNING IN THE *KHOZRASCHET* ECONOMY

In discussions of economic reform two extreme points of view are encountered. On the one hand some people argue that the transition to the *khozraschet* economy would introduce into the Soviet economy the negative features of capitalism and should therefore be avoided. On the other hand, some people treat the transition to the *khozraschet* economy as a panacea.

Economic reform has been criticised on the ground that it might have an adverse effect on personal consumption, that like capitalism it would lead not to consumers' sovereignty but to 'the evils of imperfect competition'. This line of argument reveals profound ignorance of the subject. A major reason for the transition to the *khozraschet* economy is to overcome the adverse effects on personal consumption of the administrative economy. Throughout this period in many provincial towns meat was unavailable in state shops for most of the day, as a result of low production in agriculture, the retail price policy of the state and the distribution policy adopted (to favour the principal cities). In this case the effect of the transition to the *khozraschet* economy would be to redistribute real income away from the principal cities and people with non-working female relatives and in favour of people with high nominal incomes in provincial towns. 'The evils of imperfect competition' are a much discussed phenomenon, whose importance is doubtful. The long queues in factory canteens because plates are a scarce good are only too real and quite unnecessary. It has been argued that 'No-one who has lived in the capitalist world is deceived by the pretence that the market system ensures consumers' sovereignty. It is up to the socialist countries to find some way of giving it reality.' (Robinson [1964] p. 521.) This ignores the fact that the market system, although it does not bring about 'consumers' sovereignty' (an ideological mirage) has some solid advantages (absence of shortages, absence of production for plan rather than for use) over the administrative system.

In some quarters the opposite extreme is encountered, the idea that the transition to the *khozraschet* economy would automatically overcome all the economic problems of the USSR and ensure a steady growth in consumer welfare. The transition from War Communism to NEP, the transition in Hungary to the NEM, the abortive transition from the administrative economy in Czechoslovakia, and the transition from a war economy to a peace economy in the UK in 1948–55 all seem to me to have exhibited more positive than negative aspects. It would however be quite absurd to regard the post reform economic mechanism as being devoid of economic problems. The NEM offers some useful cautionary lessons in this respect. In order to prevent excessive wage increases, leading to higher prices, one of the features of the NEM was that a limit was imposed on average wage increases for each enterprise. As a result the enterprises hired additional low paid workers, which lowered average wages and allowed scarce members of the former staff to receive wage increases. The system had to be altered to prevent this. Similarly, although two of the objects of the reform in the field of price formation were to ensure that world market prices influenced the prices of competitive products on the domestic market and to maintain stable prices, the problem of how to ensure the achievement of the first objective without importing inflation remains unsolved. In addition, the transition from one economic mechanism to another would leave unchanged the problem caused for the USSR by the facts of economic geography (the size of the country and the inclement climate prevailing over much of it) and the distribution of the national income (with its high shares of defence, investment – much of it 'political investment' – space and security).

Moreover, while it is clear that the transition to the *khozraschet* economy would have a beneficial effect on personal consumption by widening the assortment pattern of consumer good production and ending production for plan, by itself it would be quite insufficient to ensure a steady rise in living standards. The possibility of a steady rise in living standards is largely determined by state policy in the fields of economic growth, agriculture, housing, medical care, education and transfer payments. The USSR has a very good record in the field of economic growth, medical care, education and transfer payments; the successful agricultural policies followed in 1953–8 and in 1964–70, and the immense housing programme launched in the 1950s, have played a major role in raising living standards. The immense increase in living standards in the past twenty years has only been possible as a result of the successful growth strategy pursued by the party. These are fields in which it would be desirable not to expand *khozraschet*, but to expand social control over the decisions that are made and end the insulation of the leadership from the effects of its policies on living standards.

I take it for granted that after the reform, as before it, the Soviet economy will be a socialist planned economy. This results from the state ownership of the means of production and the leading role of the party.[1] The latter ensures that the economy will be powerfully influenced by measures aimed at the attainment of the economic, social and political objectives of the party. These depend on the concrete situation, but in general are likely to include a high and stable rate of economic growth, full employment, equitable regional development and a fair distribution of income.

The creation of the administrative economy was simply one aspect of

[1] Both the state ownership of the means of production and the leading role of the party would have a different significance in the *khozraschet* economy than in the administrative economy. The former question was discussed on p. 149 above. The 'leading role of the party' would have a very different social content, and require a very different style of work, both within the party and in the relations between the party and the population at large, in the *khozraschet* economy than in the administrative economy. The emphasis would have to shift from *administrirovanie* to political mobilisation, from the use of the party as an administrative machine to enforce decisions made at the top, to the realisation of the traditional self image of the party as the most self conscious group in a long run process of economic and social transformation. (These questions were much discussed in Czechoslovakia in 1968 where this was a burning issue.)

the strategy chosen by the party for the attainment of its objective, the building of socialism in backward Russia. Under NEP the USSR was in a position similar to that of many contemporary LDCs. The rate of growth of industry was constrained by the capital stock in industry, technology, the terms on which the peasants would sell grain and the real wage rate.[1] Both the society and the growth rate that would have resulted from the maintenance of this economic mechanism was unacceptable to the party. Therefore, after an extensive debate, the party adopted a strategy which enabled it to achieve a breakthrough from the constraints of NEP. The break-through enabled the share of accumulation in the national income to be raised from 14.4 % in 1928 to 36 % in 1931,[2] by pushing down to the left the peasants offer curve (by collectivisation) and lowering the real wage rate in industry (by statising the unions and inflation). The abolition of market relations between town and country was essential to the success of this strategy. The use of value relations within industry would have been very difficult at a time of rapid inflation. (Between 1928 and 1940 average money wages almost sextupled.) *Khozraschet* could only have a limited role to play in an economy characterised by (what amounted to) a tax in kind on the collective farms, rationing of basic consumer goods in the towns, wage increases of c 15 % p.a., a tenfold rise in the prices of consumer goods in state stores in 12 years (17 fold for food products sold on the collective farm market) and stable prices for producer goods (combined with subsidies) in 1928–35.[3] The success of this strategy has been extensively described in the literature,[4] and its chief features much analysed.[5]

Accordingly it might seem logical to base the case for a reform in the economic mechanism on the thesis of the diminishing relevance of this strategy to the present and future stages of development of the Soviet economy.[6] In this study I do not do this, nor do I recommend a strategy of development for the USSR, nor do I work out the implications of this strategy for the economic mechanism. Elaboration of these

---

[1] A good analysis of this type of situation can be found in Findlay [1962]. I applied it to the Soviet case in Ellman [1965].

[2] The figures for both years are in 1928 prices. See Vainshtein [1969] p. 98.

[3] For these figures see Holzman [1960].

[4] A clear introduction is Powell [1968]. The standard works are Bergson [1961], Becker [1969] and Vainshtein [1969].

[5] See for example Davies [1965], [1966], Berliner [1966], Dodge and Wilber [1970].

[6] The classic exposition of this thesis was by Lange, who repeated it on several occasions. A convenient English source is Lange [1958]. A similar thesis, though based on a more technical argument, was put forward by Bergson at the 1971 Nato conference (Symposium [1971] pp. 21–31). The thesis of the extensive and intensive stages of development, and the different economic mechanisms supposedly appropriate for them, has been elaborated and repeated by numerous authors. For critiques of the thesis see Milenkovitch [1971] and Zielinski [1973].

questions would require an independent study, which would take up wholly disproportionate space in a critical analysis of the work of the Soviet school of mathematical economists. For the purposes of this study it is sufficient to put forward concrete reform proposals designed to overcome the problems described in chapters 1 and 2, and to provide a basis for them other than the theorem of the characteristics of an optimal plan.

I would, however, like to draw attention to one aspect of the relationship between the economic mechanism and the strategy of development, namely the increasing number of persons with higher education. In 1928 there were only 233,000 such persons. By 1971 there were more than 7,000,000 and their number was rising at the rate of 500,000 per year. I suggest that this increase in the numbers of the white-collar intelligentsia, resulting from industrialisation, helps to explain the debate which has taken place (by providing the reformers with a social basis). At the same time, the fact that the white-collar intelligentsia is still only a small proportion of the labour force (7% in 1971) helps to explain why it has been unsuccessful (because the economic policies advocated by the reformers had little appeal for the mass of the population).

The reason for the failure of the Cadets in 1917 was the immense gulf between their programme (civil liberties, a parliamentary regime, maintenance of private property, continuation of the war) and the aspirations of the masses (expressed in the famous Bolshevik slogan: land, peace and bread). Similarly, Mikhailov has argued that the reason for the failure of the contemporary liberal movement up till now has been the failure of the liberal intellectuals 'to create a realistic and at the same time attractive social ideal . . . to find a common language with the masses and express their interests and demands'. (Mikhailov [1971].) I hope that the programme I have outlined above meets Mikhailov's criticism and would be acceptable both to the white-collar intelligentsia (which would have to abandon its aspirations for an increase in incomes relative to manual workers) and to the workers on the ground that the gains which it promises would be greater than the losses which its implementation might bring.

A major obstacle to economic reform is an intellectual one, the fact that planning is widely conceived of as the determination of all economic activity by instructions from above. As E. G. Liberman has pointed out (E. Liberman [1970] p. 74):

We sometimes wrongly, without the necessary bases, blame gosplans, ministries and supply-marketing organisations for annoying misunderstandings, disproportions, losses in production and the violation of the interests of consumers. When one encounters so many people making mistakes, it is necessary to look for the reason not only in their individual qualities, but in that system, or more precisely in that 'theory', which conceives of planning as the management from the centre of an all embracing extremely detailed nomenclature of commodities.

In 1966–7 some of the optimal planners tried to overcome this obstacle by adapting the Lausanne school's 'proof' of the optimality of competition to Soviet conditions. I consider that this approach is wholly undesirable, for two reasons. First, it fails to explain why reform is necessary (this requires an analysis of the economic and social problems of the administrative economy), and secondly it renders the cause of economic reform vulnerable to theoretical attacks. For example, Volkonsky's 'scientific' basis for economic reform enabled Karagedov to use the arguments developed in the 1930s by the Keynesians in their struggle with the Lausanne school to criticise the reform. Similarly, Fedorenko's use of ideas drawn from the subjective school to provide a 'scientific' basis for greater attention to personal consumption provided a platform for Bachurin to defend the traditional planning system on theoretical grounds. Karagedov's critique of Volkonsky is perfectly logical, but the policy conclusions that he draws ignore the crucial fact that there is a perfectly good case for economic reform based on ideas entirely different to those developed by Volkonsky. I am of the opinion that what is required to overcome the intellectual resistance to reform is an account of the problems of the administrative economy, which explains that they are not accidental, that it is not possible to eliminate them by changing the personnel, and that their elimination requires a major change in the economic mechanism. This account should be complemented by a carefully thought out set of policies aimed at the further development of the Soviet economy and of Soviet society. This is what I offer in chapters 1, 2 and 7 of this study.

CONCLUSION

In this chapter I have outlined the economic reform which, in my opinion, the Soviet economy requires. This reform embraces both technical-economic changes (such as the development of wholesale trade, alterations in the financial relations between the enterprises and the state budget) and socio-economic ones (publicising, and as far as possible eliminating, administrative privilege as a source of consumption benefits, the determination of the major decisions of enterprises or associations by elected committees, a major role for representative organisations in the determination of national economic policy). The aim of such a reform is both to overcome the problems of the administrative economy and in particular to improve the position of personal consumption, and to form part of a major change in the productive relations of socialism comparable to the transition from War Communism to NEP. The purpose of the latter is to establish civil liberties and self-management.

The dual character of the October Revolution, in part the completion of the bourgeois revolution and in part the beginning of the socialist revolution, has long been a central theme of Marxist analysis of the prospects and results of the revolution. Considered from this angle the reform advocated in this chapter aims to combine the maintenance of the established features of socialism (the state ownership of the means of production, national economic planning) with the fulfilment of part of the old bourgeois liberal programme (civil liberties) and that part of the socialist programme which remains unfulfilled (self-management).

8. CONCLUSION

For many years a debate has been going on in the Soviet Union about the importance of the efficient allocation of resources, in which a tiny group of economists has urged that the methods of economic calculation and the economic mechanism should be such as to ensure the efficient allocation of resources, and policy makers have failed to accept this argument. This debate flared up in the 1960s when concrete proposals were put forward by TSEMI aimed at transforming the Soviet economic system into an optimally functioning economic system. The views of the economists concerned with the efficient allocation of resources were clearly explained by Yushkov in his 1928 paper.

It would be a serious mistake to suppose that the existence of a planning apparatus, by itself, is sufficient to resolve the question of the transition to a higher stage of the utilisation of resources. The latter will be achieved only on the basis of a difficult struggle for the creation of the methodology of planning.

(Yushkov [1928] pp. 32–3.)

Liberals believe that the efficient allocation of resources is impossible under socialism, and market socialists that it is possible only by mimicking perfect competition. Marxists have traditionally believed that socialist planning is bound to be more efficient than the anarchy of production prevailing under capitalism, because the socialist mode of production eliminates the conflict between the social character of the productive forces and the individualistic nature of the capitalist mode of production[1]. Yushkov, arguing against this last position, accepted that

[1] The reader unfamiliar with the idea of the capitalist system as an obstacle to efficiency may find the following argument helpful. The essential theoretical novelty of *The General Theory* was the idea that under capitalism the volume of output is not normally determined by the quantity of scarce resources and the efficiency with which they are used, but by the level of effective demand, which may well establish an equilibrium level of output which involves substantial waste, and that therefore central regulation of the level of demand is necessary in order to ensure the efficient allocation of resources. This is simply one specific example of the Marxist idea of the inefficiency resulting from the conflict between the social character of the productive forces and the individualistic nature of the capitalist mode of production.

it is possible to have greater efficiency under socialism than under capitalism (i.e. to make 'the transition to a higher stage of the utilisation of resources'). He insisted, however, that to turn this possibility into a reality required a difficult struggle to work out and utilise the appropriate methods of economic calculation and to establish the appropriate economic mechanism – precisely the position taken by TSEMI forty years later.

The arguments of the Lausanne school have traditionally been used as arguments for unlimited private enterprise. Many of the Soviet optimal planners regard the valid kernel of the doctrines of the Lausanne school (the propositions that the rational organisation of production is important, and that value relations have a useful role to play in the economy) as an argument for the use of techniques for obtaining optimal solutions to planning problems and for the use of value relations in running the economy, in a socialist economy where the main proportions of the economy are decided by the party in accordance with its political and social objectives. This was true for Yushkov and is true for Kantorovich. The latter has explained (Kantorovich [1960a] p. 200) that:

If in the question of what to produce (final product) economic calculation plays a secondary role, then in the question of how to produce, in the choice of the most economic methods of obtaining the required product these indices are highly important.

In this way the basic character and direction of long term investment can be determined only in the plan by the general political and economic decisions.

At the same time, in the process of working out the plan, resulting from the general line [of the party], the calculation of efficiency should play a very important role, in particular in the consideration of more partial, but also important, questions such as the choice of which raw materials and technological processes to use, the type of enterprise, the degree of concentration and specialisation and so on. Of course these questions also must be solved taking into account the general plan.

In the introduction to this study the history of the current discussion in the USSR was outlined, and the chief issues explained. The study began by describing some of the non-optimalities of the existing system of planning. These are important in themselves. In addition they explain the references by the optimal planners to the 'unscientific' nature of the traditional planning techniques and the need to make the transition from the first to the third stages of planning. Moreover, they provide an explanation of the views of those supporters of the theory of the optimally functioning socialist economy who consider that

The widespread recognition of the need for an 'incomes policy' by economists and governments in capitalist countries, and the attempts to implement one in various capitalist countries, can be regarded as the general recognition that in another important area, the determination of prices and incomes, there exists a conflict between the requirements of national economic development and the individualistic nature of the capitalist mode of production.

it is at least as important to optimise the economic mechanism as to attempt to introduce optimal methods of economic calculation in an otherwise unchanged economic mechanism. Only in an economy with the waste generated by the use of the balance method for the planning of current production could a large scale campaign for the efficient allocation of resources come into existence.

In chapter 3 the theory of the optimally functioning socialist economy was outlined, and it was explained that this theory provides a framework for a large volume of research, both on improving the methods of economic calculation and on improving the economic mechanism. The relationship between this research and the development of the OGAS was explained. In chapter 4 some of the work done by the optimal planners in improving the techniques of planning was surveyed. It was concluded that they had made a useful contribution to improving the methods of economic calculation. The rapidity with which the work of the mathematical economists was incorporated into planning practice is a tribute both to the talent and ability of the research workers in this field, and also to the willingness of the authorities to adopt new methods.

In chapter 5 the validity of the conclusions about the economic mechanism which have been drawn from the theorem of the characteristics of an optimal plan were considered. It was concluded that the theorem provided a theoretical basis for the utilisation of value relations which was invaluable pedagogically and which carried more weight with engineers and practical men (because of its mathematical basis) than either Yushkov's arguments or the arguments put forward in the discussion of the law of value which took place in the 1950s. It is important to realise that in the USSR the abolition of value relations is a traditional goal of the party, whose current Programme aims at building a society in which 'value relations will be outdated economically and will wither away'. This objective is repeated from time to time in authoritative articles in the party press (e.g. Kuz'minov [1969]). Nevertheless, to base the case for economic reform on this theorem creates a number of difficulties.

From the standpoint of economic theory the main problem with drawing policy conclusions from the theorem of the characteristics of an optimal plan is that there is a danger of the hypertrophy of propositions which are valid in allocation models at the expense of propositions that are valid in growth models and macro-economic models. For example, profit, which in many allocation models is a guide to efficiency, in many growth models is a value reflection of investment. Similarly, whereas the theorem of the characteristics of an optimal plan leads to an emphasis on the use of scarce natural resources and capital intensity as price forming factors, the study of macro-economic models leads to an emphasis on the share of consumption in the national income as a price forming factor for consumer goods.

A neo-Keynesian may well ask, why is it that, at a time when Western economics is undergoing a paradigm shift from allocation to growth, the allocation paradigm has become of great importance in the USSR and so little work has been done in developing further the fruitful Soviet work of the 1920s on inter-industry accounts and economic growth? The answer appears to be fourfold.

First, it simply is not true that multi-sectoral growth models have been neglected. There has been considerable work done, particularly at Gosplan's Research Institute and IEOPP, on dynamic multi-sectoral models for medium and long term planning.

Secondly, in the administrative economy the waste resulting from the use of administrative rather than value relations is very striking (some aspects of it were discussed in chapters 1, 2 and 6) and economists naturally put forward proposals aimed at overcoming them.

Thirdly, in an economy where policy is decided by the party, economists are largely confined to sub-optimisation. The decision to build a giant car plant was made in the central organs of the party. The choice of the most efficient location for it (Tol'yatti), however, was one on which TSEMI's advice was sought and on which the result of the joint TSEMI–SOPS research was adopted.

Fourthly, the allocation model can be used to provide a 'scientific' basis for policies aimed at eliminating shortages and queues, widening the assortment pattern of consumer goods available and reducing the role of government officials in society. The discussion of optimal planning in the USSR in the 1960s provided a striking demonstration of the importance of ideology in economics. In part, the challenge posed to political economy by mathematical economics represented a clash between the ideology of Soviet society and the ideology of capitalism adapted to Soviet conditions by writers such as Volkonsky. In 1966–7 these writers were the theoretical representatives on the economic front of what turned out to be an abortive process of social change. Up till now the policy objectives of the Soviet state, the economic mechanism which gives effect to them and the social order which sustains it have proved stronger than the social groups which challenge them. Hence the optimal planners are confined to the solution of particular planning problems and the formulation of proposals for reforming particular parts of the economic mechanism, and of the transition to the optimally functioning socialist economy there are few signs. It was precisely because of the crucially important social issues of which the discussion of optimal planning was, in part, an ideological reflection, that this discussion generated so much heat. What was ultimately at stake was the fulfilment of the programme of the October Revolution by combining the maintenance of the established features of socialism (the state ownership of the means of production, the planned development of the national economy) with the accomplishment of the progressive part of the liberal programme (civil liberties) and the unfulfilled part of the socialist programme (self-management). The discussion of the 1960s was both allusive and abortive, but the issues implicit in it have not yet been resolved and the discussion will inevitably be resumed.

A Marxist may well ask, why is it that at a time when there is increased interest in, and application of, political economy in the leading capitalist countries, has there been such a striking neglect of political economy in the USSR? The reasons for this are the use of political economy from 1929 onwards as a Panglossian ideology, and the difficulties in the way of, and the penalties attaching to, the publication of works at variance with the policies being pursued by the authorities. Relative to the use of political economy as the false consciousness of Stalinist society, research aimed at improving the organisation of the productive forces is undoubtedly progressive, as Yoroshenko and Kowalik long ago noted.

From the standpoint of economic policy the main problem with drawing policy conclusions from the theorem of the characteristics of an optimal plan is that they throw no light on such central problems of economic policy as how to maintain steady economic growth at full employment. Instead, they consist of proposals to raise efficiency by the use of value relations, which are often unhelpful.

For understanding the logic of the administrative economy, the problem with the approach via the theorem of the characteristics of an optimal plan is that it ignores the role of the administrative economy as a part of the social order which has existed in the USSR since 1929 and of the economic strategy which that social order has pursued.

Considered as a contribution to the discussion of economic reform, the theorem of the characteristics of an optimal plan is much less helpful than the ideas worked out in the Institute of Economics of the Hungarian Academy of Sciences in 1954–5, which were based on a study of the problems of the administrative economy, the analysis of alternative allocation models carried out by Polish economists and the work of sociologists such as Machonin and Parkin. It is, however, important to remember that Kornai's ideas were developed more than a decade after Kantorovich's, after the persistence of the law of value under socialism had been explicitly recognised by Stalin, and in a country where the idea of the ultimate disappearance of value relations was not deep-rooted.

In chapter 6 the usefulness of the suggestions of the optimal planners for improving the economic mechanism was considered. It was concluded that TSEMI is playing a useful, but minor, role in improving the economic mechanism. It was suggested that an important reason for the limited applicability of many of the ideas of the optimal planners is their confusion of the Kantorovich algorithm for solving linear programming problems, which both enables optimal solutions to be found and uses shadow prices to find them, with the operation of economies, where different groups rank ways of organising the economy differently, the conception of an uncontroversial objective function is inapplicable and the plan formulation process is one of interaction between the aspirations of the authorities and the set of explored plans, where prices have a variety of functions to perform and a large number of non-price factors are relevant to determining the most suitable way of organising the economy. In chapter 7 I outlined the economic reform which I advocate for the USSR, and noted numerous points of contact between my ideas and those of the optimal planners. In my analysis of the economic reform which the USSR needs, an important part was played by a brief consideration of the social issues at stake.

TSEMI's approach is derived not from the study of society but mainly from linear programming and systems engineering. It is true that TSEMI has always stressed the need to create an effective system of incentives. It is also true that optimal planners such as I. Ya. Birman have repeatedly emphasised that 'strictly centralised planning and management, when all the details are calculated and planned in one centre, is hardly desirable, even if it were feasible. Economic activity is the activity of people, and it is foolish to deprive them of the possibility of showing initiative, independence and creativity.' (I. Birman [1968] p. 163.) Similarly Novozhilov has more than once argued that the optimisation of planning is concerned not only with choosing the best from all the feasible plan variants, but also with improving the productive relations of socialism. In addition, Petrakov has explicitly recognised that the economy is a sub-system of society as a whole (Petrakov [1971] p. 56). Nevertheless it remains true that none of TSEMI's work has thrown any light on the crucial questions of how to enlist the support of workers, engineers, managers and scientists for raising efficiency, and how to develop the productive relations of socialism. Up till now, to my knowledge, the only concrete work which has been done by TSEMI in this direction is the proposal to replace incentives for adopting a taut plan by incentives for high results, which is being experimented with at Glavmosavtotrans. Meanwhile Rakitsky, who is not a mathematical economist, has put forward proposals for reducing the role of one man management (Rakitsky

[1968] chapter 5). Whereas TSEMI considers that correct policy conclusions can only be derived by studying the conditions for the maximisation of the national economic objective function, I consider that a full understanding of many economic policy questions, such as reform, requires an analysis of their social basis.

What does it mean to talk about an 'optimal plan' in a society with conflicting social groups? Soviet writers on optimal planning usually avoid this question, preferring to concentrate on methods for solving extremal problems given the constraints and the objective function. As one writer on optimal planning puts it: 'It should be emphasised that at every given moment the aim of production and the criterion of optimality must be given from outside, from beyond the boundaries of the model of the national economy (who should formulate this criterion and the system of constraints is a special question which does not relate to our theme).' (I. Birman [1968 *b*] p. 222.) The problem has been recognised by Volkonsky, who read a paper entitled 'On the possibilities and difficulties of applying the concept of the optimum to society as a whole' at a conference on economic-mathematical models in April 1969. The paper has remained unpublished, but its delivery has been described as follows:

The speaker based his theses on the fact that there exists a contradiction between the necessity to work out the principles of optimal, or rational from the point of view of society as a whole, decisions, and the fact that the interests of the members of society and of various social groups diverge. In this connection he made an attempt to describe several systems, regulating the life of society and enumerated the concepts and categories which, in his opinion, are necessary for the discussion of optimality. Among these the speaker included the democratic mechanism for the self regulation of social life, the 'value' orientation of society, the role of science (i.e. of the specialists) and so on.   (*Simpoziyum* [1969] p. 791.)

It so happens, however, that the authorities consider that specialists should be 'on tap but not on top', and to 'the democratic mechanism for the self regulation of social life' they counterpose 'the Leninist principle of democratic centralism'. As a result, although there are numerous areas in which the work of the optimal planners does have an impact, the economic policy of the Soviet state is not primarily concerned with the transition to an optimally functioning socialist economy.

In some quarters the work of the optimal planners is regarded as a vindication of the neo-classical emphasis on the efficient allocation of resources and a powerful criticism of Marxism for ignoring it. If the argument of this book is accepted it follows that the concept of efficient allocation of resources does have considerable normative usefulness in some areas (as explained in chapter 4) but not in others (such as the level of employment, the rate of growth, the price level, the distribution of income, the relations between social classes). Nor is it very useful as a descriptive theory of an economy (as argued in chapters 6 and 7). Simultaneously, however, the argument of this book vindicates the Marxist emphasis on the usefulness of political economy as a guide to understanding the social processes unfolding on our planet and supports the thesis that it is the class historical approach, rather than the study of efficient allocation, which throws most light on such topics as economic reform in the European socialist countries.

The relationship between the proposals of the optimal planners aimed at establishing an optimally functioning economic system and the economic reform which is actually being implemented in the USSR is a complex one, in which the work of the optimal planners is not without influence on the economic reform, but in which the main features and pace of the latter are decided on other grounds.

The optimal planners strongly supported the programme announced at the September (1965) Plenum as a step in the right direction. They approved its stress on the need to reduce the number of obligatory indices in the *tekhpromfinplan* and to expand the autonomy of enterprises, the greater emphasis on value relations and profit, its promise of a transition from supply to trade and the recognition of capital intensity as a factor in price formation. These measures were announced after a prolonged public discussion in which the optimal planners were one of the groups, an influential one but not the only one, pressing for them. On the other hand, such important features of the reform as the re-establishment of the ministries, and the transition from incentives for plan fulfilment and overfulfilment to incentives for adopting a taut plan, were a natural response to the problems of the existing system of planning and management and owed nothing to the ideas of the optimal planners. Subsequently many optimal planners became rather dissatisfied with the progress of the reform. A greater role for profit without concomitant changes in other parts of the economic mechanism was criticised by TSEMI at the 1966 debate. The greater independence of the enterprises turned out to be largely illusory and the enterprise in any case is often not suitable as a *khozraschet* unit. The transition from supply to trade was very slow. The decisions of the December (1969) Plenum, with its stress on the need to overcome the problems of the economic mechanism by greater discipline, were entirely alien to the position of the optimal planners. The enterprise incentive fund system, which was an important part of the reform, seemed most unsatisfactory to the mathematical economists. From 1966 onwards the optimal planners persistently argued the need to deepen the reform. By the end of the period the position was that the views of the optimal planners were taken into account when measures for improving the economic mechanism were being formulated (for example Fedorenko was a member of the Commission working out the Statute of the Association), but the idea that economic policy should be concerned with the gradual implementation of the theory of the optimally functioning socialist economy had not been accepted. An example of what this meant in practice is that the idea that in general prices should be determined by marginal costs was not accepted when the 1967 price reform was being prepared, but in the special circumstances of the oil and natural gas industry it was accepted and TSEMI was invited to calculate the magnitude of the rent payments. The reasons why the ideas of the optimal planners about an optimally functioning economic system had not been accepted *in toto* and implemented at once appeared to be threefold, that they were of secondary importance and were often either impracticable or politically unacceptable.

As explained in the Introduction, the official view in the USSR is that 'growth' is more important than 'choice'. Hence the main policy variables are the allocation of investment, technical progress, training the labour force and geological exploration; and not prices, profit, rent and quasi rent. For example, in an article in *Pravda* at the end of the period on economic aspects of the development of agriculture, by the deputy head of the agricultural department of the CC, emphasis was placed on the need to expand output by introducing new methods, new seeds and better machinery, but the proposal to raise efficiency by introducing rent payments was ignored (Kuznetsov [1972]).

The ideas of Kantorovich and TSEMI on optimal functioning (as opposed to optimal planning) are widely thought, by practical administrators, to be quite impracticable. Even such a limited step as the introduction of rent payments has encountered serious practical difficulties. Chapter 8 of Ellman [1971] made clear the immense gulf between the problems of the enterprise incentive fund system (which concerned such questions as the type of incentive system, the division of the net income between profits and turnover tax, the system of managerial bonuses, and the stability of the norms) and the ideas propounded by TSEMI in 1966–7. The practicability of using shadow prices in the way advocated by Kantorovich remains to be demonstrated.

The reasons for the political unacceptability of 'market socialism', 'a major change in the productive relations of socialism comparable to the transition from War Communism to NEP', a 'new economic mechanism', 'the *khozraschet* economy' and kindred ideas, are that experience of the new economic model in other socialist countries suggests that it might bring unemployment and open inflation, accentuate regional disparities, have adverse effects on the distribution of income, and above all that it might weaken the role of the socialist state and the party of the working class in the management of the economy.

In the administrative economy national economic policy is decided in the central organs of the party, and a large part of the time of the local party organisations is devoted to operational questions of plan fulfilment, such as securing supplies. Both party theory and many local party officials are opposed to such officials spending a large part of their time acting as *tolkachi*, a role they are often pushed into by the inconsistencies of the plans, the pleading of enterprise management and the overwhelming importance of current plan fulfilment. On the other hand, the party considers that policy questions must be decided by the party, and that to suppose that major issues ought to be decided by 'purely economic' considerations is unacceptable. The reforming economists would like to replace the 'arbitrary' decisions of officials by rational calculations or market decisions. Although the party is opposed to voluntarism and in favour of calculating optimal solutions to planning problems, it considers that to leave basic policy issues to be decided by 'economic criteria' is unacceptable. Novozhilov, who in the 1960s played such a prominent role in the development of the theory of optimal planning, in the 1920s proposed dealing with 'the goods famine' by raising prices. The Bolshevik solution was to launch an immense industrialisation programme. A. M. Birman has proposed that enterprises which are unable to cover their costs should face liquidation. The party considers that its commitment to full employment prevents the use of this lever for raising efficiency. I. Ya. Birman supposes that cost minimising calculations can be decisive in deciding investment policy for an industry, which entirely ignores wider issues.

The problem which Yushkov posed, ensuring the efficient attainment of given output targets, did exist and was important, and it is possible that if more attention had been paid at that time to investment criteria waste might have been reduced. Yushkov's problem was not, however, relevant to the economic mechanism. The administrative economy was created following a debate within the party on the building of socialism in backward Russia. In 1928, when Yushkov's article was published, the central question of economic policy was the grain problem, how to extract from the peasants sufficient grain to feed the towns and the army, and to finance the imports necessary for the industrialisation programme of the party. This problem arose because of the combination of the growth strategy of the party and the social structure of the USSR. The economic analysis most relevant to the economic mechanism at that time was Preobrazhensky's analysis of primitive socialist accumulation.

Neo-classical economics has traditionally argued that both the methods of economic calculation and the institutional arrangements of an economy should be determined by the requirements of efficient resource allocation. Soviet experience corroborates the idea that obtaining optimal solutions to planning problems is important, but also corroborates the party argument that it is the strategy of economic development, and/or socio-political objectives, that ought to determine the economic mechanism.

Given the policy objectives of the party, it makes little sense to criticise the authorities for ignoring the views of those who advocated full *khozraschet* at the time of the grain crisis, explained the merits of *khozraschet* during the Great Patriotic War,[1] advocated greater reliance on profit in 1955–65, and, when the reform ran into difficulties, recommended that profit maximising enterprises should implement the optimal plans worked out by a multi-level tâtonnement process. On the other hand, it is clear that the authorities are open to criticism for being extremely dilatory in the large scale application of techniques for ensuring the efficient allocation of resources. Although linear programming was discovered in the 1930s by a Soviet mathematician in order to solve a production scheduling problem, the first large scale application of linear programming to production scheduling in the USSR was three decades later and followed, rather than preceded, similar work in the United States. Similarly, it is clear that the problems of the administrative economy are serious problems and that measures are required to overcome them. Shortages are a great nuisance and Novozhilov was quite right to argue that they are not inevitable, that by suitable measures of economic policy they can be overcome.

There were three factors which account for the fact that the ideas of the optimal planners played an important part in Soviet economic discussion in the 1960s, while Yushkov's paper seems to have been entirely ignored when it was published.

First, the development of computers made possible the large scale application of optimal planning techniques. In a vivid passage Kendall ([1960] p. 1) has stated that:

As a boy I was much impressed by a picture in one of my school-books showing James Watt staring thoughtfully at a kettle on the family hob. This, we were told, portrayed one of the great moments in the history of mankind, the conception of the steam engine. I cannot remember whether the picture was by a well known artist, and even the central figure in it has, I find, become inextricably confounded in my recollection with 'Bubbles' and 'The Boyhood of Raleigh'. But the message to be conveyed by the rapt gaze of concentration was clear. It was the idea that mattered, not the technique. All that remained to bring the steam locomotive to life was for Watt and a few rude mechanicals to go out and build the thing.

[1] The 'Great Patriotic War' is the Soviet phrase for the Soviet–German war 1941–5.

The absurdity of the whole notion did not strike me until much later. For at least two thousand years man had appreciated the possibilities of steam power. The significance of James Watt was not that he did too, but that he lived at a time when fuel was available and engineering skill had developed far enough to make the construction of locomotive engines possible. It is technology, not inspiration, which dictates the pace of progress, even in the sciences, and even, I would contend, in philosophy. Imagination and vision are as important as ever they were to provide the initial ideas and the motive force; but to work out their consequences requires an adequate technical equipment.

The Soviet experience with linear programming, its discovery in the late 1930s by a gifted mathematician and its first large scale application to current planning in the 1960s, bears this out.

Secondly, after the 20th Congress the authorities accepted that economists are able to contribute to the improvement of the methods of economic calculation. The evidence for this was of the type which carries most weight with the Soviet authorities, the large scale and apparently successful application of the new techniques in the United States. Whereas in *Economic problems of socialism in the USSR* Stalin expressed his scepticism about the very existence of a problem of the rational organisation of production, at the present time the authorities do recognise the existence of this problem. The recognition by the authorities of the contribution which the mathematical economists can make to improving the methods of economic calculation has taken on concrete organisational form in the development of an automated system of plan calculations. Even in the field of methods of economic calculation, however, the ideas of the mathematical economists have only been partially accepted. For example, one of the areas in which the mathematical economists have worked longest is that of investment criteria, but throughout this period the official method for determining investment efficiency was based on an approach which they rejected (the recoupment period), rather than one which they supported (present value).

Thirdly, whereas when Yushov's paper was published, the Soviet Union was living through the break-through, the bitter struggle to impose collectivisation on the peasants and build the foundations of an advanced socialist industrialised state, after the 22nd Congress the views of those economists concerned with the need to enlarge the role of value relations became relevant to the real situation which existed in the country and to the policy options open to the party.

TSEMI of course is not advocating a new economic mechanism, but is concerned with the optimisation of planning. Nevertheless, to the extent that TSEMI's proposals have elements in common with the unacceptable theories (wholesale trade, emphasis on value relations as guides to efficiency) they have met, and are likely to meet in the future, considerable resistance. The fact that the wind in favour of mathematical economics veered after the 1968 events in Czechoslovakia was no accident. If some economists believe that 'our criticism of command plans will carry little weight until it is aimed at the root of the matter, against the absence of optimal planning',[1] it is quite natural that the authorities should respond by believing that 'our criticism of "market socialism" will carry little weight until it is aimed at the root of the matter, i.e. against the theory of optimal planning'. Nevertheless it would be a mistake to suppose that orthodoxy is immutable. Seven years after Nemchinov called for the transition from supply to trade the overwhelming bulk of materials was still allocated, but wholesale trade did exist and was growing. In Czechoslovakia the party eventually came to the view (expressed in the May 1968 Action programme) that the further development of a socialist society required a far reaching process of social change, of which economic reform was a part, and it is not wholly impossible that the CPSU may one day come to the view that the same applies to the USSR. This appears to have been the position of the *Politicheskii Dnevnik* group.

It would clearly be an exaggeration to state that Soviet mathematical economics has been imported, lock, stock and barrel, from the West, as a number of Western economists are inclined to do. This ignores not only the early Soviet work on input–output and linear programming, but also the fact that the evolution of mathematical economics in the USSR has been profoundly influenced by the Soviet economic mechanism, the methods of economic calculation used in the USSR and the official doctrine of the USSR – Marxism–Leninism. The influence of the economic mechanism is shown, for example, in the proposals which have been put forward, and the calculations which have been made, for the introduction of rent payments in agriculture and the extractive industries and in the work done by TSEMI in improving the system of distributing the profit of an enterprise. The influence of the methods of economic calculation is shown, for example, by Kantorovich's work for Soyuzglavmetal on optimal production scheduling, the work done by Aganbegyan, I. Ya. Birman and others on optimal plans for the development and location of industries, and the work done in Gosplan's Research Institute and IEOPP on utilising input–output in medium term planning. The influence of Marxism–Leninism is shown, for example, in the work of Novozhilov, who devoted great efforts to demonstrating that the theory of optimal planning fits into Marxist–Leninist political economy.[2]

---

[1] See p. 139 above.

[2] In the USA economists working on modern planning techniques have to argue that their work fits into Walrasian orthodoxy and far from being incompatible with free enterprise

On the other hand, it is undoubtedly true that Soviet work in this field has been heavily influenced by Western work. This is not an isolated phenomenon. One finds the same in other fields, such as sociology. Western mathematical (and non-mathematical) economics is, of course, profoundly influenced by liberal ideology and in taking over some techniques from the West some Soviet economists have taken over ideas which are no more valid in their new setting than they were in the old. At the 1966 debate Fedorenko stated that the 'logical basis for constructing the optimality criterion [for the national economy] is the assumption that the behaviour of the consumer reflects his conscious or unconscious striving for the fullest possible satisfaction of his needs' (*Diskussiya* [1968] p. 10), a formulation which has a familiar ring. It is encouraging to see that by the end of this period some Soviet economists had advanced beyond simple reaction against Marxism–Leninism and enthusiasm for novelties imported from the West, and were deeply engaged in a series of research programmes aimed at improving the economic decisions being made in the USSR.

SUMMARY

Since before the creation of the administrative economy there have existed in the USSR economists who have rejected the view that a socialist planned economy is bound to be more efficient than capitalism. They have agreed that socialism creates the possibility of a more efficient allocation of resources than is possible under capitalism, by eliminating the conflict between the social character of the productive forces and the individualistic nature of the capitalist mode of production which characterises capitalism. They have argued, however, that this possibility will only become a reality when the appropriate methods of economic calculation are used and the appropriate economic mechanism has been established.

Stalin ignored this line of argument in practice and rejected it in theory. After the 20th Congress a new direction, the economic-mathematical direction, rapidly emerged within Soviet economic science. The mathematical economists have already made three important contributions to Soviet economic thought, planning practice and the organisation of the economy. First, they have provided a theoretical basis for the use of value relations. Secondly, they have made an important contribution to improving the techniques of planning. Thirdly, they have lent their weight to a number of progressive policy

actually helps to raise profits. In the USSR economists working on modern planning techniques have to argue that their work fits into Marxist–Leninist orthodoxy and far from being incompatible with socialist planning helps to raise its efficiency.

measures such as the recognition of capital intensity as a factor in price formation. Their work is continuing and is likely to make a useful contribution to Soviet economic science in fields as diverse as long-term forecasting, production scheduling, investment planning, the calculation of rent payments in agriculture and the extractive industries and support for the transition from the planning of supply to wholesale trade.

BIBLIOGRAPHY

This bibliography is intended neither as an exhaustive bibliography of the subject nor as a complete list of the works consulted in writing it, but as a list of the works referred to in the text and of the most useful works consulted while writing it.

Notes

1 Books in Russian are published in Moscow unless otherwise stated. Books in English are published in London unless otherwise stated.

2 Russian words are transliterated into English according to the *Soviet Studies* transliteration system, with the exception that when proper names end in 'ii' the last two letters are sometimes transliterated by a 'y'.

3 Works marked with an asterisk are unpublished.

4 A complete bibliography of the Soviet literature for 1958–66 is provided by: I. V. Romanovskii and K. I. Shafranovskii (eds) *Matematiko-ekonomicheskie metody i modeli. Bibliographicheskii ukazatel'* (Moscow-Leningrad 1964). This covers 1958 to May 1963 (and includes some important earlier works). I. V. Romanovskii (ed) *Matematiko-ekonomicheskie metody i modeli. Bibliographicheskii ukazatel'* (Iyun' 1963g – dekabr' 1966g) (Leningrad 1968).

5 I have surveyed some of the Soviet literature in the review articles, 'Optimal planning', *Soviet Studies* July 1968, 'Optimal planning revisited', *Soviet Studies* October 1969, and, 'From the first stage of planning to the second', *Ost Europa Wirtschaft* 1970 No. 4.

6 For a dictionary of Soviet mathematical economics see *Matematika i kibernetika v ekonomike. Slovar'-spravochnik* ed N. P. Fedorenko *et al* (1971).

BOOKS AND ARTICLES IN RUSSIAN

Adirim [1969] I. G. Adirim, *Optimal'noe planirovanie razvitiya i razmeschcheniya otrasli promyshlennosti* (Riga 1969).

Aganbegyan [1961] A. G. Aganbegyan et al, *Primenenie matematiki i elektronnoi tekhniki v planirovanii* (1961).

Aganbegyan [1964] A. G. Aganbegyan, 'K sozdaniyu optimal'noi sistemy planirovaniya i upravleniya narodnym khozyaistvom', *Vestnik Akademii Nauk SSSR* 1964 no. 6.

*Aganbegyan [1965] A. G. Aganbegyan (ed.), *Modeli i metody optimal'nogo razvitiya i razmeshcheniya proizvodstva* (Novosibirsk 1965) NGU nauchnye trudy seriya ekonomicheskaya vol. 3.

*Aganbegyan [1966]   A. G. Aganbegyan and K. K. Val'tukh (eds), *Problemy narodnokhozyaistvennogo optimuma* (Novosibirsk 1966). This is the first (mimeo) edition of Aganbegyan [1969b].

Aganbegyan [1968]   A. G. Aganbegyan and A. G. Granberg, *Ekonomiko-matematicheskii analiz mezhotraslevogo balansa SSSR* (1968).

Aganbegyan [1969a]   A. G. Aganbegyan and D. M. Kazakevich (eds), *Optimal'noe territorial'no-proizvodstvennoe planirovanie* (Novosibirsk 1969).

Aganbegyan [1969b]   A. G. Aganbegyan and K. K. Val'tukh (eds), *Problemy narodnokhozyaistvennogo optimuma* (1969).

Aganbegyan [1972]   A. G. Aganbegyan, K. A. Bagrinovskii, A. G. Granberg, *Sistema modelei narodnokhozyaistvennogo planirovaniya* (1972).

Albegov [1968]   M. A. Albegov, 'Raschet zamykayushchikh zatrat na toplivo na osnove modeli toplivno-energeticheskogo balansa strany', in *Primenenie* [1968] q.v.

Albegov [1969]   M. A. Albegov, 'O lokalizatsii zadach razvitiya i razmeshcheniya proizvodstva', in *Ekonomicheskie* [1969] q.v.

Aleshin [1972]   A. V. Aleshin, I. E. Krichenskii, E. P. Shchukin, *Khimizatsiya i optimal'nye proportsii* (1972).

Allakhverdyan [1969]   D. Allakhverdyan, 'Leninskie printsipy khozyaistvennogo rascheta', *Pravda*, 26 September 1969.

Amalrik [1969]   A. Amalrik, *Prosushestvuet li sovetskii soyuz do 1984 goda?* (Amsterdam 1969). An English translation *Will the Soviet Union survive to 1984?* was published in 1970.

Andreev [1966]   B. P. Andreev, Yu. A. Kuznetsov, A. A. Makarov, 'Issledovanie, svoistv zamykayushchego topliva i zamykayushchikh zatrat', chapter 6–11 of Melent'ev [1966] q.v.

Andreev [1967]   B. P. Andreev, A. A. Makarov, L. A. Melent'ev, A. A. Beschinsky, A. G. Vigdorchik, L. O. Saatchyan, 'Osnovnye polozheniya opredeleniya zamykayushchikh zatrat na toplivo', *Teploenergetika* 1967 no. 8.

Aven [1968]   O. Aven, A. Lerner, A. Mamikonov, 'Postroeniya avtomatizirovannoi sistemy upravleniya snabzheniem metalloproduktsiei', *Material'no-technicheskoe snabzhenie* 1968 no. 3.

Bachurin [1969]   A. Bachurin, 'V. I. Lenin i sovremennye problemy planirovaniya narodnogo khozyaistava', *Planovoe khozyaistvo* 1969 no. 11.

Baibakov [1968]   N. K. Baibakov, 'Zadachi sovershenstvovaniya planirovaniya i uluchsheniya ekonomicheskoi raboty v narodnom khozyaistve', *Planovoe khozyaistvo* 1968 no. 7.

Bakaev [1966]   A. A. Bakaev, *Tsifrovye vychislitel'nye mashiny v planirovanii raboty transporta* (Kiev 1966).

*Baranov [1964]   E. F. Baranov, *Osobennosty razrabotki raionykh mezhotraslevykh balansov i metody raschetov na ikh osnove (na opyte rabot po Latviiskoi, Litovskoi i Estonskoi SSR)* (1964). Candidate's thesis.

*Baranov [1970]   E. F. Baranov, V. I. Danilov-Danil'yan, M. G. Zavel'skii, *Problemy razrabotki sistemy optimal'nogo planirovaniya narodnogo khozyaistva* (1970) TSEMI.

Baranov [1971]   E. F. Baranov, V. I. Danilov-Danil'yan, M. G. Zavel'skii, 'O sisteme optimal'nogo perspektivnogo planirovaniya', *Ekonomika i matematicheskie metody* 1971 No. 3. (This paper, together with the previous work, are discussed in Malkin [1972] q.v.)

Bazarova [1968]   G. V. Bazarova, *Pribyl' v ekonomicheskom stimulirovanii proizvodstva* (1968).

Belkin [1964]   V. D. Belkin and I. Ya. Birman, 'Samostoyatel'nost' predpriyatiya: ekonomicheskie stimuly', *Izvestiya* 4 December 1964.

Belkin [1969]   V. D. Belkin and V. V. Ivanter, *Ekonomicheskoe upravlenie i bank* (1969).

Belyaev [1968]   V. Belyaev, 'Kakoi y tonny ves?', *Pravda* 6 December 1968.

Berri [1968]   L. Ya. Berri (ed.), *Planirovanie narodnogo khozyaistva* (1968).

Berg [1968]   A. I. Berg and E. Kol'man (eds.) *Kilbernetika ozhidaemaya i kibernetika neozhidannaya* (1968).

A. Birman [1967]   A. M. Birman, 'Neotvratimost'', *Literaturnaya Gazeta* 1967 no. 2.

A. Birman [1968]   A. M. Birman, 'Sut' reformy', *Novyi Mir* 1968 no. 12.

I. Birman [1963]   I. Ya. Birman and L. E. Mints (eds), *Mathematicheskie metody i problemy razmeshchenya proizvodstva* (1963).

*I. Birman [1966]   I. Ya. Birman, *Spornye voprosy otraslevogo planirovaniya*, paper delivered at the all-Union conference on the use of economic-mathematical methods in the planning and management of industries (1966).

I. Birman [1968a]   I. Ya. Birman, 'Kogda ekonomiya ubytochna', *Izvestiya* 21 January 1968.

I. Birman [1968b]   I. Ya. Birman, *Optimal'noe programmirovanie* (1968).

I. Birman [1970]   I. Ya. Birman (ed.), *Optimal'nyi plan otrasli* (1970).

I. Birman [1971]   I. Ya. Birman, *Metodologiya optimal'nogo planirovaniya* (1971).

Blyakhman [1969]   L. S. Blyakham, *Shagi reformy* (Leningrad 1969).

Bogachev [1966]   V. N. Bogachev, *Srok okupaemosti* (1966).

Bogachev [1969]   V. N. Bogachev and L. V. Kantorovich, 'Tsena vremeni', *Kommunist* 1969 no. 10. A translation is in *Problems of Economics* vol. 12.

Bogachev [1970]   V. N. Bogachev, 'Optimal'nyi plan i polnyi khozraschet', in Zhamin [1970] q.v.

Bor [1969]   M. Z. Bor, 'Ekonomicheskaya reforma i voprosy teorii planirovaniya narodnogo khozyaistva', in Bor and Poltorygin [1969] q.v.

Bor and Poltorygin [1969]   M. Z. Bor and V. K. Poltorygin (eds), *Planirovanie i khozyaistvennaya reforma* (1969).

Boruk [1972]   A.Ya. Boruk, *Bonitirovka i ekonomicheskaya otsenka zemel'* (1972).

Boyarsky [1961]   A.Ya. Boyarsky, 'K voprosu o primenenii matematiki v ekonomike', *Voprosy ekonomiki* 1961 no. 2.

Boyarsky [1962]   A.Ya. Boyarsky, *Matematiko-ekonomicheskie ocherki* (1962).

Bronshtein [1966]   M. L. Bronshtein, 'Zemlya i ekonomicheskie rychagi', *Pravda* 26 July 1966.

Bronshtein [1967]   M. L. Bronshtein, 'Ekonomicheskaya otsenka zemli i vyravnivanie uslovii vosproizvodstva v kolkhozakh', chapter 7 of *Zemel'nyi* [1967] q.v.

Brudno [1963]   A. L. Brudno, 'Primer tsen optimal'nogo planirovaniya', *Problemy kibernetiki* vol. 9 (1963).

Bukharin [1928]   N. I. Bukharin, 'Zametki ekonomista', *Pravda* 30 September 1928.

Bunich [1970]   P. G. Bunich, *Problemy khozyaistvennogo rascheta i finansov v usloviyakh reformy* (1970).

Burkov [1970]   V. N. Burkov and A. Ya. Lerner,' Printsip otkrytovogo upravleniya aktivnymi sistemami', *Avtomatika i telemekhanika* 1970 no. 8.

Cheremushkin [1963]   S. D. Cheremushkin, *Teoriya i praktika ekonomicheskoi otsenki zemli* (1963).

Cheremushkin [1967]   S. D. Cheremushkin, 'O stoimostnoi otsenke zemli', *Ekonomika sel'skogo khozyaistva* 1967 no. 12.

Chernyavsky [1962]   V. O. Chernyavsky, 'Optimizatsiya toplivno-energeticheskogo balansa', *Planovoe khozyaistvo* 1962 no. 2. A translation is in *Problems of Economics* vol. 5.

Chernyavsky [1967]   V. O. Chernyavsky, *Effektivnaya ekonomika* (1967).

Chernyavsky [1969]   V. O. Chernyavsky, 'Sovershenstvovanie i optimizatsiva otraslevogo planirovaniya', *Voprosy ekonomiki* 1969 no. 7.

Chernyavsky [1970]   V. O. Chernyavsky, 'Matematicheskie metody v praktike otras-levogo planirovaniya', *Ekonomika i organizatsiya promyshlennogo proizvodstva* 1970 no. 4.
Chernyavsky [1971]   V. O. Chernyavsky, 'Voprosy optimizatsii planirovaniya', *Voprosy ekonomiki* 1971 no. 5.
Diskussiya [1968]   *Diskussiya ob optimal'nom planirovanii* (1968) compilers L.Ya. Kazakevich and L. V. Levshin.
Diskussiya po problemam [1971]   'Diskussiya po problemam optimal'nogo upravleniya i stimulirovaniya nauchno-tekhnicheskogo progressa', *Ekonomika i matematicheskie metody* 1971 no. 2 pp. 302–9.
Dobrov [1969]   G. M. Dobrov, *Prognozirovaniya nauki i tekhniki* (1969).
Dorovskikh [1967]   A. Dorovskikh, 'Nekotorye voprosy teorii i praktiki mezho-traslevogo balansa', *Planovoe khozyaistvo* 1967 no. 12. A translation is in *Problems of Economics* vol. 11.
Dmitriev [1904]   V. K. Dmitriev, *Ekonomicheskie ocherki* (1904).
Drogichinsky [1968]   N. E. Drogichinskii and D. I. Tsarev, *Khozyaistvennaya reforma: opyt, perspektivy* (1968).
Drogichinsky [1971]   N. E. Drogichinskii and V. G. Starodubrovskii (eds), *Osnovy i praktika khozyaistvennoi reformy v SSSR* (1971).
Dudkin [1965]   L. Dudkin and E. Yershov, 'Mezhotraslevoi balans i material'nye balansy otdel'nykh produktov', *Planovoe khozyaistvo* 1965 no. 5.
Dudkin [1966]   L. M. Dudkin, *Optimal'nyi material'nyi balans narodnogo khozyaistva* (1966).
Dudkin [1968]   L. M. Dudkin, 'Agregirovanie i dezagregirovanie . . .', Fedorenko [1968c] q.v.
Dudkin [1971]   L. Dudkin, Ya. Radchenko, V. Trigubenko, B. Shchennikov and V. Ul'yanov, 'Puti k optimal'nomu planirovaniyu', *Pravda* 12 October 1971.
Efimov [1957]   A. N. Efimov *Perestroika upravleniya promyshlennostiyu i stroitel'stvom* (1957).
Efimov [1965]   A. N. Efimov and L. Ya. Berri (eds), *Metody planirovaniya mezhot-raslevykh proportsii* (1965).
Efimov [1969a]   A. N. Efimov (ed.), *Mezhotraslevoi balans i planirovanie v strahakh – chlenakh SEV* (1969).
Efimov [1969b]   A. N. Efimov (ed.), *Mezhotraslevoi balans i proportsii narodnogo khozyaistva* (1969).
Eidelman [1966]   M. R. Eidelman, *Mezhotraslevoi balans obshchestvennogo produkta* (1966).
*Eikhin [1966]   E. A. Eikhin, *Metody issledovaniya i planirovaniya struktury proizvodst-vennykh osnovnykh fondov soyuznoi respubliki* (Talinn 1966). Candidate's thesis.
Ekonomicheskaya [1970]   *Ekonomicheskaya semiotika* (1970).
Ekonomicheskie [1969]   *Ekonomicheskie problemy razmeshcheniya proizvoditel'nykh sil SSSR* (1969).
Ekonomika [1963]   *Ekonomika material'no tekhnicheskogo snabzheniya* 2nd ed. (1963).
Ekonomisty i matematiki [1965]   *Ekonomisty i matematiki za kruglym stolom* (1965). Another report on this round table is in *Voprosy ekonomiki* 1964 no. 9.
Emdin [1966]   A. Ya. Emdin, *Metodologiya planirovaniya i organizatsiya material'no-tekhnicheskogo snabzheniya* (1966).
Faerman [1971]   E. Yu. Faerman, *Problemy dolgosrochnogo planirovaniya* (1971).
Fedorenko [1964]   N. P. Fedorenko, 'O rabote tsentral'nogo ekonomiko-mate-maticheskogo instituta', *Vestnik AN SSSR* 1964 no. 10.
Fedorenko [1965a]   N. P. Fedorenko, 'Vazhnaya ekonomicheskaya problema', *Pravda* 17 January 1965.
Fedorenko [1965b]   N. P. Fedorenko, 'O razrabotke nauchnykh metodov uprav-leniya narodnym khozyaistvom', *Ekonomika i matematicheskie metody* 1965 no. 3.

Fedorenko [1966a]   N. P. Fedorenko, 'Optimal'noe planirovanie i tsenoobrazo-vanie', *Vestnik AN SSSR* 1966 No. 2.

Fedorenko [1966b]   N. P. Fedorenko, 'Tsena i optimal'noe planirovanie', *Kommunist* 1966 no. 8.

Fedorenko [1967a]   N. P. Fedorenko, 'Reforma v promyshlennosti', *Planovoe khozyaistvo* 1967 no. 4. A translation is in *Problems of Economics* vol. 10.

Fedorenko [1967b]   N. P. Fedorenko (ed.), *Sistemy ekonomicheskoi informatsii* (1967).

Fedorenko [1967c]   N. P. Fedorenko, 'Problemy sozdaniya avtomatizirovannoi sistemy upravleniya snabzheniem', *Material'no-tekhnicheskoe snabzhenie* 1967 no. 2.

Fedorenko [1968a]   N. P. Fedorenko, *O razrabotke sistemy optimal'nogo funktsionirovaniya ekonomiki* (1968).

Fedorenko [1968b]   N. P. Fedorenko, 'Ob ekonomicheskoi otsenka prirodnykh resursov', *Voprosy ekonomiki* 1968 no. 3.

Fedorenko [1968c]   N. P. Fedorenko (ed.), *Ekonomicheskie problemy razvitiya i razmeshcheniya khimicheskoi promyshlennosti* (1968).

Fedorenko [1969a]   N. P. Fedorenko (ed.), *Ekonomiko-matematicheskie modeli* (1969).

Fedorenko [1970a]   N. P. Fedorenko, P. G. Bunich, S. S. Shatalin (eds), *Sotsialisticheskie printsipy khozyaistovovaniya i effektivnost' obshchestvennogo proizvodstva* (1970).

Fedorenko [1970b]   N. P. Fedorenko, 'Nauchno-tekhnicheskaya revolyutsiya i upravlenie', *Novyi Mir* 1970 no. 10.

Fedorenko [1970c]   N. P. Fedorenko, 'Printsipy optimal'nogo funktsionirovaniya sotsialisticheskoi ekonomiki v svete leninskogo naslediya', *Ekonomika i matematicheskie metody* 1970 no. 2.

Fedorenko [1971a]   N. P. Fedorenko, 'Nekotorye voprosy optimal'nogo planirovaniya ekonomiki v usloviyakh razvitogo sotsializma', *Rabochii klass i sovremennyi mir* 1971 no. 5–6.

Fedorenko [1971b]   N. P. Fedorenko, 'Ekonomisty-matematiki – narodnomu khozyaistvu', *Vestnik AN SSSR* 1971 no. 1.

Fedorenko [1971c]   N. P. Fedorenko, 'Sovershenstvovat' sistemy sotsialisticheskogo planirovaniya', *Ekonomika i matematichesie metody* 1971 no. 4.

Fedorenko [1971d]   N. P. Fedorenko, 'K voprosu o postroeniya sistemy optimal'-nogo perspektivnogo planirovanoya narodnogo khozyaistva', *Vestnik AN SSSR* 1971 no. 5.

Fedorenko [1972a]   N. P. Fedorenko, Yu. R. Leibkind, E. Z. Maiminas, A. A. Modin, S. S. Shatalin, O. M. Yun', 'Sistema kompleksnogo planirovaniya', *Ekonomika i matematicheskie metody* 1972 No. 3.

Fedorenko [1972b]   N. P. Fedorenko, 'Ot eksperimentov – k sisteme', *Ekonomicheskaya Gazeta* 1972 no. 23.

Fedorenko [1972c]   N. P. Fedorenko, 'Sotsial'no- ekonomicheskie tsely i planirovanie', *Kommunist* 1972 no. 5.

Fedorenko [1972d]   N. P. Fedorenko, 'O sostoyanii i perspektivakh sozdaniya avtomatizirovannykh sistem upravleniya promyshlennymi predpriyatiyami', *Ekonomika i matematicheskie metody* 1972 no. 2.

Fedorenko [1972e]   N. P. Fedorenko, 'O razrabotke sistemy optimal'nogo funktsionirovaniya sotsialisticheskoi ekonomiki', *Voprosy ekonomiki* 1972 no. 6.

Fedorenko [1972f]   N. P. Fedorenko (ed.), *Problemy optimal'nogo funktsionirovaniya sotsialisticheskoi ekonomiki* (1972).

Fedorenko [1972g]   N. P. Fedorenko (ed.), *Informatsiya i modeli struktur upravleniya* (1972).

Friss [1968]   I. Friss (ed.), *Reforma khozyaistvennogo mekhanizma v Vengrii* (Budapest 1968).

Friss [1970]   I. Friss, 'Nekotorye soobrazheniya o planirovanii na 15 let vengerskogo narodnogo khozyaistva', *Acta Oeconomica* 1970 Fasc 1–2.
Garetovsky [1969]   N. V. Garetovsky, *Finansy i kredit v usloviyakh khozyaistvennoi reformy* (1969).
Gatovsky [1967]   L. M. Gatovsky (ed.), *Teoriya i praktika khozyaistvennoi reformy* (1967).
Gatovsky [1971a]   L. M. Gatovsky, *Ekonomicheskie problemy nauchno-tekhnicheskogo progressa* (1971).
Gatovsky [1971b]   L. M. Gatovsky and S. A. Kheinman (eds), *Metodologiya prognozirovaniya ekonomicheskogo razvitiya SSSR* (1971).
Gerchuk [1965]   Ya. P. Gerchuk, *Granitsy primeneniya lineinogo programmirovaniya* (1965).
Gerchuk [1969]   Ya. P. Gerchuk, 'K voprosu o primenenii ekonomiko-matematicheskikh metodov na praktike', *Voprosy ekonomiki* 1969 no. 4. Translated in *Problems of Economics* vol. 12.
Gerchuk [1972]   Ya. P. Gerchuk, 'Ob odnom vazhnom svoistve modelei lineinogo programmirovaniya', *Ekonomika i matematicheskie metody* 1972 no. 1.
Glezerman [1969]   G. Glezerman, 'Leninskii printsip sootnosheniya politiki i ekonomiki', *Pravda* 29 January 1969.
Gol'shtein [1969]   E. G. Gol'shtein and D. B. Yudin, *Zadachi lineinogo programmirovaniya transportnogo tipa* (1969).
Gol'shtein [1970]   E. G. Gol'shtein, *Vypukloe programmirovanie (elementy teorii)* (1970).
Gol'shtein [1971]   E. G. Gol'shtein, *Teoriya dvoistvennosti v matematicheskom programmirovanii i ee prilozheniya* (1971).
Golubeva [1969]   V. Golubeva, 'Khozyaistvennaya reforma v Vengrii', *Planovoe khozyaistvo* 1969 no. 9.
Gorfan [1972]   K. L. Gorfan, 'Sovershenstvovanie planirovaniya i upravleniya narodnym khozyaistvom', *Vestnik AN SSSR* 1972 no. 4.
*Granberg [1963]   A. G. Granberg, *Problemy planovogo mezhotraslevogo balansa v natural'nom virazhenii* (1963). Candidate's thesis.
Granberg [1969]   A. G. Granberg, 'Tselevaya funktsiya obshchestvennogo blagosostoyaniya i kriterii optimal'nosti v prikladnykh narodnokhozyaistvennykh modelyakh', Aganbegyan [1969b] q.v.
Grebtsov [1960]   G. I. Grebtsov and P. P. Karpov (eds), *Material'nye balansy v narodnokhozyaistvennom plane* (1960).
Greshnev [1969]   A. Greshnev, 'O sovershenstvovanii organizatsii metallosnabzheniya', *Material'no-tekhnicheskoe snabzhenie* 1969 no. 8.
Grigor'ev [1969]   S. I. Grigor'ev and K. M. Skovoroda, *Planirovanie fondov tovarov narodnogo potrebleniya* (1969).
Gromov [1967]   V. I. Gromov and V. Ya. Kamenetskii, *Proizvodstvennye ob"edineniya v SSSR* (1967).
Gukov [1969]   N. V. Gukov, *Organizatsiya material'no-tekhnicheskogo snabzheniya predpriyatii bytovogo obsluzhivaniya naseleniya* (1969).
Gurvich [1969]   F. G. Gurvich, 'Problemy sozdaniya avtomatizirovannykh sistem planovykh raschetov', *Ekonomika i matematicheskie metody* 1969 no. 5.
Gusarev [1969]   A. Gusarev, 'Tsena – instrument plana', *Ekonomicheskaya Gazeta* 1969 no. 40.
Integrirovannye [1970]   *Integrirovannye sistemy obrabotki dannykh* (1970).
Ioffe [1971]   V. M. Ioffe and B. K. Khazanov, *Metodologiya optimizatsii perspektivnogo otraslevogo planirovaniya* (1971).
Iotkovskii [1970]   A. A. Iotkovskii and N. D. Fasolyak (eds), *Ekonomika organizatsiya i planirovanie material'no-tekhnicheskogo snabzheniya i sbyta* (1970).
Isaev [1969]   B. L. Isaev, *Integrirovannye balansovye sistemy v analize i planirovanie ekonomiki* (1969).

*Isaev [1971] B. L. Isaev, *Integrirovannaya balansovaya sistema dlya opisaniya finan-
sovykh rezul'tatov khozyaistvovaniya (tezisy doklada)* (1971). For a brief summary in
English of Isaev's proposals see Isaev [1967].

Issledovanie [1968] *Issledovanie potokov ekonomicheskoi informatsii* (1968).

Ivanov [1969] N. V. Ivanov, E. Yu. Lokshin, G. M. Demichev, *Ekonomika i
planirovanie material'no-tekhnicheskogo snabzheniya promyshlennosti* (1969).

Kaitsa [1965] E. O. Kaitsa, *Snabzhenie i proizvodstvenno-khozyaistvennaya deyatel'nost
promyshlennogo predpriyatiya* (Tartu 1965).

Kantorovich [1939] L. V. Kantorovich, *Matematicheskie metody organizatsiya i
planirovaniya proizvodstva* (Leningrad 1939). The English translation is Kantorovich
[1960b].

Kantorovich's achievement, in this and subsequent writings, was that he realised
that the problem of the efficient allocation of resources is a general problem of production planning with a large number of applications, that he provided an algorithm
for deriving numerical solutions, and that he emphasised the economic significance of
the optimality conditions.

The importance of the problem of the efficient allocation of resources, within the
field of railway freight transport, was already familiar to Soviet planners, and
methods for achieving it had been worked out. See *Planirovanie* [1930] a collection of
papers based on the work of the Interdepartmental office for the planning and rational-
isation of transport, Tolstoi [1939], [1941]. Tolstoi's position in the development of
l.p. in the USSR is analogous to that of Stigler in the USA. Both were concerned with
concrete economic problems (the most efficient organisation of railway freight
movements in Tolstoi's case, the most efficient diet in Stigler's case) and both obtained
quite good answers without the help of l.p. In the USA the solution of Stigler's
problem by l.p. (by Laderman in 1947) was used as a test of the simplex method. In
the USSR Kantorovich [1949a] used Tolstoi's problem as an example of the practical
problems which the new method he had discovered could be used to solve.

A pair of linear programmes is equivalent to a game, and hence it is possible to
derive the theorem of the characteristics of an optimal plan from von Neumann's 1928
proof of the existence of a saddle point for certain games. In addition, in a comment on
his growth model, published in 1938, von Neumann drew attention to the duality of
the physical and value variables. Nevertheless, it is still true that if one is interested in
linear programming as a technique for generating numerical optimal solution to problems of the organisation of production, and in shadow prices as instruments for the
solution of practical problems, then Kantorovich is the pioneer.

Kantorovich [1940] L. V. Kantorovich, 'A new method of solving of some classes
of extremal problems', *Comptes Rendues (Doklady) de l'Academie de l'URSS* 1940 vol.
XXVIII no. 3.

Kantorovich [1942] L. V. Kantorovich, 'On the translocation of masses', *Comptes
Rendues (doklady) de l'Adademie des Sciences de l'URSS* 1942 vol. 37 no. 7–8. This is
reprinted in *Management Science* 1958.

Kantorovich [1948] L. V. Kantorovich, 'Ob odnoi probleme Monzha', [On a
problem of Monge] *Uspekhi matematicheskikh nauk* 1948 vol. 3 no. 2 pp. 225–6.

Kantorovich [1949a] L. V. Kantorovich and M. K. Gavurin, 'Primenenie matematicheskikh metodov v voprosakh analiza gruzopotokov', *Problemy povisheniya
effektivnosti raboty transporta* (1949).

Kantorovich [1949b] L. V. Kantorovich, 'Podbor postavov, obespechivayushchikh
maksimal'nyi vykhod piloproduktsii v zadannom assortimente', *Lesnaya promyshlennost'* 1949, no. 7 pp. 15–17 and no. 8 pp. 17–18.

Kantorovich [1957] L. V. Kantorovich, 'O metodakh analiza nekotorykh ekstre-
mal'nykh planovo-proizvodstvennykh zadach', *Doklady akademii nauk SSSR* 1957

vol. 115 no. 3. (There is a correction by the author in *Doklady akademii nauk SSSR* vol. 118 (1958) p. 1054.) For an 'improved translation' by Isbell and Marlow see *Management Science* October 1961.

Kantorovich [1959]   L. V. Kantorovich, 'Matematicheskie metody organizatsii i planirovaniya proizvodstva', in Nemchinov [1959] q.v. (This is a reprint, with a few alterations of Kantorovich [1939].)

Kantorovich [1960a]   L. V. Kantorovich, *Ekonomicheskii raschet nailuchshego ispol'-zovanie resursov* (1960). (This is a reprint of the 1959 edition.) The English translation is Kantorovich [1965b].

Kantorovich [1960c]   L. V. Kantorovich, 'Ob ischislenii proizvodstvennykh zat-rat', *Voprosy ekonomiki* 1960 no. 1. A translation is in *Problems of Economics* vol. 3.

Kantorovich [1964]   L. V. Kantorovich, 'Dinamicheskaya model' optimal'nogo planirovaniya' [A dynamic optimal planning model], in *Planirovanie i ekonomiko-matematicheskie metody* (1964). A translation is in *Matekon* vol. 1 no. 2.

Kantorovich [1965a]   L. V. Kantorovich and V. L. Makarov, 'Optimal'nye modeli perspektivnogo planirovaniya' [Optimisation models of perspective planning], in Nemchinov [1965a] q.v.

Kantorovich [1965c]   L. V. Kantorovich, 'Matematika i ekonomika', *Pravda* 24 August 1965. A translation is in *Problems of Economics* vol. 8.

Kantorovich [1965d]   L. V. Kantorovich, 'Printsip optimal'nosti', *Ekonomicheskaya Gazeta* 1965 no. 45.

Kantorovich [1965e]   L. V. Kantorovich and I. V. Romanovskii, 'Amortizat-sionnye platezhi pri optimal'nom ispol'zovanii oborudovaniya', *Doklady akademii nauk SSSR* 1965 vol. 162 no. 5.

Kantorovich [1966a]   L. V. Kantorovich, 'Matematicheskie problemy optimal'nogo planirovaniya', *Matematicheskie modeli i metody optimal'nogo planirovaniya* ed. L. V. Kantorovich (Novosibirsk 1966).

Kantorovich [1966b]   L. V. Kantorovich, 'Razvitie matematicheskikh metodov ekonomicheskogo analiza', *Vestnik akademii nauk SSSR* 1966 no. 10.

Kantorovich [1966c]   L. V. Kantorovich and I. V. Romanovskii, 'Struktura amortizationnykh otchislenii pri statsionarnoi nagruzke mashinnogo parka', *Doklady akademii nauk* 1966 vol. 166 no. 2.

Kantorovich [1966d]   L. V. Kantorovich, 'Amortizatsionnye otchisleniya i otsenki effektivnosti novoi tekhniki v sisteme optimal'nogo planirovaniya', *Matematiko* [1966] q.v.

Kantorovich [1967a]   L. V. Kantorovich, 'Matematicheskie optimal'nye modeli v planirovanii i razvitiya otrasli i tekhnicheskoi politike', *Voprosy ekonomiki* 1967 no. 10. A translation is in *Problems of Economics* vol. 11.

Kantorovich [1967b]   L. V. Kantorovich and A. L. Vainshtein, 'Ob ischislenii normy effektivnosti na osnove odnoproduktovi modeli razvitiya khozyaistva', *Ekonomika i matematicheskie metody* 1967 no. 5. A translation is in *Matekon* vol. VII no. 2.

Kantorovich [1967c]   L. V. Kantorovich and I. G. Globenko, 'Odnoproduktovaya dinamicheskaya model' pri nalichii mgnovenoi prevrashchaemosti fondov'[A one product dynamic model assuming the malleability of capital], *Doklady akademii nauk SSSR* 1967 vol. 174 no. 3. A translation is in *Soviet mathematics* vol. 8 1967.

Kantorovich [1967d]   L. V. Kantorovich and I. G. Globenko, 'Dinamicheskaya model' economiki', *Doklady akademii nauk SSSR* 1967 vol. 176 no. 5. A translation is in *Soviet mathematics* vol. 8 1967.

Kantorovich [1967e]   L. V. Kantorovich, 'Dinamicheskaya model' optimal'nogo planirovaniya', *Optimal'noe planirovanie* no. 8.

Kantorovich [1967f]   L. V. Kantorovich and V. L. Makarov, 'Voprosy razrabotki i ispol'zovaniya krupnoagregirovannoi modeli optimal'nogo perspektivnogo planirovaniya', *Optimal'noe planirovanie* no. 8.

Kantorovich [1968]   L. V. Kantorovich and A. B. Gorstko, *Mathematicheskoe optimal' noe programmirovanie v ekonomike* (1968).

Kantorovich [1969]   See Bogachev [1969].

Kantorovich [1970a]   L. V. Kantorovich, 'Opyt optimal'noi zagruzki prokatnykh stanov', *Material'no- tekhnicheskoe snabzhenie* 1970 no. 4.

Kantorovich [1970b]   L. V. Kantorovich, V. N. Bogachev, V. L. Makarov, 'Ob otsenke effektivnosti kapital'nykh zatrat', *Ekonomika i matematicheskie metody* 1970 no. 6. A translation is in *Matekon* vol. viii no. 1.

Kantorovich [1970c]   L. V. Kantorovich and V. L. Makarov, 'Differentsial'nye i funktsional'nye uravneniya, voznikayushcheie v modelyakh ekonomicheskoi dinamiki' [Differential and functional equations arising in dynamic economic models] *Sibirskii matematicheskii zhurnal* 1970.

Kantorovich [1971]   L. V. Kantorovich and V. A. Zalgaller, *Ratsional'nyi raskroi promyshlennykh materialov* [The rational cutting of industrial materials] 2nd ed. (Novosibirsk 1971). (The first edition was published in 1951.)

The above list is a selective one, and excludes all Kantorovich's writings on purely mathematical topics.

*Karagedov [1970a]   R. G. Karagedov, *Rentabel'nost' i ekonomicheskii optimum (kriticheskii obzor nemarksistskoi literatury)* (Novosibirsk 1970).

Karagedov [1970b]   R. G. Karagedov, 'K voprosu o sootnoshenii kategorii ekonomicheskoi effektivnosti i rentabel'nosti', *Izvestiya sibirskogo otdeleniya akademii nauk SSSR: seriya obshchestvennykh nauk* 1970 no. 1. A translation is in *Problems of Economics* vol. 13.

Karagedov [1970c]   R. G. Karagedov, 'Effektivnost', rentabel'nost' i fond pooshchreniya', *Planovoe khozyaistvo* 1970 no. 9.

*Karagedov [1971]   R. G. Karagedov, *Rentabel'nost' i effektivnost' sotsialisticheskogo predpriyatiya* (Novosibivsk 1971).

Karnaukhova [1970]   E. S. Karnaukhova and I. A. Borodin (eds), *Ekonomika sotsialisticheskogo sel'skogo khozyaistva* (1970).

Karpov [1972]   P. P. Karpov, *Raspredelenie sredstv proizvodstva v novykh usloviyakh khozyaistvovaniya* (1972).

Kats [1970]   A. I. Kats, *Dinamicheskii ekonomicheskii optimum* (1970).

Katsenelinboigen [1969a] A. I. Katsenelinboigen, Yu. V. Ovsienko, E. Yu. Faerman, 'Nekotorye metodologicheskie voprosy optimal'nogo funksionirovaniya sotsialisticheskoi ekonomiki kak bol'shoi sistemy', *Problemy funktsionirovaniya bol'shikh ekonomicheskikh sistem* (1969).

Katsenelinboigen [1969b]   A. I. Katsenelinboigen, I. L. Lakhman, Yu. V. Ovsienko, 'Optimal'noe upravlenie i tsennostnoi mekhanizm' [Optimal control and the price mechanism], *Ekonomika i matematicheskie metody* 1969 no. 4. A translation is in *Matekon* vol. vi no. 3.

Katsenelinboigen [1972]   A. I. Katsenelinboigen, A. M. Movshovich, Yu. V. Ovsienko, *Vosproizvodstva i ekonomicheskii optimum* (1972).

Kazakevich [1972]   D. M. Kazakevich, *Proizvodstvenno-transportnye modeli v perspektivnom otraslevom planirovanii* (1972).

Khanin [1967a]   G. I. Khanin, 'Ekonomicheskii rost i vybor', *Novyi Mir* 1967 no. 12.

Khanin [1970]   G. I. Khanin, 'Logika ekonomicheskogo mekhanizma', *Novyi Mir* 1970 no. 5.

Khozyaistvennaya reforma [1968]   *Khozyaistvennaya reforma i problemy realizatsii* (1968).

Khozyaistvennaya reforma [1969] *Khozyaistvennaya reforma v SSSR* (1969) (the *Ekonomicheskaya Gazeta* book).

Klarov [1969] Yu. Klarov, 'Sudebnaya oshibka', *Literaturnaya Gazeta* 1969 no. 27 p. 10.

Kobrinskii [1969] A. and N. Kobrinskii, *Mnogo li cheloveku nuzhno?* (1969).

Kobrinskii and Matlin [1968] N. E. Kobrinskii and A. M. Matlin, *Ekonomiko matematicheskie modeli v planirovanii* (1968).

Koldomasov [1959] *Metod material'nykh balansov v planirovanii narodnogo khozyaistva* (1959).

Komin [1971] A. N. Komin, *Problemy planovogo tsenoobrazovaniya* (1971).

Kondrashev [1969] D. D. Kondrashev and G. D. Kondrashev, *Pribyl' tsena, khozraschet* (1969).

Konenko [1970] V. Konenko, 'Stakan v defitsite', *Sotsialisticheskaya Industriya* 15 September 1970 p. 3.

*Konferentsiya [1967] *Konferentsiya molodykh uchenykh. Tezisy dokladov* (TSEMI 1967).

Konüs [1924] A. A. Konüs, 'Problema istinnogo indeksa stoimosti zhizni', *Ekonomicheskii byulleten' kon"yunkturnogo instituta* 1924 no. 11–12. A translation is in *Econometrica* 1939.

Konüs [1964] A. A. Konüs, 'Trudovaya teoriya stoimosti i ekonometrika', *On political economy and econometrics: Essays in honour of Oskar Lange* (Warsaw 1964).

Kotov [1969] V. F. Kotov, *Planirovanie realizatsii produktsii pribyli i rentabel'nosti* (1969).

Kovalev [1964] N. I. Kovalev, 'Ekonomiko-matematicheskaya model' planirovaniya ratsional'noi struktury proizvodstva ekonomicheskogo raiona', *Voprosy ekonomiki* 1964 no. 2.

Kovalev [1970] N. I. Kovalev, 'Politicheskaya ekonomiya sotsializma i ekonomiko-matematicheskie metody', *Planovoe khozyaistvo* 1970 no. 5.

Kovalevskii [1968] A. M. Kovalevskii, *Tekhpromfinplan v novykh usloviyakh i tipovaya metodika ego razrabotki* (1968).

*Kozlov [1965] L. A. Kozlov and D. M. Kazakevich (eds), *Optimal'noe planirovanie razmeshcheniya proizvodstva* NGU nauchnye trudy seriya ekonomicheskaya vol. 7. (Novosibirsk 1965.)

Kozlov [1969] L. A. Kozlov and D. M. Kazakevich, 'Metodologicheskie i metodicheskie problemy optimizatsiya perspektivnykh planov proizvodstva v promyshlennosti', *Izvestiya sibirskogo otdeleniya akademii nauk SSSR: seriya obshchestvennykh nauk* 1969 no. 1.

Kozlov [1970] L. A. Kozlov, *Optimal'noe planirovanie razvitiya i razmeshcheniya otraslei promyshlennosti* (Novosibirsk 1970).

Krasovsky [1967] V. P. Krasovsky, *Problemy ekonomiki kapital'nykh vlozhenii* (1967).

Krylov [1969] P. Krylov, 'Tsentralizovannoe planirovanie v novykh usloviyakh', *Ekonomicheskaya Gazeta* 1969 no. 45.

Kuz'michev [1968] B. Kuz'michev, 'Psikhologicheskii bar'er', *Pravda* 3 June 1968.

Kuz'minov [1969] I. Kuz'minov, 'Lenin i problemy ekonomicheskoi teorii sotsializma', *Pravda* 16 April 1969.

Kuznetsov [1972] I. Kuznetsov, 'S ekonomicheskim raschetom', *Pravda* 19 January 1972.

Kvasha [1961] Kvasha and Krasovsky, 'Planirovanie kapital'nykh vlozhenii i novaya tekhnika', *Voprosy ekonomiki* 1961 no. 8. A translation is in *Problems of Economics* vol. 4.

Kvasha [1971] Ya. B. Kvasha, *Rezervnye moshchnosti* (1971).

Lagutkin [1970] V. M. Lagutkin (ed.), *Nekotorye problemy sovershenstvovaniya material' nogo tekhnicheskogo snabzheniya* (1970).

Laptev [1944]   I. D. Laptev, 'Kolkhoznye dokhody i differential'naya renta', *Bol'shevik* 1944 no. 16.
Lashchinsky [1968]   I. T. Lashchinskii, 'Izuchenie zakonomernosti formirovaniya potrebitel'skogo sprosa', *Vestnik akademii nauk SSSR* 1968 no. 12.
Lebed' [1969]   A. N. Lebed', M. Sh. Dovetov, Yu. M. Aristakov, *Material'no tekhnicheskoe snabzehnie i sbyt v sovremennykh usloviyakh* (1969).
*Leibkind [1971]   Yu. R. Leibkind and L. N. Svirin, *Struktura sistemy utverzhdaemykh pokazatelei godovogo norodnokhozyaistvennogo plana* (TSEMI 1971).
Lemeshev [1968]   M. Lemeshev, *Mezhotraslevye svyazi sel'skogo khozyaistva* (1968).
Lerner [1969]   A. Ya. Lerner and F. Kh. Tsel'man, 'Ob evristicheskikh metodakh resheniya nekotorykh zadach upravleniya material'no-teknicheskim snabzheniem', *Avtomatika i telemekhanika* 1969 no. 2. A translation is in *Automation and remote control* 1969 no. 2.
Leontief [1925]   W. W. Leontief, 'Balans narodnogo khozyaistva SSSR; metodologicheskii obzor raboty TsSU', *Planovoe khozyaistvo* 1925 no. 12. (This is a translation of a review originally published in Germany.)
Leshchevskii [1970]   I. Leshchevskii, 'V put' za farforovoi tarelkoi', *Sotsialisticheskaya industriya* 16 August 1970.
Levental' [1970]   G. B. Levental' and L. S. Popyrin, *Optimizatsiya teploenergeticheskikh ustanovok* (1970).
E. Liberman [1950]   E. G. Liberman, *Khozyaistvennyi raschet mashinostroitel'nogo zavoda* (1950).
E. Liberman [1970]   E. G. Liberman, *Ekonomicheskie metody povisheniya effektivnosti obshchestvennogo proizvodstva* (1970). The English translation is E. G. Liberman, *Economic methods and the effectiveness of production* (New York 1972).
Ya. Liberman [1968]   Ya. G. Liberman, 'Optimal'noe upravlenie ekonomiki i effektivnost' material'nogo stimulirovaniya', *Ekonomika i matematicheskie metody* 1968 no. 5.
Ya. Liberman [1970]   Ya. G. Liberman, *Gosudarstvennyi byudzhet SSSR v novykh usloviyakh khozyaistvovaniya* (1970).
Lisichkin [1966]   G. S. Lisichkin, *Plan i rynok* (1966).
Livshitz [1971]   V. N. Livshitz, *Vybor optimal'nykh reshenii v tekhnikoekonomicheskikh raschetakh* (1971).
Loginov [1968]   Z. I. Loginov and L. Yu. Astanskii, 'Skhema optimal'nogo razmeshcheniya tsementnoi promyshlennosti', *Primenenie* [1968] q.v.
Lur'e [1964]   A. L. Lur'e, *O matematicheskikh metodakh resheniya zadach na optimum pri planirovanii sotsialisticheskogo khozyaistva* (1964).
Lur'e [1968]   A. L. Lur'e, 'O znachenii nelineinosti pri analize sotsialisticheskoi ekonomiki' [The significance of non linearity for the analysis of a socialist economy], *Ekonomika i matematicheskie metody* 1968 no. 1.
Lur'e [1969a]   A. L. Lur'e, 'O raschetakh normy effektivnosti i ob odnoproduktovoi nepreryvnoi modeli narodnogo khozyaistva', *Ekonomika i matematicheskie metody* 1969 no. 3.
Lur'e [1969b]   A. L. Lur'e, 'O probleme tselevoi funktsii sotsialisticheskogo khozyaistva', *Optimal'noe* [1969] q.v.
A. Makarov [1964]   A. A. Makarov, 'Matematicheskaya model' dlya planirovaniya razvitiya toplivno-energeticheskogo khozyaistva SSSR', *Energetika i transport* 1964 no. 3.
(A. A. Makarov is a co-author of Andreev [1966].)
V. Makarov [1962]   V. L. Makarov, 'Ob uslovii ravnovesiya v modeli Neimana' [On the equilibrium conditions for the Neumann model], *Sibirskii matematicheskii zhurnal* 1962 vol. 3 no. 3.

V. Makarov [1965a] V. L. Makarov, 'Asimptotika reshenii lineinykh dinamich-eskikh modelei ekonomicheskikh sistem s diskretnym vremenem', *Doklady akademii nauk SSSR* 1965 vol. 165 no. 4. An English translation is in *Soviet Mathematics* 1965 pp. 1515–18.

V. Makarov [1965b] V. L. Makarov, 'Sostoyaniya ravnovesiya zamknutoi lineinoi modeli rasshiryayushcheisya ekonomiki' [On the equilibrium conditions for a closed linear model of a growing economy] *Ekonomika i matematicheskie metody* 1965 no. 5.

V. Makarov [1965c] See Kantorovich [1965a].

V. Makarov [1966a] V. L. Makarov, 'Asimptoticheskoe povedenie optimal'nykh traektorii lineinykh modelei ekonomiki', *Sibirskii matematicheskii zhurnal* 1966 vol. 7 no. 4.

V. Makarov [1966b] V. L. Makarov, 'Lineinye dinamicheskie modeli proizvod-stva', *Optimal'noe planirovanie* vol. 5 (Novosibirsk 1966).

V. Makarov [1966c] 'Optimal'noe funktsionirovanie lineinykh modelei ekonomiki na beskonechnom vremennom intervale', *Optimal'noe planirovanie* vol. 5 (Novosibirsk 1966).

V. Makarov [1966d] V. L. Makarov, 'O postroenii optimal'noi modeli perspek-tivnogo razvitiya energetiki i toplivnoi promyshlennosti SSSR', *Matematicheskie modeli i metody optimal'nogo planirovaniya* ed. L. V. Kantorovich (Novosibirsk 1966).

V. Makarov [1969a] V. L. Makarov, 'Modeli optimal'nogo rosta ekonomiki', *Ekonomika i matematicheskie metody* 1969 no. 4. A translation is in *Matekon* vol. VI no. 4.

V. Makarov [1969b] V. L. Makarov, 'O modeli konkurentnogo ekonomicheskogo ravnovesiya' [On the model of competitive equilibrium], *Kibernetika* 1969 no. 5.

V. Makarov [1970a] See Kantorovich [1970c].

V. Makarov [1970b] V. L. Makarov and A. M. Rubinov, 'Superlineinye mnozhest-vennye otobrazheniya i modeli ekonomicheskoi dinamiki' [Superlinear point set mappings and models of economic dynamics], *Uspekhi matematicheskikh nauk* no 5. 1970.

V. Makarov [1971] V. L. Makarov, 'Sushestvovanie magistrali v modeli s diskontom' [The existence of a turnpike in a model with interest], *Optimizatsiya* 2 (19) 1971.

Manaseryan [1967] N. M. Manaseryan, *Differentsial'naya renta i rentabel'nost' kolkhozov* (Yerevan 1967). (The author was awarded a Doctorate in 1971 for his work on this subject.)

Matematiko [1966] *Matematiko-ekonomicheskie problemy* (Leningrad 1966). (Vol. 58 of the *Trudy* of the Leningrad economic-engineering Institute named after Tol'yatti.)

Matlin [1968] A. M. Matlin, *Tseny i ekonomicheskaya effektivnost'mashin* (1968).

Matlin [1970] A. M. Matlin, *Plan, tsena i effektivnost' proizvodstva* (1970).

Medvedev [1971] A. G. Medvedev, L. N. Surovyi, G. M. Okrut, V. S. Zhmako, *Kachestvennaya otsenka zemel' v kolkhozakh i sovkhozakh BSSR* (Minsk 1971).

Melent'ev [1966] L. A. Melent'ev and L. S. Belyaev (eds) *Metody matematicheskogo modelirovanie v energetike* (Irkutsk 1966).

Metodicheskie [1967] *Metodicheskie polozheniya po optimal'nomu otraslevomu planiro-vaniyu v promyshlennosti* (Novosibirsk 1967).

Metodicheskie [1969] *Metodicheskie ukazaniya k sostavleniyu gosudarstvennogo plana razvitiya narodnogo khozyaistva* (1969).

Metodika [1968] *Metodika kratkosrochnykh i dolgosrochnykh prognozov raspredeleniya rabochykh i sluzhashchikh po razmeram zarabotnoi platy* (TSEMI 1968).

Mikhalevsky [1964] B. N. Mikhalevskii, *Perspektivnye raschety na osnove prostykh dinamicheskikh modelei* (1964).

Mikhalevskii [1971] B. N. Mikhalevskii, 'Ekonomicheskie modeli mekhaniko-organicheskogo tipa i modeli otkrytoi mnogourovnevoi dinamicheskoi sistemy', *Ekonomika i matematicheskie metody* 1971 no. 1. A French translation is in *Economie* (1972) q.v., and an English one in *Matekon* Fall 1972.

Mikhno [1971] M. Mikhno and L. Lobanov, 'O modelirovanii osnovnykh protsessov upravleniya metallosnabzheniem', *Material'no-tekhnicheskoe snabzhenie* 1971 no. 12.

L. Mints [1966] L. E. Mints (ed.) *Ekonomiko-matematicheskie metody:* vol. 3 *Ekonomiko-matematicheskie modeli narodnogo khozyaistva* (1966).

A. Mints [1972] A. A. Mints, *Ekonomicheskaya otsenka estestvennykh resursov* (1972).

*Model' [1964] *Model' dlya rascheta sbalansirovannogo i optimal'nogo perspektivnogo plana na 1965–70gg* (TSEMI 1964).

Narkhoz [19xx] *Narodnoe khozyaistvo SSSR v 19xx* g (19xx + 1).

Nauchno [1970] 'Nauchno-tekhnicheskii progress i upravlenie ekonomikoi', *Ekonomika i matematicheskie metody* 1970 no. 4.

Nemchinov [1957] V. S. Nemchinov, 'Statisticheskie i ekonomicheskie voprosy postroeniya balansa narodnogo khozyaistva', *Uchenie zapiski po statistike* vol. 3 *Voprosy balansa narodnogo khozyaistva i proizvoditel'nosti truda* (1957).

Nemchinov [1959] V. S. Nemchinov (ed.), *Primenenie matematiki v ekonomicheskikh issledovaniyakh* (1959). (The English translation is Nove [1964b].)

Nemchinov [1960] V. S. Nemchinov (ed.), *Trudy nauchnogo soveshaniya o primenenii matematicheskikh metodov v ekonomicheskikh issledovaniyakh i planirovanii* (4–8 aprelya 1960 goda) in 7 volumes.

Nemchinov [1961] V. S. Nemchinov (ed.), *Primenenie matematiki v ekonomicheskikh issledovaniyakh* vol. 2 (1961).

Nemchinov [1962] V. S. Nemchinov (ed.), *Matematicheskii analiz rasshirennogo vosproizvodstva* (1962) vol. 2 of Nemchinov [1960] q.v.

Nemchinov [1965a] V. S. Nemchinov (ed.), *Primenenie matematiki v ekonomicheskikh issledovaniyakh* vol. 3 (1965).

Nemchinov [1965b] V. S. Nemchinov, *O dal'neishem sovershenstvovanii planirovaniya i upravleniya narodnym khozyaistvom* 2nd ed. (1965).

Nemchinov [1967a] V. S. Nemchinov, *Izbrannye proizvedeniya* vol. 1 (1967). (The subsequent volumes are referred to as Nemchinov [1967b] etc.)

Nesterov [1971] E. P. Nesterov, *Transportnye zadachi lineinogo programmirovaniya* (1971).

Novozhilov [1926] V. V. Novozhilov, 'Nedostatok tovarov', *Vestnik Finansov* 1926 no. 2.

Novozhilov [1939] V. V. Novozhilov, 'Metody soizmereniya narodnokhozyaist-vennogo effektivnosti planovykh i proektnykh variantov', *Trudy Leningradskogo Industrial'nogo institituta* 1939 no. 4.

Novozhilov [1946] V. V. Novozhilov, 'Prakticheskie metody soizmereniya sebes-toimosti i vlozhenii', *Trudy Leningradskogo Politekhnicheskogo instituta* 1946. (There is an English translation – Novozhilov [1956].)

Novozhilov [1959] V. V. Novozhilov, 'Izmerenie zatrat i ikh rezul'tatov v sotsial-isticheskom khozyaistve', in Nemchinov [1959] q.v.

Novozhilov [1963] V. V. Novozhilov, 'K diskussii o printsipakh planovogo tsenoobrazovaniya', *Primenenie matematiki v ekonomike*, vol. 1 (Leningrad 1963).

Novozhilov [1965] V. V. Novozhilov, 'Zakonomernosti razvitiya sistemy upravleniya sotsialisticheskim khozyaistvom', *Ekonomika i matematicheskie metody* 1965 no. 5.

Novozhilov [1966] V. V. Novozhilov, 'Problemy planovogo tsenoobrazovaniya i reforma upravleniya promyshlennost'yu', *Ekonomika i matematicheskie metody* 1966 no. 3.

Novozhilov [1967] V. V. Novozhilov, *Problemy izmereniya zatrat i rezul'tatov pri optimal'nom planirovanii* (1967). (There is an English translation, Novozhilov [1970].)

Novozhilov [1969]   Novozhilov and Gdalevich, 'Khozraschetnaya sistema planirovaniya', *Optimal'noe* [1969] q.v.

O rabote [1972]   'O rabote partiinoi organizatsii instituta ekonomiki', *Kommunist*
1972 no. 1.

Optimal'noe [1969]   *Optimal'noe planirovanie i sovershenstvovanie upravlenie narodnym
khozyaistvom* (1969).

Optimizatsiya [1971]   *Optimizatsiya energeticheskogo khozyaistva* (Tallinn 1971).
Institute of Thermophysics and Electrophysics, Estonian Academy of Sciences.

Osada[1969]   Osada, Spivakovsky, Nizhgeredov, 'Truby, rezervy, planirovanie',
Pravda 6 March 1969.

Osnovnye [1968]   *Osnovnye polozheniya optimal'nogo planirovaniya razvitiya i razmeshcheniya proizvodstva* (Moscow-Novosibirsk 1968) TSEMI, IEOPP, SOPS.

Osnovnye [1969]   *Osnovnye polozheniya optimizatsii razvitiya i razmeshcheniya proizvodstva*
(Moscow-Novosibirsk 1969) TSEMI, IEOPP, SOPS.

Pashkov [1967]   A. Pashkov, 'Razvitie v SSSR politicheskoi ekonomii sotsializma',
Voprosy ekonomiki 1967 no. 10.

Perevedentsev [1966]   V. I. Perevedentsev, *Migratsiya naseleniya i trudovye problemy
Sibiri* (Novosibirsk 1966).

Petrakov [1964]   N. Ya. Petrakov, *Rentabel'nost' i tsena* [1964].

Petrakov [1966]   N. Ya. Petrakov, *Nekotorye aspekty diskussii ob ekonomicheskikh
metodakh khozyaistvovaniya* (1966).

Petrakov [1970]   N. Ya. Petrakov, 'Upravlenie ekonomikoi i ekonomicheskie
interesy', *Novyi Mir* 1970 no. 8. In an article in *Pravda* the chairman of the Committee on the Press of the Council of Ministers cited this article as an example of how
the economic literature sometimes fails to meet the requirements of the 24th Congress and sometimes contains 'serious methodological errors, incorrect treatment of
certain political-economic questions'. (B. Stukalin, *Pravda* 10 November 1971 p. 3.)

Petrakov [1971]   N. Ya. Petrakov, *Khozyaistvennaya reforma: plan i ekonomicheskaya
samostoyatel'nost'* (1971).

Planirovanie [1930]   *Planirovanie perevozok* (1930).

Plenum [1969]   'Plenum nauchnogo soveta AN SSSR po kompleksnoi probleme
"Optimal'noe planirovanie i upravlenie narodnyn khozyaistvom"', *Ekonomika
i matematicheskie metody* 1969 no. 3.

Poltorygin [1969]   V. K. Poltorygin, 'Napryazhennyi plan predpriyatiya i khozyaistvennaya reforma', in M. Z. Bor and V. K. Poltorygin (eds), *Planirovanie i
khozyaistvennaya reforma* (1969).

Popov [1926]   P. I. Popov (ed.), *Balans narodnogo khozyaistva SSSR 1923/24 goda*
(1926) TsSU.

Primenenie [1968]   *Primenenie matematicheskikh metodov v razmeshchenii proizvodstva* (1968)
SOPS.

Primenenie matematiki [1964]   *Primenenie matematiki pri razmeshchenii proizvoditel'nykh sil*
(1964) SOPS.

Problemy [1971]   'Problemy sozdaniya avtomatizirovannoi sistemy upravleniya
material'no-tekhnicheskim snabzheniem', *Ekonomika i matematicheskie metody* 1971
no. 2, pp. 309–14.

Problemy funktsionirovaniya [1969]   *Problemy funktsionirovaniya bol'shikh ekonomicheskikh
sistem* (1969).

Probst [1967]   A. E. Probst, 'Znachenie rezervov dlya narodnokhozyaistvennogo
planirovaniya', *Sovershenstvovanie planirovaniya i upravleniya narodnym khozyaistvom* (the
Strumilin festschrift) (1967).

Pugachev [1966]   V. F. Pugachev, 'Lokal'nyi kriterii i stimulirovanie rabotnikov v
optimal'noi ekonomicheskoi sisteme', *Ekonomika i matematicheskie metody* 1966 no. 5.

Pugachev [1967]   V. F. Pugachev, 'Lokal'nyi kriterii narodnokhozyaistvennogo effektivnosti i reshenie chastnykh zadach optimizatsii', *Ekonomika i matematicheskie metody* 1967 no. 5.

Pugachev [1968]   V. F. Pugachev, *Optimizatsiya planirovaniya* (1968).

Rakhmanin [1969]   G. D. Rakhmanin and G. V. Shalabin, *Optimal'noe razmeshchenie predpriyatii otrasli* (1969).

Rakitsky [1968]   B. V. Rakitskii, *Formy khozyaistvennogo rukovodstva predpriyatiyami* (1968).

Rakitsky [1969]   B. V. Rakitskii, *Chto takoe ekonomicheskie metody khozyaistvovaniya* (1969).

Razvitie [1970]   'Razvitie issledovaniya v oblasti ekonomiki', *Vestnik Akademii Nauk SSSR* 1970 no. 2.

Reforma [1968]   *Reforma stavit problemy* (1968) compilers Yu. V. Yakovlets and L. S. Blyakhman.

Romanchenko [1969]   G. Romanchenko, 'Otsenka zemli i differentsial'naya renta', *Ekonomika sel'skogo khozyaistva* 1969 no. 9.

Rumyantsev [1969]   A. M. Rumyantsev and P. G. Bunich (eds), *Ekonomicheskaya reforma: ee osushestvlenie i problemy* (1969).

Rybalkin [1969]   V. E. Rybalkin, E. I. Kobzar', N. G. Cherkasov, *Plata za proizvodstvennye fondy v evropeiskikh sotsialisticheskikh stranakh* (1969).

Sakharov [1968]   A. D. Sakharov, *Razmyshleniya o progresse mirnom sosushchestvovanii i intellektual'noi svobode* (Frankfurt 1968).

Salimzhanov [1969]   I. K. Salimzhanov, B. A. Neroslavskaya, P. Rychin, *Tseny na tovary kul'turnogo-bytovogo i khozyaistvennogo naznacheniya* (1969).

Sarychev [1970]   V. G. Sarychev (ed.) *Problemy vnutrennogo rynka pri sotsializme* (Leningrad 1970). Vol. 35 of the *Trudy* of the Leningrad Institute of Soviet trade.

Salivanovsky [1971]   V. M. Salivanovskii (ed.) *Spravochnik po material'no tekhnicheskomu snabzeniyu i sbytu na promyshlennykh predpriyatiyakh* (Kiev 1971).

Samokhin [1967]   Yu. M. Samokhin and D. V. Yurin, 'Vsesoyuznoe soveshchanie po voprosam mekhanizatsii i avtomatizatsii planovykh raschetov', *Ekonomika i matematicheskie metody* 1967 no. 3.

Selyunin [1968]   V. Selyunin, 'Vedomstvennyi bar'er', *Ekonomicheskaya Gazeta* 1968 no. 25.

Seminar [1970]   'Seminar po nauchno-metodicheskim voprosam razrabotki i vnedreniya ASPR', *Ekonomika i matematicheskie metody* 1970 no. 5.

Shaposhnikov [1914]   N. N. Shaposhnikov, *Pervyi russki ekonomist-matematik Vladimir Karpovich Dmitriev* (1914).

Shchennikov [1966]   B. Shchennikov, 'Primenenie metodov iterativnogo agregirovaniya dlya resheniya sistem lineinykh uravnenii', *Ekonomika i matematicheskie metody* 1966 no. 5.

Shkatov [1969]   V. K. Shkatov and B. S. Suponitskii, *Optovye tseny na produktsiyu tyazheloi promyshlennosti* (1969).

Shkurko [1970]   S. I. Shkurko, *Material'noe stimulirovanie v novykh usloviyakh khozyaistvovaniya* (1970).

Shokin [1971]   N. A. Shokin, 'Razmeshchenie i ekonomicheskaya otsenka toplivno-energeticheskikh resursov po raionam SSSR', N. A. Shokin, *Metodologicheskie problemy razmeshcheniya otrasli promyshlennosti* (1971) pp. 186–9.

Simpozium [1969]   'Simpozium po ekonomiko-matematicheskim metodam v terskole', *Ekonomika i matematicheskie metody* 1969 no. 5 pp. 791–2.

Simpozium [1971]   'Simpozium po problemam sozdaniyu ASU MTS', *Material'noe tekhnicheskoe snabzehniya* 1971 no. 1.

V. K. Sitnin [1969]   V. K. Sitnin, 'Tsenoobrazovanie v novykh usloviyakh planirovaniya i stimulirovaniya', Rumyantsev [1969] q.v.

V. V. Sitnin [1969]   V. V. Sitnin, *Problemy pribyli i khozyaistvennogo rascheta v pro-myshlennosti* (1969).

Sovershenstvovanie [1969]   *Sovershenstvovanie planirovaniya i uluchshenie ekonomicheskoi raboty v narodnom khozyaistve* (*Materialy Vsesoyuznogo ekonomicheskogo soveshchaniya* (1969).

Smekhov [1968]   B. M. Smekhov, 'Khozyaistvovaniya reforma i stabil'nost' planov', in B. M. Smekhov (ed.) *Problemy sovershenstvovaniya planirovaniya* (1968) (vol. 59 of the *Trudy* of the Plekhanov Institute).

Solomonovich [1970]   I. Solomonovich, 'Monografiya po material'no-tekhniches-komu snabzheniyu', *Material'no-tekhnicheskoe snabzhenie* 1970 no. 5.

Stalin [1929a]   J. V. Stalin, 'O pravom uklone v VKP (b)', printed in full in Stalin [1955] q.v. The passage referred to is on pp. 79–80.

Stalin [1929b]   J. V. Stalin, 'K voprosam agrarnoi politikoi v SSSR', *Pravda* 29 September 1929. Reprinted in Stalin [1955] q.v.

Stalin [1929c]   J. V. Stalin, 'Telegramma V. I. Leninu', *Pravda* 21 December 1929. Reprinted in Stalin [1947] p. 261.

Stalin [1947]   J. V. Stalin, *Sochineniya* vol. 4 (1947).

Stalin [1950]   J. V. Stalin, *Sochineniya* vol. 10 (1950).

Stalin [1955]   J. V. Stalin, *Sochineniya* vol. 12 (1955).

Strumilin [1925]   S. Strumilin, 'Na planovom fronte', *Planovoe khozyaistvo* 1925 no. 1.

Strumilin [1967]   S. Strumilin, 'O tsene "darovykh blag" prirody', *Voprosy ekonomiki* 1967 no. 8. A translation is in *Problem of Economics* vol. 10.

Strumilin [1968]   S. Strumilin, 'O kriteriyakh v optimal'nom planirovanii', *Voprosy ekonomiki* 1968 no. 4.

Sukhotin [1970]   Yu. V. Sukhotin, 'Ekonomicheskaya reforma i narodnokhozy-aistvennyi optimum', in Zhamin [1970] q.v.

Surovyi [1972]   L. Surovyi, 'O sozdanii ravnykh ekonomicheskikh uslovii vos-proizvodstva v kolkhozakh na osnove differentsiatsii podokhodnogo naloga (po materialam zemel'nogo kadastra BSSR)', *Finansy SSSR* 1972 no. 3.

Surovyi is one of the co-authors of Medvedev [1971].

Tanchuk [1965]   I. A. Tanchuk, *Pravoe regulirovanie material'no-tekhnicheskogo snab-zheniya promyshlennosti* (1965).

Terekhov [1967]   L. L. Terekhov, *Otsenki v optimal'nom plane* (1967).

Terent'ev [1971]   M. L. Terent'ev, *Gosudarstvennoe planirovanie kolkhoznogo proiz-vodstva* (1971).

Tolstoi [1939]   A. N. Tolstoi, 'Metody ustraneniya neratsional'nykh perevozok pri planirovanii', *Sotsialisticheskii transport* 1939 no. 9.

Tolstoi [1941]   A. N. Tolstoi, *Metody ustraneniya neratsional'nykh perevozok pri sostavlenii operativnykh planov* (1941).

Trotsky [1932]   L. D. Trotsky, 'Sovetskoe khozyaistvo v opasnosti', *Byulleten' oppozitsii* (Berlin) no. 31 November 1932.

Turchins [1969]   Ya. B. Turchins, *Otsenka zemli i sovershenstvovanie ekonomicheskikh otnoshenii v sel'skom khozyaistve* (Riga 1969).

Udachin [1970]   S. A. Udachin, 'Zemel'nyi fond SSR i ego ispol'zovanie v sel'skom khozyaistve', chapter 4 of Karnaukhova [1970] q.v.

Vaag [1962]   L. A. Vaag and S. N. Zakharov, *Metody ekonomicheskoi otsenki v ener-getike* (1962).

Vainshtein [1966]   A. L. Vainshtein, 'Vozniknovenie i razvitie primeneniya lineinogo programmirovaniya v SSSR (k 25 letiyu lineinogo programmiro-vaniya)', in L. Mints [1966] q.v.

Vainshtein [1969]   A. L. Vainshtein, *Narodnyi dokhod rossii i SSSR* (1969).

Vainshtein [1970]   A. L. Vainshtein, 'Kriterii optimal'nogo razvitiya sotsialisticheskogo narodnogo khozyaistva', *Voprosy ekonomiki* 1970 no. 5. Translated in *Problems of Economics* vol. 13.

*Val'tukh [1965]   K. K. Val'tukh and I. N. Khokhlushkin, 'K metodologii ekonomiko-matematicheskogo modelirovaniya protsessov razvitiya otdel'nykh otraslei proizvodstva sredstv proizvodstva (na primere promyshlennosti plastmass)', in *Aganbegyan [1965] q.v.

*Val'tukh [1969]   K. K. Val'tukh (ed.), *Problemy narodnokhozyaistvennogo optimuma* vol. 2 (Novosibirsk 1969).

Val'tukh [1970a]   K. K. Val'tukh, 'O predel'nykh otsenkakh vosproizvodimykh resursov v dinamicheskom optimal'nom plane' [On the marginal values of reproducible resources in a dynamic optimal plan], *Ekonomicheskie nauki* 1970 no. 7.

Val'tukh [1970b]   K. K. Val'tukh, 'Sootnoshenie tsen i staticheskie ekonomiko-matematicheskie otsenki' [The relationship between prices and static shadow prices] in Sh. Ya. Turetskii (ed.), *Tseny i vosproizvodstva* (1970). (Vol. 90 of the *Trudy* of the Plekhanov institute.)

*Val'tukh [1970c]   K. K. Val'tukh (ed.), *Problemy postroeniya i ispol'zovaniya modelei ekonomiki* (Novosibirsk 1970).

*Val'tukh [1970d]   K. K. Val'tukh, 'Teorema Erro-Debre o konkurentnom ravnovesii i problemy ekonomikeskoi teorii' [The Arrow-Debreu theorem of competitive equilibrium and problems of economic theory], *Problemy narodnokhozyaistvennogo optimuma* vol. 3 (Novosibirsk 1970).

Veselkov [1968]   F. S. Veselkov, *Stimuly vysokikh planovykh zadanii* (1968).

Veselkov [1969]   F. S. Veselkov, 'Analiz metodov obrazovaniya fondov material'nogo pooshchreniya c tochki zreniya stimulirovaniya rosta effektivnosti proizvodstva', *Voprosy ekonomiki* 1969 no. 12.

Volchkov [1970]   B. A. Volchkov, *Avtomatizirovannaya sistema planovykh raschetov* (1970).

Volkonsky et al [1965]   V. A. Volkonskii *et al*, 'Po povody stat'i N. Kovaleva', *Voprosy ekonomiki* 1965 no. 1.

Volkonsky [1967a]   V. A. Volkonskii, *Model' optimal'nogo planirovaniya i vzaimosvyazi ekonomicheskikh pokazatelei* (1967).

Volkonsky [1967b]   V. A. Volkonskii, 'Ekonomiko-matematicheskie metody i teoriya planirovaniya i upravleniya narodnym khozyaistom', *Voprosy ekonomiki* 1967 no. 3. A translation is in *Problems of Economics* vol. 10.

Volkonsky [1967c]   V. A. Volkonskii, 'Tovarno-denezhnyi mekhanizm v optimal'nom upravlenii khozyaistvom i tsenoobrazovanie', *Ekonomika i matematicheskie metody* 1967 no. 4.

Voprosy [1968]   'Voprosy ekonomicheskoi otsenki zemli i prirodnykh resursov', *Vestnik AN SSSR* 1968 no. 2.

Vorob'ev [1970]   G. Vorob'ev, 'Problemy intensifikatsii zernovogo proizdstva', *Voprosy ekonomiki* 1970 no. 10.

Vystupleniya [1968]   'Vystupleniya uchastnikov zasedaniya sektsii', *Material'no tekhnicheskoe snabzhenie* 1968 no. 8.

Yakovets [1964]   Yu. V. Yakovets, *Metodologiya tsenoobrazovaniya v gornodobyvayushchei promyshlennosti* (1964).

Yasin [1971]   E. Yasin, 'Chego ne vidit elektronnyi glaz', *Literaturnaya Gazeta* 1971 no. 31.

Yegiazaryan [1970]   G. A. Yegiazaryan and L. S. Kheifets, *Problemy material'nogo stimulirovaniya v promyshlennosti* (1970).

Yudin [1969]   D. B. Yudin and E. S. Gol'shtein, *Lineinogo programmirovanie (teoriya, metody i prilozheniya)* (1969).

Yudina [1969]   V. Yudina, 'Stimuly ili simboly?' *Novyi Mir* 1969 no. 9.

Yushkov [1928]   L. P. Yushkov, 'Osnovnoi vopros planovoi metodologii', *Vestnik finansov* 1928 no. 10.
This article was printed with a note to say that it was a discussion article, i.e. that the views expressed in it were the responsibility of the author alone.
Yushkov is not just a forgotten forerunner of later developments. His article is referred to in their books by Kantorovich ([1960a] p. 261), Lur'e ([1964] p. 222), Bogachev ([1966] pp. 56–8), and Zalesski ([1968] p. 4 and p. 10).
The importance of Yushkov's paper was noticed by Collette ([1965] pp. 40–1). Collette, however, and following after him Zauberman ([1966] p. 91) treat Yushkov as a precursor of linear programming, rather than as the economist who adapted neo-classical ideas to a socialist planned economy, emphasising both the importance of optimal solutions to planning problems and the usefulness of value relations.
*Yusupov [1963]   M. Kh. Yusupov, *Ekonomiko-matematicheskie i vychislitel'nye voprosy mezhotraslevykh balansov* (1963). Candidate's thesis.
Zaifert [1970]   E. Zaifert (ed.) *Pribyl' v sotsialisticheskoi promyshlennosti* (1970). (Translated from German.)
Zakharov [1967]   A. K. Zakharov, 'K voprosu o staticheskom narodnokhozyaistvennom optimume', *Mir glazmi molodogo uchenogo: Ekonomika* (1967).
Zakruzhnyi [1966]   A. A. Zakruzhnyi, *Organizatsiya i planirovanie material'no-tekhnicheskogo snabzheniya* (Minsk 1966).
Zemel'naya [1952]   'Zemel'naya renta', *Bolshaya Sovetskaya Entsiklopediya* 2nd ed. vol. 16 (1952).
Zemel'naya [1959]   *Zemel'naya renta v sotsialisticheskom sel'skom khozyaistve* (1959).
Zemel'nyi [1967]   *Zemel'nyi kadastr v SSSR* (1967).
Zhamin [1970]   V. A. Zhamin (ed.), *Voprosy effektivnosti obshchestvennogo proizvodstva* (1970).

SOVIET SERIALS

Occasional Papers

Matematicheskie metody v ekonomike (Institute of Economics, Latvian Academy of Sciences, Riga)
Modelirovanie ekonomicheskikh protsessov (Economic cybernetics section, Economics Faculty, Moscow State University, Moscow)
Nauchnye trudy: seriya ekonomicheskaya (Laboratory for economic-mathematical research of the Siberian branch of the Academy of Sciences, and the Laboratory for economic-mathematical research of Novosibirsk State University, Novosibirsk)
Optimal'noe planirovanie (Institute of Mathematics of the Siberian branch of the Academy of Sciences, Novosibirsk)
Optimizatsiya (Institute of Mathematics of the Siberian branch of the Academy of Sciences, Novosibirsk)
Primenenie matematicheskikh metodov v ekonomicheskikh issledovaniyakh i planirovanii (Institute of Cybernetics, Ukrainian Academy of Sciences, Kiev)
Primenenie matematiki v ekonomike (Department and laboratory of economic-mathematical methods, Economics Faculty, Leningrad State University, Leningrad)
Trudy (Plekhanov Institute [department of national economic planning], Moscow)

Journals

Avtomatika i telemekhanika (IPU)
Doklady akademii nauk SSSR (Academy of Sciences)
Ekonomicheskie nauki (Ministry of Higher Education)
Ekonomika i matematicheskie metody (TSEMI)
Ekonomika i organizatsiya promyshlennogo proizvodstva (IEOPP)

Ekonomika sel'skogo khozyaistva   (Ministry of Agriculture)
Finansy SSSR   (Ministry of Finance)
Izvestiya AN SSSR: *Energetika i transport*   (Section on physical-technical energy problems, Academy of Sciences)
Izvestiya AN SSSR: seriya ekonomicheskaya   (Economics section, Academy of Sciences)
Izvestiya sibirskogo otdeleniya AN SSSR: seriya obshchestvennykh nauk   (Siberian branch, Academy of Sciences)
Kibernetika   (Cybernetics centre, Ukranian Academy of Sciences)
Kommunist   (CC)
Novyi Mir   (Union of writers)
Material'no-tekhnicheskoe snabzhenie   (Gossnab)
Planovoe khozyaistvo   (Gosplan)
Sibirskii matematicheskii zhurnal   (Institute of Mathematics, Siberian branch, Academy of Sciences)
Teploenergetika   (Academy of Sciences, Gostekhnika, and Central board of the scientific-technical societies of the energy and electrical industry)
Vestnik AN SSSR   (Presidium, Academy of Sciences)
Vestnik MGU: Ekonomika   (Economics Faculty, Moscow State University)
Vestnik Statistiki   (TsSU)
Voprosy ekonomiki   (Institute of Economics)

Weeklies

Ekonomicheskaya Gazeta   (CC)
Literaturnaya Gazeta   (Union of writers)

Dailies

Pravda   (CC)
Sotsialisticheskaya industriya   (CC)

Translation journals

Automation and remote control   (NY)   A complete English translation of *Avtomatika i telemekhanika*
Current Digest of the Soviet Press   (Columbus, Ohio)   Articles from the Soviet press
Matekon   (NY)   Soviet and East European papers in mathematical economics
Problems of Economics   (NY)   Papers from Soviet economics journals
Soviet automatic control   (NY)   A complete translation of *Avtomatika*, the journal of the Ukrainian Cybernetics Institute (published in Ukrainian)
Soviet mathematics   (Providence, Rhode Island, USA)   Translation of mathematics section of *Doklady AN SSSR*

BOOKS AND ARTICLES IN LANGUAGES OTHER THAN RUSSIAN

Acton [1964]   R. A. Acton, D. Robinson and N. R. Tobin, 'Developing an automatic scheduling system for a new integrated steel works', *Proceedings of the 3rd international conference on operational research* (Paris 1964).
Ahluwalia [1965]   S. S. Ahluwalia, 'Balancing versus input–output techniques in ensuring the internal consistency of a plan', *Essays* [1965] q.v.
Ames [1965]   E. Ames, *Soviet economic processes* (Homewood, Illinois 1965).

Amey [1968]   L. Amey, 'On opportunity costs and decision making', *Accountancy* vol. 79, no. 899 July 1968 pp. 442–51.

Arrow [n.d.]   K. Arrow and L. Hurwicz, 'Decentralisation and computation in resource allocation', Pfouts [n.d.] q.v.

Arrow [1971]   K. Arrow and F. Hahn, *General Competitive Analysis* (San Francisco and Edinburgh 1971).

Barron [1972]   M. J. Barron, 'The application of linear programming prices in management accounting – some cautionary observations', *Journal of Business Finance* vol. 4 no. 1 (Spring 1972).

Basic [1971]   *Basic principles of the system of balances of the national economy* (UN NY 1971). ST/STAT/SER.F/17.

Baumol [1964]   W. J. Baumol and T. Fabian, 'Decomposition, Pricing for Decentralization and External Economies', *Management Science* September 1964.

Baumol [1967]   W. J. Baumol and R. C. Bushnell, 'Error produced by linearization in mathematical programming', *Econometrica* 1967.

Becker [1961]   A. S. Becker, *Soviet national income 1958–64* (Berkeley 1969).

Bergson [1961]   A. Bergson, *The real national income of Soviet Russia since 1928* (Cambridge, Mass. 1961).

Bergson [1964]   A. Bergson, *The economics of Soviet planning* (New Haven 1964).

Berliner [1957]   J. S. Berliner, *Factory and manager in the USSR* (Cambridge, Mass. 1957).

Berliner [1966]   J. C. Berliner, 'The economics of overtaking and surpassing', H. Rosovsky (ed.), *Industrialisation in two systems* (New York 1966).

Bliss [1972]   C. J. Bliss, 'Prices, markets and planning', *Economic Journal* March 1972.

Boornstein [1962]   M. Boornstein, 'The Soviet price system', *American Economic Review* March 1962.

Boornstein [1966]   M. Boornstein, 'Soviet price theory and policy', *New Directions* [1966] q.v.

Boyarsky [1930]   A. Ya. Boyarsky, 'On the theory of diminishing growth rates of the Soviet economy', Spulber [1964] q.v. This is a translation of an article first published in *Planovoe khozyaistvo* 1930 no. 10–11.

Broekmeyer [1970]   M. J. Broekmeyer, *Yugoslav workers' self management* (Dordrecht, Holland 1970).

Bronson [1970]   D. W. Bronson and B. S. Severin in *Economic performance and the military burden in the USSR* (Washington DC 1970).

Campbell [1958a]   R. Campbell, 'A comparison of Soviet and American inventory-output ratios', *American Economic Review* September 1958.

Campbell [1958b]   R. Campbell, 'Accounting for cost control in the Soviet economy', *Review of Economics and Statistics* February 1958.

Campbell [1961]   R. Campbell, 'Marx, Kantorovich and Novozhilov – *Stoimost*' versus reality', *Slavic Review* October 1961.

Cartwright [1961]   W. F. Cartwright and G. W. Thomas, 'The integration of production planning, electronic data processing and process control', *Journal of the iron and steel institute* vol. 198 1961.

*Chandra [1965]   N. K. Chandra, *Some problems of investment planning in a socialist economy with special reference to the USSR and Poland* (PhD thesis London 1965).

Chandra [1970]   N. K. Chandra, 'Theory and practice of Soviet price reforms', *Yearbook of East-European Economics* Band 1 (Munich-Vienna 1970).

Charnes [1962]   A. Charnes and W. W. Cooper, 'On some works of Kantorovich, Koopmans and others', *Management Science* April 1962. Immediately following this paper is a comment by Koopmans.

Chelnokov [1967]   V. Chelnokov and V. Rybin, 'Economic reflections: PARTNER

OF THE ENTERPRISE', *Current digest of the Soviet Press* vol. 19 no. 5 p. 31. (This is a translation of an article in *Izvestiya* 5 February 1967 p. 2.)

Collette [1965] J. M. Collette, *Politique des investissements et calcul economique: L'experience sovietique* (Paris 1965).

Csikos-Nagy [1968] B. Csikos-Nagy, *Pricing in Hungary* (1968) IEA.

Csikos-Nagy [1969] B. Csikos-Nagy, 'First experiences gained in the implementation of the economic reform in Hungary', *Acta Oeconomica* 1969 fasc. 1.

Dantzig [1963] G. B. Dantzig, *Linear programming and extensions* (Princeton 1963).

Davies [1965] R. W. Davies, 'Planning for rapid growth in the USSR', *Economics of Planning* 1965 no. 1–2.

Davies [1966] R. W. Davies, 'The Soviet planning process for rapid industrialisation', *Economics of Planning* vol. 6 no. 1.

Devons [1950] E. Devons, *Planning in practice* (1950).

Dickinson [1963] H. D. Dickinson, Note on the article by Johansen, 'Labour theory of value and marginal utilities', *Economics of Planning* 1963 no. 3.

Djordjevic [1966] J. Djordjevic, 'A contribution to the theory of social property', *Socialist thought and practice* no. 24 (October–December 1966).

Dmitriev [1968] V. K. Dmitriev, *Essais Economiques* (Paris 1968). (This is a translation of Dmitriev [1904] q.v.)

Dobb [1960] M. Dobb, *An essay on economic growth and planning* (1960).

Dobb [1964] M. Dobb, 'Some further comments on the discussion about socialist price policy', Lange [1964] q.v.

Dobb [1966] M. Dobb, *Soviet economic development* (1966).

Dobb [1967] M. Dobb, *Papers on capitalism, development and planning* (1967).

Dobb [1969] M. Dobb, *Welfare economics and the economics of socialism* (Cambridge 1969).

Dodge and Wilber [1970] N. T. Dodge and C. K. Wilber, 'The relevance of Soviet industrial experience for less developed countries', *Soviet Studies* January 1970.

DOSSO [1958] R. Dorfman, P. A. Samuelson and R. Solow, *Linear programming and economic analysis* (New York 1958).

ECE [1960] ECE UN, 'A note on the introduction of mathematical techniques into Soviet planning', *Economic Bulletin for Europe* no. 1 1960.

ECE [1969] ECE UN, *Automation in the iron and steel industry* (New York 1969).

Economie [1972] *Economie mathematique en URSS* Cahiers de l'ISEA, série G no. 30 Economies et societies vol. 6 no. 1 January 1972.

Ellman [1965] Michael Ellman, 'The logic of collectivisation', *Ost Europa Wirtschaft* 1965 no. 4.

Ellman [1966] Michael Ellman, 'Individual preferences and the market', *Economics of Planning* 1966 no. 3.

Ellman [1968] Michael Ellman, 'The use of input–output in regional economic planning: The Soviet experience', *Economic Journal* December 1968.

Ellman [1969] Michael Ellman, 'Aggregation as a cause of inconsistent plans', *Economica* 1969 no. 1.

Ellman [1971] Michael Ellman, *Soviet planning today: proposals for an optimally functioning economic system* (Cambridge 1971).

Emery [1969] J. C. Emery, *Organisational planning and control systems* (1969).

Essays [1965] *Essays on planning and economic development* (Warsaw 1965).

Fedorenko [1969b] N. P. Fedorenko, 'The role of economico-mathematical methods in the planning and management of the economy of the Union of Soviet Socialist Republics', *Journal of development planning* 1969 no. 1.

Feinstein [1967] C. H. Feinstein (ed.), *Socialism, capitalism and economic growth* (Cambridge 1967).

Findlay [1962]   R. Findlay, 'Capital theory and development planning', *Review of Economic Studies* 1962.

Fiszel [1966]   H. Fiszel, *Investment efficiency in a socialist economy* (Oxford 1966).

Friss [1969]   I. Friss (ed.), *Reform of the economic mechanism in Hungary* (Budapest 1969).

Gale [1960]   D. Gale, *The theory of linear economic models* (New York 1960).

Georgescu-Roegen [1971]   N. Georgescu-Roegen, *The entropy law and the economic process* (Cambridge, Mass. 1971).

Glushkov [1970]   'Development of cybernetics and computers in the Ukraine', *Soviet Automatic Control* vol. 15 no. 2.

Gomory [1960]   R. E. Gomory and W. J. Baumol, 'Integer programming and prices', *Econometrica* 1960.

Goodwin [1951]   R. M. Goodwin, 'Iteration, automatic computers and economic dynamics', *Metroeconomica* 1951.

Grossman [1960]   G. Grossman (ed.), *Value and plan* (Berkeley 1960).

Hardt [1967]   J. P. Hardt, M. Hoffenberg and H. S. Levine, *Mathematics and computers in Soviet economic planning* (New Haven 1967).

Hayek [1939]   F. von Hayek, 'Pricing versus Rationing', and 'The economy of Capital', *The Banker* September and October 1939.

Heady [1971]   E. O. Heady (ed.), *Economic models and quantitative methods for decisions and planning in agriculture*. Proceedings of an East–West seminar (Ames, Iowa 1971).

Henderson [1958]   J. M. Henderson, *The Efficiency of the coal industry* (Cambridge, Mass. 1958).

Hicks [1960]   J. R. Hicks, 'Linear theory', *Economic Journal* 1960.

Hitch [1960]   C. J. Hitch and R. N. McKean, *The economics of defence in the nuclear age* (Cambridge, Mass. 1960).

Hodge [1969]   B. Hodge and R. N. Hodgson, *Management and the computer in information and control systems* (New York 1969).

Holesovsky [1968]   V. Holesovsky, 'Planning reforms in Czeckoslovakia', *Soviet Studies* April 1968.

Holzman [1960]   F. D. Holzman, 'Soviet inflationary pressures 1928–57: causes and cures', *Quarterly Journal of Economics* 1960.

Hough [1969]   J. F. Hough, *The Soviet prefects: the local party organs in industrial decision making* (Cambridge, Mass. 1969).

Ijiri [1965]   Y. Ijiri, *Management goals and accounting for control* (Amsterdam 1965).

Isaev [1967]   B. I. Isaev, 'Block matrix of financial flows', *Econometrica* 1967 supplementary issue pp. 65–8.

Johansen [1963a]   L. Johansen, 'Marxism and mathematical economics', *Monthly Review* January 1963.

Johansen [1963b]   L. Johansen, 'Labour theory of value and marginal utilities', *Economics of Planning* vol. 3 1963 no. 2.

Johansen [1966]   L. Johansen, 'Soviet mathematical economics', *Economic Journal* 1966.

Joravsky [1970]   D. Joravsky, *The Lysenko affair* (Cambridge, Mass. 1970).

Kabaj [1968]   M. Kabaj, 'Shift working and employment expansion: Towards an optimum pattern', *International Labour Review* 1968 vol. 98 no. 3.

Kahn [1949]   R. Kahn, 'Professor Meade on planning', *Economic Journal* 1949.

Kantorovich [1958]   L. V. Kantorovich, 'On the translocation of masses', *Management Science* 1958 vol. 5 no. 1. (This is a reprint of Kantorovich [1942].)

Kantorovich [1960b]   L. V. Kantorovich, 'Mathematical methods for the organisation and planning of production', *Management Science* July 1960. This is a translation of Kantorovich [1939]. (There is an introductory note by Koopmans.) The relationship between this paper and subsequent Western work is considered in Charnes [1962] q.v.

Kantorovich [1965b]   L. V. Kantorovich, *The best use of economic resources* (Oxford 1965). This is a translation of Kantorovich [1960a].

Karol [1965]   K. Karol, 'Reflections on the people's democracies', *The Socialist Register* 1965 (eds Miliband and Saville).

Kendall [1960]   M. Kendall, *New prospects in economic analysis* (1960).

Kendrick [1967a]   D. A. Kendrick, *Programming investment in the process industries* (Cambridge, Mass. 1967).

Kendrick [1967b]   D. A. Kendrick, 'Investment planning and economic integration', *Economics of Planning* 1967 no. 1.

Koopmans [1951a]   T. C. Koopmans, 'Analysis of production as an efficient combination of activities', Koopmans [1951b] q.v.

Koopmans [1951b]   T. C. Koopmans (ed.), *Activity analysis of production and allocation* (New York 1951).

Koopmans [1951c]   T. C. Koopmans, 'The efficient allocation of resources', *Econometrica* 1951.

Koopmans [1957]   T. C. Koopmans, *Three essays on the state of economic science* (New York 1957).

Kornai [1959]   J. Kornai, *Overcentralisation in economic administration* (1959).

Kornai [1965]   J. Kornai and T. Liptak, 'Two level planning', *Econometrica* 1965.

Kornai [1967]   J. Kornai, *Mathematical planning of structural decisions* (Amsterdam 1967).

Kornai [1969]   J. Kornai, 'Multi-level programming – A first report on the model and on the experimental computations', *European Economic Review* vol. 1 no. 1.

Kornai [1970]   J. Kornai, 'A general descriptive model of planning process', *Economics of Planning* 1970 no. 1–2.

Kornai [1971]   J. Kornai, *Anti-equilibrium: On economic systems theory and the tasks of research* (Amsterdam and London 1971).

Kouba [1969]   K. Kouba, 'The plan and the market in a socialist economy', *Czechoslovak Economic Papers* 11 (1969).

Kowalik [1964]   T. Kowalik, 'Three conceptions of the political economy of socialism', Lange [1964] q.v.

Kuhn [1956]   H. W. Kuhn and A. W. Tucker (eds), *Linear inequalities and related systems* (Princeton 1956).

Kuron [n.d.]   J. Kuron and K. Modzelewski, *An open letter to the party* (n.d. 1968?).

Labedz [1962]   L. Labedz (ed.), *Revisionism* (1962).

Lakatos [1966]   I. Lakatos, 'Proofs and refutations', *British Journal for the Philosophy of Science* 1966.

Lancaster [1968]   K. Lancaster, *Mathematical economics* (1968).

Lane [1970]   D. Lane, *Politics and society in the USSR* (1970).

Lane [1971]   D. Lane, *The end of inequality? Stratification under state socialism* (1971).

Lane [1973]   D. Lane and G. Kolankiewicz (eds), *Social groups in Polish society* (1973).

Lange [1937]   O. Lange, 'On the economic theory of socialism', *Review of Economic Studies* February 1937.

Lange [1958]   O. Lange, 'The role of planning in a socialist economy', *Indian Economic Review* 1958.

Lange [1962]   O. Lange (ed.), *Problems of political economy of socialism* (New Delhi 1962). This is a translation of a revised version of a book published in Warsaw in 1959.

Lange [1964]   *On political economy and econometrics: Essays in honour of Oskar Lange* (Warsaw 1964).

Leibenstein [1966]   H. Leibenstein, 'Allocative efficiency versus X efficiency', *American Economic Review* June 1966.

Lerner [1949]   A. Lerner, *The economics of control* (1949).

Levine [1959]   H. S. Levine, 'The centralised planning of supply in Soviet industry', Joint Economic Committee US Congress, *Comparisons of the United States and Soviet economies* (Washington DC 1959).

Machonin [1969a]   P. Machonin, 'The social structure of contemporary Czechoslovak society', *Czechoslovak Economic Papers* no. 11.

Machonin [1969b]   P. Machonin, *Československá Společnost* (Bratislava 1969). For a review article see E. G. Gellner, 'The pluralist anti-levellers of Prague', *Government and Opposition* vol. 7 no. 1 Winter 1972.

Machonin [1970]   P. Machonin, 'Social stratification in contemporary Czechoslovakia', *American Journal of sociology* vol. 75.

Malinvaud [1967]   E. Malinvaud, 'Decentralized procedures for planning', E. Malinvaud and M. Bacharach (eds), *Activity analysis in the theory of growth and planning* (1967).

Malkin [1972]   D. Malkin and J. Muguet, 'Modelisation regionale et systeme de planification optimale', in *Economie* [1972] q.v.

Manove [1971]   M. Manove, 'A model of Soviet-type economic planning', *American Economic Review* June 1971.

Marglin [1969]   S. A. Marglin, 'Information in price and command systems of planning', J. Margolis and H. Guittons (ed.), *Public Economics* (1969).

Margolis [1965]   J. Margolis (ed.), *The public economy of urban communities* (Washington 1965).

Marschak [1959]   T. Marschak, 'Centralization and decentralization in economic organisation', *Econometrica* 1959.

Meade [1945]   J. E. Meade, 'Mr Lerner on "the economics of control"', *Economic Journal* 1945.

Meade [1965]   J. E. Meade, *The stationary economy* (1965).

Medvedev [1972]   R. A. Medvedev, *Let history judge* (1972).

Mesarovic [1970]   M. D. Mesarovic, D. Macho and Y. Takahara. *The theory of hierarchical, multi-level, systems* (New York and London 1970).

Mikhailov [1971]   A. Mikhailov (pseudonym), 'Thoughts on the liberal campaign of 1968', *A chronicle of current events* 1971 no. 17.

Milenkovitch [1971]   D. D. Milenkovitch, *Plan and market in Yugoslav economic thought* (New Haven 1971).

Miliband [1969]   R. M. Miliband, *The state in capitalist society* (1969).

Montias [1959]   J. M. Montias, 'Planning with material balances in Soviet type economies', *American Economic Review* December 1959.

Montias [1962a]   J. M. Montias, 'On the consistency and efficiency of central plans', *Review of Economic Studies* October 1962.

Montias [1962b]   J. M. Montias, *Central planning in Poland* (New Haven 1962).

Multi level planning [1970]   *Multi level planning and decision making* (UN New York 1970). This contains an important paper by Margolis and Trzeciakowski.

Nerlove [1959]   M. Nerlove, 'On the efficiency of the coal industry', *Journal of Business* 1959 pp. 271–8.

New Directions [1966]   *New directions in the Soviet economy* (Washington DC 1966).

Normativni [1970]   *Normativni aktove za prilozhenie na ikonomicheskaya mekhaniz"m prez perioda 1971–1975g* (Sofia 1970).

Nove [1958a]   A. Nove, 'The politics of economic rationality', *Social Research* 1958, reprinted in Nove [1964a] q.v.

Nove [1958b]   A. Nove, 'The problem of success indicators in Soviet industry', *Economica* 1958. Reprinted in Nove [1964a] q.v.

Nove [1964a]   A. Nove, *Was Stalin really necessary?* (1964).

Nove [1964b]   A. Nove (ed.), *The use of mathematics in economics* (Edinburgh 1964). This is a translation of Nemchinov [1959] q.v.

Nove [1969a]   A. Nove, 'History, Hierarchy and Nationalities: Some observation on the Soviet Social Structure', *Soviet Studies* July 1969.

Nove [1969b]   A. Nove, Internal economies, *Economic Journal* December 1969.

Novozhilov [1956]   V. V. Novozhilov, 'On choosing between investment projects', *International Economic Papers* 1959 no. 6. (This is a translation of Novozhilov [1946] q.v. and part of Novozhilov [1939] q.v.)

Novozhilov [1970]   V. V. Novozhilov, *Problems of cost benefit analysis in optimal planning* (New York 1970).

Nuti [1970]   M. Nuti, 'Investment reforms in Czechoslovkia', *Soviet Studies* January 1970.

Nuti [1971]   M. Nuti, 'Discounting methods in Polish planning', *Soviet Studies* October 1971.

Parfenov [1971]   V. Parfenov, 'Economic survey: THE FOURTH PROCESS' *Current digest of the Soviet press* vol. 23 no. 42 p. 11. (This is a translation of an article in *Pravda* 19 October 1971 p. 2.)

Parkin [1969]   F. Parkin, 'Class stratification in socialist societies', *British Journal of Sociology* 1969.

Parkin [1971]   F. Parkin, *Class Inequality and Political Order* (1971).

Parkin [1972]   F. Parkin, 'System contradiction and political transformation', *European Journal of Sociology* 1972 no. 1. For a review article on Parkin and other Marxisant writing, with special reference to the UK, see J. Goldthorpe, 'Status and Party in modern Britain: some recent interpretations Marxist and *Marxisant*', *European Journal of Sociology* 1972.

Pfouts [n.d.]   Pfouts R. (ed.), *Essays on economics and econometrics* (Chapel Hill n.d.).

Powell [1968]   R. Powell, 'Economic growth in the USSR', *Scientific American* December 1968.

Richman [1963]   B. Richman, Formulation of enterprise operating plans in Soviet industry, *Soviet Studies* vol. 15.

Riddell [1968]   D. S. Riddell, 'Social self-government: the background of theory and practice in Yugoslav socialism', *British Journal of Sociology* 1968.

Robinson [1960]   J. Robinson, *Exercise in economic analysis* (1960).

Robinson [1964]   J. Robinson, 'Consumer's sovereignty in a planned economy', Lange [1964] q.v.

Robinson [1967]   J. Robinson, 'Socialist affluence', Feinstein [1967] q.v.

Russell [1903]   B. Russell, *The principles of mathematics* (Cambridge 1903).

*Samuelson [1949]   P. Samuelson, *Market mechanisms and maximisation* (RAND 1949) reprinted in Samuelson [1966].

Samuelson [1966]   *The collected scientific papers of Paul A. Samuelson* ed. J. E. Stiglitz vol. 1 (Cambridge, Mass. 1966).

Sanders [1970]   D. H. Sanders, *Computers and management* (New York 1970).

Scherer [1964]   F. M. Scherer, *The weapons acquisition process: Economic incentives* (Boston 1964).

Sen [1970]   A. K. Sen, *Collective choice and social welfare* (San Francisco 1970).

Siroyezhin [1968]   I. Siroyezhin, 'Man-machine systems in the USSR', *Management Science* 1968 vol. 15 no. 2.

Skilling [1971]   H. G. Skilling and F. Griffiths (eds), *Interest groups and Soviet politics* (Princeton 1971).

Spulber [1964]   N. Spulber (ed.), *Foundations of Soviet strategy for economic growth* (Bloomington, Indiana 1964).

Stalin [1952]   J. Stalin, *Economic problems of socialism in the USSR* (Moscow 1952).

Symposium [1971]   *Symposium – Soviet economic growth 1970–1980* (Brussels 1971).

TLS [1972]   The rising planometrician of Moscow, *Times Literary Supplement* 11 February 1972. This is a review of Ellman [1971].

Treml [1967]   V. Treml, Input–output analysis and Soviet planning, in Hardt [1967] q.v.

Tucker [1959]   A. W. Tucker and R. D. Luce (eds), *Contributions to the theory of games* vol. IV Annals of Mathematics (Princeton 1959).

Vanek [1970]   J. Vanek, *The general theory of labour-managed market economies* (New York 1970).

Von Neumann [1945]   J. von Neumann, 'A model of general economic equilibrium', *Review of Economic Studies* 1945.

Von Neumann [1959]   J. von Neumann, 'On the theory of games of strategy', Tucker [1959] q.v. This is a translation of a paper first published in German in 1928.

Wadsworth [1969]   J. Wadsworth, 'Appraisal of an integrated management and work control computer system before and after implementation', *Systems in action* (Report of the third automation conference organised by the plant engineering and energy division of BISRA) (1969).

Waker [1963]   A. Waker and J. G. Zielinskii, 'Socialist operational price systems', *American Economic Review* March 1963.

Walras [1954]   L. Walras, *Elements of pure economics* (1954). This is a translation of a book the first edition of which was published in Lausanne in 1874.

Ward [1960]   B. Ward, 'Kantorovich on economic calculation', *Journal of Political Economy* December 1960.

Ward [1967a]   B. Ward, *The socialist economy* (New York 1967).

Ward [1967b]   B. Ward, 'Linear programming and Soviet planning', Hardt [1967] q.v.

Weitzman [1971]   M. Weitzman, 'Material balances under uncertainty', *Quarterly Journal of Economics* May 1971.

Wigley [1968]   K. Wigley, *The demand for fuel 1948–1975* (1968), no. 8 in A programme for growth.

Wilczynski [1969]   J. Wilczynski, 'Towards rationality in land economics under central planning', *Economic Journal* September 1969.

Wiles [1962]   P. Wiles, *The political economy of communism* (Oxford 1962).

Zauberman [1960a]   A. Zauberman, 'Law of value and price formation', Grossman [1960] q.v.

Zauberman [1960b]   A. Zauberman, 'New winds in Soviet planning', *Soviet Studies* July 1960.

Zauberman [1962]   A. Zauberman, 'Revisionism in Soviet economics', in Ladedz [1962] q.v.

Zauberman [1966]   A. Zauberman, 'Forty years of the time factor in Soviet economics', *Soviet Studies* vol. 18.

Zauberman [1967]   *Aspects of planometrics* (1967) by A. Zauberman, with contributions by A. Bergstrom, T. Kronsjo and E. J. Mishan, and editorial assistance by M. J. Ellman.

Zielinski [1967]   J. G. Zielinski, 'On the theory of success indicators', *Economics of Planning* 1967 no. 1.

Zielinski [1969]   J. G. Zielinski, 'Economics and politics of economic reform in Eastern Europe', *Economics of Planning* 1969 no. 3.

Zielinski [1970]   J. G. Zielinski, 'Planification et gestation au niveau de la branche industrielle on Europe de l'Est', *Revue de l'Est* 1970 vol. 1 no. 1.
Zielinski [1971]   J. G. Zielinski, 'On the effectiveness of the Polish economic reforms', *Soviet Studies* January 1971.
Zielinski [1973]   J. G. Zielinski, *Economic reforms in Polish industry* (Oxford 1973).

Non-Soviet journals

Acta Oeconomica (Budapest)
The ASTE Bulletin (Philadelphia)
Czechoslavak Economic Papers (Prague)
Economics of Planning (Oslo)
Soviet Studies (Glasgow)

INDEX